BISMARCK

THE MAN AND THE STATESMAN
BEING THE REFLECTIONS AND REMINISCENCES OF
OTTO, PRINCE VON BISMARCK

*WRITTEN AND DICTATED BY HIMSELF AFTER
HIS RETIREMENT FROM OFFICE*

VOLUME II

Elibron Classics
www.elibron.com

Elibron Classics series.

© 2006 Adamant Media Corporation.

ISBN 0-543-98348-X (paperback)
ISBN 0-543-98347-1 (hardcover)

This Elibron Classics Replica Edition is an unabridged facsimile
of the edition published in 1898 by Smith, Elder, & Co., London.

BISMARCK

VOL. II.

F. von Lenbach. pinx.   Walker & Boutall ph. sc.

By permission of the Berlin Photographic Co. London. W.

London. Published by Smith, Elder & Co. 15, Waterloo Place.

BISMARCK

THE MAN AND THE STATESMAN

BEING THE REFLECTIONS AND REMINISCENCES OF

OTTO PRINCE VON BISMARCK

WRITTEN AND DICTATED BY HIMSELF AFTER
HIS RETIREMENT FROM OFFICE

TRANSLATED FROM THE GERMAN UNDER THE SUPERVISION OF

A. J. BUTLER

LATE FELLOW OF TRINITY COLLEGE, CAMBRIDGE

WITH TWO PORTRAITS AND A FACSIMILE OF
HANDWRITING

IN TWO VOLUMES—VOL. II.

LONDON
SMITH, ELDER, & CO., 15 WATERLOO PLACE
1898

CONTENTS

OF

THE SECOND VOLUME

———•⊙•———

CHAPTER XIX

SCHLESWIG-HOLSTEIN

CHAPTER XX

NIKOLSBURG

CHAPTER XXI

THE NORTH GERMAN *BUND*

CONTENTS OF VOLUME II ix

CHAPTER XXII

THE EMS TELEGRAM

                            CHAPTER XXIII

                              VERSAILLES

CHAPTER XXIV

THE *CULTURKAMPF*

CHAPTER XXV

RUPTURE WITH THE CONSERVATIVES

CHAPTER XXVI

INTRIGUES

CHAPTER XXVII

THE GOVERNMENT DEPARTMENTS

CHAPTER XXVIII

THE BERLIN CONGRESS

CHAPTER XXIX

THE TRIPLE ALLIANCE

CHAPTER XXX

THE FUTURE POLICY OF RUSSIA

CHAPTER XXXI

THE COUNCIL OF STATE

CHAPTER XXXII

THE EMPEROR WILLIAM I

CHAPTER XXXIII

THE EMPEROR FREDERICK III

BISMARCK

CHAPTER XIX

SCHLESWIG-HOLSTEIN

MY successor at Paris was Count Robert von der Goltz, who had been since 1855 ambassador at Athens, Constantinople, and St. Petersburg. My expectation that office would have disciplined him, that the transition from literary to business activity would have made him more sober and practical, and that the summons to what was then the most important post in Prussian diplomacy would have gratified his ambition, was not to be immediately or fully realised. At the end of the year 1863 I found myself obliged to have a written explanation with him, the whole of which is unfortunately no longer in my possession; of his letter of December 22, which was the immediate occasion of the correspondence, only a fragment [1] remains, and in the copy of my reply the beginning is missing. But even so this document has its value as a sketch of the situation at the time, and as illustrating the development that proceeded from it.

'Berlin: December 24, 1863.

'. . . . As to the Danish matter, it is not possible that the King should have two Ministers of Foreign Affairs;

[1] See *Bismarck-Jahrbuch*, v. 231.

I mean that the post most important in the critical question of the day should represent towards the King a policy opposed to that of his ministers. The friction of our state machine, already excessive, must not be still further increased. I can put up with any contradiction to myself personally, as long as it proceeds from so competent a source as yourself; but I cannot officially share with any one the task of advising the King in this matter; and if his Majesty were to call on me to do any such thing, I should have to resign my post. I told the King this on the occasion of our reading one of your latest dispatches; his Majesty considered my point of view very natural, and I can but hold to it. Nobody expects reports to be only the reflection of ministerial views; yours, however, are not reports in the usual sense, but assume the nature of ministerial proposals recommending to the King a policy opposed to that upon which he has already resolved with his assembled ministry in council, and has already followed for four weeks. What I may well call a sharp, if not hostile, criticism of this decision constitutes, however, a fresh ministerial programme, and is no longer an ambassadorial report. A view which so directly traverses ours may certainly do *harm*, but cannot do good; for it may elicit hesitation and indecision, and I prefer any policy to one that is vacillating.

'I entirely echo your observation that a "question of Prussian policy quite simple in itself" is obscured by the dust arising from the Danish business, and the mirage attaching thereto. The question is whether we are a Great Power or a state in the German Federation; and whether we are, conformably to the former quality, to be governed by a monarch or, as in the latter case would be at any rate admissible, by professors, district judges, and the gossips of the small towns. The pursuit of the phantom of popularity "in Germany" which we have been carrying on for the last forty years has cost us our position in Germany and in Europe; and we shall not win this back again by allowing ourselves to be carried away by the stream in the persuasion that we are directing its course, but only by standing firmly upon our legs, and being *first of all* a Great Power, and German Federal state *afterwards*. That is what Austria, to our injury, has always recognised as right for herself, and she will not allow herself to be wrested away, by the comedy she is playing with German sympathies, from her European alliances—if indeed she has any. If we go too far for her, she will pretend to go along with us a little way, especially will sign what we do; but the twenty per cent. of Germans that she has in her population are not in the last resort to be an element constraining her to let herself be carried away by us against her own interest. At the proper moment she will stay behind us, and will know how to find her proper line towards a European situation as soon as we give it up. Schmerling's policy, the counterpart of which appears to you to be an ideal one for Prussia, has ended in a *fiasco* for Austria. Our policy, which was so briskly opposed by you in the spring, has been verified in the Polish question, while the Schmerling policy has borne bitter fruit for her. Is it not indeed the most signal victory we could win that Austria, two months after the reform attempt, should be glad when nothing more is said about it, should be writing identical notes with us to her former friends, and joining in our threats towards her pet, the majority in the Federal Diet, to the effect that she will not allow herself to be bullied by majorities? We have won this summer what we have been vainly striving after for twelve years, the split-up of the Bregenz coalition; Austria has adopted the very policy of ours that she openly scoffed at in October last; she has chosen the Prussian instead of the Würzburg alliance, and receives her assistance from us; and if we now turn our back upon her to-day we upset the ministry. Never before has the policy of Vienna been controlled to such a degree *en gros et en détail* from Berlin. Add to this that we are sought after by France—Fleury offers more than the King wants; our voice has, in London and St. Petersburg, the weight it had lost for twenty years; and all this eight months after you prophesied to me the most dangerous isolation as a result of our Polish policy. If we now turn our back upon the Great Powers in order to throw ourselves into the arms of the policy of the minor states—enmeshed as it is in the net of club-democracy—that would be the most wretched position, either at home or abroad, to which the monarchy could be brought. We should be pushed instead of pushing; we should lean for support upon elements which we do not control, which are necessarily hostile to us, and to which we should have to devote ourselves unconditionally. You believe that there is some hidden virtue in " German public opinion," Chambers, newspapers, and suchlike, which might support or help us in a " Union " or " Hegemony " policy. I consider that a radical error, a product of the fancy. Our strength cannot proceed from a press and parliamentary policy, but only from the policy of a great military Power, and we have not so much staying power that we can afford to fritter it away by fronting in the wrong direction for the sake of phrases and Augustenburg. You attach a great deal too much importance to the whole Danish question, and allow yourself to be blinded

by the fact that it has become the general rallying-cry of
the democracy which controls the speaking trumpet of
the press and the clubs, and gives a sparkle to this
question, insignificant as it is in itself. Twelve months
ago the question was that of two years' service; eight
months ago it was Poland; and now it is Schleswig-
Holstein. What was your own view of the European
situation in the summer? You were dreading all sorts
of dangers for us, and at Kissingen you did not at all
conceal your views as to the incapacity of our policy:
have all these dangers suddenly disappeared with the
death of the King of Denmark? and are we now, at the
side of Pfordten, Coburg, and Augustenburg, supported
by all the chatterboxes and humbugs of the party of
movement, suddenly to be strong enough to take an off-
hand tone towards all four of the Great Powers? and have
the latter suddenly become so good-natured or so impotent
that we can boldly plunge into every sort of embarrass-
ment without having any anxiety as to what they may do?

'You call it a "marvellous" policy that we should
have been able to realise the Gagern programme without
a Constitution for the whole of Germany. I do not see
how we could have got as far as that if we had been
in the necessity of overcoming Europe in league with
the Würzburgers, and thrown upon them for support.
Either the governments would have stood by us honourably, and the reward of victory would have been one Grand
Duke more in Germany, who in his anxiety to preserve his
new sovereignty would vote in the *Bund* against Prussia—
one Würzburger more, in fact; or on the other hand we
should have been obliged (and this more probably) to cut
the ground from under the feet of our own allies *by means
of* an imperial constitution, and nevertheless have had to

reckon upon their fidelity. If this did not succeed, as was to be expected, we should have been shown up; if it succeeded, we had the Union *together with* the imperial constitution.

'You speak of a conglomeration of states of seventy million people, with a million soldiers, who are to defy Europe united and compact. Consequently you attribute to Austria a persistence, dead or alive, in a policy which must lead to the hegemony of Prussia. Yet you would not trust further than you could reach her the state which possesses thirty-five of these seventy millions. Neither would I; but I consider it our correct policy at present to have Austria with us. Whether the moment of separation comes and on whose initiative it will come, we shall see. You ask: "When on earth, then, are we to have war? What is the use of army reorganisation?" And your own reports describe to us the necessity to France of having a war in the spring and the prospect of a revolution in Galicia to boot. Russia has 200,000 men on their feet, over and above what is wanted for Poland, and she has no money to waste on fancy armaments. It looks, therefore, as if she had made up her mind for war. I am prepared for war combined with revolution. Then you say that "we by no means expose ourselves to war." I cannot make that fit in with your own reports during the last three months. I am at the same time by no means shy of war—quite the reverse; I am also as indifferent to "revolutionary" or "Conservative" as I am to all phrases. Perhaps you will very soon be convinced that war is also part of my programme; but I consider your way of reaching a war the wrong one from the statesman's point of view. The fact that with regard to this you find yourself in agreement with Pfordten, Beust, Dalwigk, or whatever our opponents' names are, makes me look upon the side you represent not indeed as either revolutionary or Conservative, but as not the right one for Prussia. If the pothouse enthusiasm in London and Paris makes any impression, I shall be glad of it; it is part of our stock-in-trade, but it has not impressed me so far, and, in the case of a fight, furnishes us with few pence and no powder. You may call the convention of London revolutionary if you like; the Vienna treaties were ten times more so, and ten times more unjust towards many princes, estates, and countries; it is only by European treaties that European law is established. If, however, you want to apply the standard of morality and justice to these latter they must well-nigh all be abolished.

'If you were in office here instead of me, I fancy you would very soon be convinced of the impossibility of the policy you recommend to me to-day and regard as so exclusively " patriotic " that you threaten to break off our friendship over it. I can only say, " La critique est aisée ; ' it is not difficult, amid the applause of the mob, to find fault with the government, especially a government which has been obliged to lay hold of several wasps' nests into the bargain. If the result proves that the government proceeded rightly, there is no further question for blame ; if the government makes a *fiasco* over things which are in general beyond the control of human will and foresight, you have the glory of having prophesied at the right time that the government was on the " woodman's road." * I have a high opinion of your political insight, but I consider that I, too, am not stupid, though I am quite prepared to hear you say that this is self-delusion. Perhaps your opinion of my patriotism and judgement will rise when

* ['Path that goes nowhere.']

I tell you that, for the last fortnight, I have been taking my stand on the proposals made in your Report No. ——. With some difficulty I have determined Austria to convoke the Holstein Estates, in case we carry the matter through at Frankfort; we must first of all be all right in the country. The examination of the succession question at the *Bund* ensues with our consent, even if, having regard to England, we cannot vote for it. I had left Sydow without any instruction ; he is not made for carrying out delicate instructions.

'It may be that other phases of the matter will follow that do not lie very remote from your programme ; but how am I to make up my mind to let myself out frankly to you as to my latest ideas, after your declaring war against me politically, and pretty candidly acknowledging the intention to oppose the present ministry and its policy, and consequently to turn it out ? On this point I am judging merely by the contents of what you write to me, and leave out of the question everything I have learnt through *colportage* and at third hand, as to your verbal and written diatribes with regard to myself. And yet I am bound as a minister, if the interests of state are not to suffer, to be ruthlessly frank towards our ambassador at Paris with regard to my policy from first to last. The friction which every one in my position has to overcome—with ministers and councillors at Court, with occult influences, with the Chambers, the press, and foreign Courts—must not be aggravated by the substitution for the discipline of my department, of a rivalry between the minister and the ambassador, and by my having to restore the indispensable homogeneity of the service by a discussion through the post. I can seldom write at such length as I can to-day, Christmas Eve, when all the officials are on leave; and I would not write the fourth part of this to any one but you. I do so because I cannot bring myself to write to you officially and through the clerks in the same autocratic tone in which your reports to hand have been couched. I have no hope of convincing you, but I have sufficient confidence in your own official experience and impartiality to make me believe that you will grant me that only one policy can be carried out at a time, and that it must be the policy upon which the ministry and the King are at one. If you want to try to overthrow that and the ministry along with it, you must do it here in the Chamber and in the press, at the head of the Opposition, but not from your present position; in that case I should equally have to abide by your maxim that, in case of a conflict between patriotism and friendship, the former must decide. But I can assure you that my patriotism is of so pure and strong a nature that a friendship which has to give way to it may nevertheless be very cordial.'[1]

The gradations which appeared attainable in the Danish question, every one of them meaning for the duchies an advance to something better than the existing conditions, culminated, in my judgement, in the acquisition of the duchies by Prussia, a view which I expressed in a council held immediately after the death of Frederick VII. I reminded the King that every one of his immediate ancestors, not even excepting his brother, had won an increment of territory for the state; Frederick William IV had acquired Hohenzollern and the Jahde district; Frederick

---

[1] Cf. *Bismarck-Jahrbuch*, v. 232. See Goltz's answer to this letter with Bismarck's marginal remarks in *Bismarck-Jahrbuch*, v. 238.

William III the Rhine province ; Frederick William II, Poland ; Frederick II, Silesia ; Frederick William I, old Hither Pomerania ; the Great Elector, Further Pomerania and Magdeburg, Minden, &c. ; and I encouraged him to do likewise. This pronouncement of mine did not appear in the protocol. As Geheimrath Costenoble, who had drawn up the protocol, explained to me, when I asked him the reason of this, the King had opined that I should prefer what I blurted out not to be embedded in protocols. His Majesty seems to have imagined that I had spoken under the Bacchic influences of a *déjeuner*, and would be glad to hear no more of it. I insisted, however, upon the words being put in, and they were. While I was speaking, the Crown Prince raised his hands to heaven as if he doubted my sanity ; my colleagues remained silent.

If the utmost we aimed at could not be realised, we might have, in spite of all Augustenburg renunciations, have gone as far as the introduction of that dynasty, and the establishment of a new middle state, provided the Prussian and German national interests had been put on a sure footing—these interests to be protected by what was the essential part of the subsequent February conditions— that is, a military convention, Kiel as a harbour for the *Bund*, and the Baltic and North Sea canal.

Even if, taking into consideration the European situation and the wish of the King, this had not been attainable without the isolation of Prussia from all the Great Powers, including Austria—the question was in what way, whether under the form of a personal union or under some other, a provisional settlement was attainable as regards the duchies, which must in any case be an improvement in their position. From the very beginning I kept annexation steadily before my eyes, without losing sight of the other gradations. I considered the situation set up in the public opinion of our opponents as our programme to be the one which I believed must absolutely be avoided—that is to say, to fight out Prussia's struggle and war for the erection of a new grand duchy, at the head of the newspapers, the clubs, the volunteers, and the states of the *Bund* (Austria excepted), and this without the assurance that the Federal governments would carry the affair through, despite every obstacle. Moreover, the public opinion that had developed in this direction, and even the President Ludwig von Gerlach, had a childlike confidence in the assistance England would render to isolated Prussia. The partnership of France would have been much more easy to obtain than that of England, had we been willing to pay the price which it might be foreseen it would cost us. I have never wavered in the conviction that Prussia, supported only by the arms and associates of 1848—and by these I mean public opinion, Diets, political clubs, volunteers, and the small contingents as they were then constituted—would have embarked upon a hopeless course and would have only found enemies in the Great Powers, in England also. I should have regarded as a humbug and a traitor any minister who had fallen back upon the erroneous policy of 1848, 1849, and 1850, which must have prepared a new Olmütz for us. Austria once with us, however, the possibility of a coalition of the other Powers against us disappeared.

Even though German unity could not be restored by means of resolutions of Diets, newspapers, and rifle-meetings, Liberalism nevertheless continued to exercise a pressure on the princes which made them more inclined to make concessions for the sake of the *Reich*. The mood of the Courts wavered between the wish to fortify the monarchical position by separate particularistic and autocratic policy in view of the advance of the Liberals, and anxiety lest peace should be disturbed by violence at home or abroad. No German government allowed any doubt to remain as to its *German* sentiments ; but as to the way in which the future of Germany was to be shaped, neither governments nor parties were agreed. It is not probable that the Emperor William as Regent, or subsequently as King, could ever have been brought so far by the road which he had first trodden, under the influence of his consort, at the beginning of the new era, to do what was necessary to bring about unity, namely, to renounce the *Bund*, and use the Prussian army in the German cause.

On the other hand, however, it is not probable that he could have been guided into the path that led to the Danish war, and consequently to that in Bohemia, but for his previous attempts and endeavours in the direction of Liberalism, and the obligations he had thereby incurred. Perhaps we should never have succeeded in holding him aloof from the Frankfort Congress of Princes in 1863 if his Liberal antecedents had not left behind in him a certain need of popularity in the Liberal direction, which before Olmütz would have been foreign to him, but since then was the natural psychological result of the desire to seek healing and satisfaction on the field of German policy, for the wounds inflicted upon his Prussian sense of honour on the same field. The Holstein question, the Danish war, Düppel and Alsen, the breach with Austria, and the decision of the German question on the battlefield—all this was a system of adventures upon which he would, perhaps, not have entered but for the difficult position into which the new era had brought him.

Even in 1864 it certainly cost us much trouble to

loosen the threads by which the King, with the co-operation of the Liberalising influence of his consort, remained attached to that camp. Without having investigated the complicated legal questions of the succession, he stuck to his motto : ' I have no right to Holstein.' My representation that the Duke of Augustenburg had no right to the Ducal and the Schaumburg portion ; never had had, and had twice (in 1721 and 1852) renounced his claims to the Royal portion ; that Denmark had as a rule voted with Prussia in the Federal Diet ; that the Duke of Schleswig-Holstein, from fear of the preponderance of Prussia, would hold with Austria—produced no impression. Even though the acquisition of these provinces, washed by two seas, and my historical reminder in the cabinet council of December 1863, were not without effect on the dynastic sentiments of the King, on the other hand the realisation of the disapproval which, if he threw over the Augustenburger, he would have to encounter at the hands of his consort, of the Crown Prince and Princess, of various dynasties, and of those who in his estimation at that time formed the public opinion of Germany, was not without effect.

Without doubt, public opinion in the cultured middle class of Germany was in favour of the Prince of Augustenburg, with the same want of judgement as at an earlier period palmed off ' Polonism ' as the German national interest, and at a later period the artificial enthusiasm for Battenbergian Bulgaria. The press was, in these two somewhat analogous cases, worked with distressing success, and public stupidity was as receptive as ever of its operation. Criticism of the government in 1864 had only reached the level of the phrase : ' No, I don't like the new burgomaster.' I do not know if there is anybody to-day who would consider it reasonable that, after the liberation of the duchies, a new grand duchy should be formed out of them, possessing the right of voting in the Federal Diet, and as an *ipso facto* result called to go in fear of Prussia and hold with her opponents. At that time, however, the acquisition of the duchies by Prussia was regarded as an act of profligacy by all those who, since 1848, had set up to play the part of representatives of national views. My respect for so-called public opinion—or, in other words, the clamour of orators and newspapers—has never been very great, but was still further materially lowered as regards foreign policy in the two cases compared above. How strangely, up to this time, the King's way of looking at things was impregnated with vagabond Liberalism through the influence of his consort and of the pushing Beth-mann-Hollweg clique is evident from the tenacity with which he clung to the contradictory attitude in which the Austro-Frankfort-Augustenburg programme stood towards the Prussian efforts after National Unity. This policy could not have recommended itself to the King on logical grounds. He had taken it over, without making a previous chemical analysis of its contents, as an appurtenance of the old Liberalism, from the point of view of the earlier critical attitude of the heir to the throne, and of the counsellors of the Queen, Goltz, Pourtalès, &c. I will anticipate a little by here inserting the last sign of life given by the 'Wochenblatt party,' in the shape of the letter of Herr von Bethmann-Hollweg to the King, dated June 15, 1866, whose main points are as follows : [1]

' What your Majesty has constantly dreaded and avoided, what all persons of insight have foreseen, namely, that a serious quarrel with Austria would be utilised by France

---

[1] Published in full in L. Schneider's *Aus dem Leben Kaiser Wilhelms I.* i. 334 &c., also in Kohl's *Bismarck Register*, i. 287 &c.

in order to increase her territory at the expense of Germany, [where?][1]—lies patent to all the world in Louis Napoleon's openly expressed programme. . . . The whole of the Rhineland for the duchies would not be a bad exchange for him; for he certainly would not be contented in the *petites rectifications des frontières* that he formerly claimed.   And he is the omnipotent arbiter in Europe. . . . . I have no hostile feeling against the originator of this policy of ours.   I am glad to recall how in 1848 I went hand in hand with him to strengthen the King's position.   In March 1862 I advised your Majesty to select a helmsman of Conservative antecedents, possessing sufficient ambition, audacity and adroitness to steer the ship of state out of the rocks among which she had got; and I should have named Herr von Bismarck had I believed that he combined with these qualities that discretion and logical sequence of thought and action, the lack of which is scarcely pardonable in a youth, but in a man may endanger the life of a state which he guides.   As a matter of fact, all Count Bismarck's action has from the first been full of contradictions. . . . Of old a decided advocate of the alliance with France and Russia, he linked, with the help to be furnished in Prussian interest to Russia against the Polish insurrection, political projects[2] which were sure to alienate both states from him.   In 1863, when the death of the King of Denmark threw into his lap a task as fortunate as ever fell to a statesman's lot, he scorned to take advantage of it to place Prussia at the head of a unanimous rising [in resolutions][1] of Germany, whose union under the leadership of Prussia was his object; and preferred a union with Austria, the opponent in principle of this plan in order subsequently to become her irreconcilable foe.   He

[1] Marginal notes in Bismarck's own hand.   [2] Cf. vol. i. p. 340.

ill-treated * the Prince of Augustenburg—to whom your
Majesty was well-disposed, and from whom at that time
everything might have been obtained—allowing him soon
afterwards to be declared the rightful candidate by Count
Bernstorff at the London Conference. Then at the Peace
of Vienna he pledges Prussia to dispose † definitely of the
liberated duchies subject only to an understanding with
Austria ; and has arrangements inserted in it which plainly
announce the " annexation " he had in view. . . .

'Many regard these and similar measures, which
for the very reason that they were self-contradictory constantly swung round to the opposite of what was intended,
as faults of indiscretion. To others they appeared as the
steps of a man who proceeds at random, throws everything into a tangle, and brings things into a situation
from which he may make his profit, or of a gambler who
after every loss only punts higher, and finally cries *va
banque !*

'All this is bad, but what appears much worse in my
eyes is that Count Bismarck, by this mode of procedure,
should place himself in contradiction to the inclination
and aims of his King, and show his skill chiefly in leading
him step by step nearer to a goal diametrically opposed
thereto, till a return appeared impossible. According to
my opinion a minister's first duty is to give his master
loyal counsel, to provide him with the means of carrying
out his projects, and above all to keep the King's image
unspotted in the eyes of all the world. Your Majesty's
straightforward, righteous, and chivalrous sentiments are
known to all, and have won for your Majesty universal trust
and universal veneration. Count Bismarck, however,

* [Cf. the Prince's letter of December 11, 1863, *infra*, p. 28.]
† [Why not : He pledged Austria only with the consent of Prussia ?]

has brought things to such a pass that your Majesty's noblest words to your own country die away without effect because they are not believed; and any understanding with other Powers is become impossible, because the first condition thereof—I mean confidence—has been destroyed by a policy full of intrigue. Not a shot has yet been fired; an understanding is still possible on one condition. Our preparations for war must not be discontinued; nay, rather, if necessary, they must be redoubled, if we are triumphantly to encounter antagonists who aim at our annihilation, or to emerge with full honours from this complicated business. But every understanding is impossible so long as a man remains at your Majesty's side and possesses your decided confidence who has robbed your Majesty of the confidence of all the other Powers.' [1]

By the time the King received this letter he had been freed from the entanglement of the arguments repeated therein by the Gastein Convention of August 14 to 20, 1865. The difficulties I had still to encounter in dealing with them, and the caution I had still to use, are evident from my following letter to his Majesty:

' Gastein : August 1, 1865.

'Your Majesty will be gracious enough to forgive me if a perhaps too excessive care for the interests of your service induces me to revert to the communications you have just done me the honour to make to me. The thought of a partition, even in the administration of the

---

[1] King William did not open the letter till he was at Nikolsburg in July 1866. His answer began: 'I first opened your letter at Nikolsburg, and the place and date of my answer should be answer enough,' &c. Cp. Schneider, *loc. cit.* i. 341.

duchies, would, if it became notorious in the Augustenburg camp, arouse a violent storm in diplomatic circles
and in the press—because people would see in it the
beginning of a definitive partition, and would not doubt
that those portions of the country which are to fall
into the hands of exclusively Prussian administration
are lost to Augustenburg. I believe with your Majesty
that her Majesty the Queen will keep these communications secret, but if an intimation from Coblenz sent
in reliance upon the relations between kinsfolk were to
reach Queen Victoria, the Crown Prince and Princess,
Weimar or Baden, then the very circumstance that the
secret (which at his desire I told to Count Blome) had
not been kept by us would arouse the distrust of the
Emperor Francis Joseph, and wreck the negotiations.
This wreck of the negotiations would lead almost inevit-
ably to a war with Austria. Your Majesty will kindly
credit it not only to my interest on your behalf, but
also to my attachment to your person, if I say that I
am dominated by the impression that your Majesty would
embark on a war with different feelings and with a
freer courage if the necessity for the war resulted
from the nature of events and from a monarch's sense
of duty, than if there were room for any afterthought
that a premature disclosure of the intended solution of
the question restrained the Emperor of Austria from
consenting to the last expedient your Majesty could
accept. Perhaps my anxiety is foolish; and even if
it were well-grounded, and your Majesty should wish to
disregard it, I should still think that God directs your
Majesty's heart, and should therefore do my duty none
the less joyfully; but for the safeguarding of my own
conscience I should, nevertheless, respectfully suggest

whether your Majesty would not like to command me to summon back the courier from Salzburg by telegraph. (†) The ministerial dispatch-service might offer an ostensible occasion for this, and to-morrow another in place of him or the same man might start betimes. I most submissively beg to append a copy of what I have telegraphed to Werther as to the negotiations with Count Blome. I have the most respectful confidence in your Majesty's well-approved favour, in the persuasion that your Majesty, even when you do not approve of my scruples, will attribute my insistence on them to my sincere desire to serve your Majesty not only as my duty commands, but also to your personal contentment.'

Where the ' (†) ' appears in the above letter, the King wrote in the margin: 'Agreed.—I mentioned the matter because during the last twenty-four hours no mention of it had been made, and I regarded it as quite fallen out of the combination; later, the actual "seisin" had taken place. By my communication to the Queen I wished to *pave the way* for the future transition to the "seisin," which had gradually developed out of the partition of the administration. Nevertheless I can at a later time so represent this if the proprietary partition actually comes about; that, however, I still continue to doubt, inasmuch as Austria would have to draw back too abruptly, after having pushed herself too far forward in favour of Augustenburg, and against occupation though it were only *one*-sided.

'W.' [1]

After the Gastein Convention and the occupation of Lauenburg, the first addition made to the kingdom under

[1] *Bismarck-Jahrbuch,* vi. 202.

King William, his frame of mind, so far as I could observe, underwent a psychological change ; he developed a taste for conquest. This was nevertheless accompanied by a preponderating satisfaction that this increase—i.e. the harbour of Kiel, the military position in Schleswig, and right to construct a canal through Holstein—had been won in peace and amity with Austria.

I imagine that the right of absolute disposal of Kiel harbour had more weight with his Majesty than the impression produced by the newly won pleasant district of Ratzeburg and its lake.   The German fleet with Kiel harbour as the basis of its establishment had since 1848 been one of the enkindling thoughts around whose flame the German endeavours for unity were wont to centre and from which they drew their warmth. At times, however, the hatred of my parliamentary opponents for me had been stronger than their concern for the German fleet ; and it seemed to me that the Party of Progress would then rather have seen Prussia's newly won right to Kiel and the prospect of our maritime future which was bound up with it, in the hands of the auctioneer Hannibal Fischer than in those of the Bismarck ministry.[1]   The right of complaining and grumbling over this government's annihilation of German hopes would have afforded the deputies far more satisfaction than the progress already made on the way to their fulfilment. I here insert some passages from a speech I delivered on June 1, 1865, in support of the extraordinary Navy Budget : [2]

‘ Certainly in no question during the last twenty years has public opinion in Germany been so unanimous as in the question of the navy. We have seen that the political

---

[1] Cf. the speech of June 1, 1865. *Politische Reden*, ii. 356.

[2] *Politische Reden*, ii. 355.

clubs, the press, and the Diets have given expression to their sympathies; and these sympathies have resulted in the collection of comparatively quite considerable sums. Reproaches were brought against the government and against the Conservative party for the tardiness and the parsimony with which they have proceeded in this direction; the Liberal parties were particularly active in this respect. We thought, therefore, that this proposal will be a genuine pleasure to you. . . .

'I was not prepared to find in the report of the committee an indirect apology for Hannibal Fischer, who brought the German fleet to the hammer. That German fleet, too, thus came to grief because party passion was more potent than public spirit in the German domains, equally in the higher administrative circles and in the lower. I hope the same destiny is not appointed for us.

'I was further somewhat surprised that so large a space in the report was devoted to technicalities. I do not doubt there are many of you who know more about naval matters than I do, and have been to sea more than I; but, gentlemen, that is not the case with the greater number of you; and yet I have to say that I would not trust myself on technical naval details to pass an opinion such as to give a reason for my vote, and a motive for rejecting a Navy Bill. I cannot therefore occupy myself in refuting this portion of your objections. . . .

'Your doubt as to whether I shall succeed in acquiring Kiel touches my department more closely. In the duchies we possess more than Kiel; we possess in them full sovereignty in common with Austria; and I did not know who could wrest from us this pledge, which so far exceeds in value the object aimed at by us, otherwise than by a war disastrous to Prussia. But if we keep this eventuality

before our eyes, we might just as well lose *every* harbour
actually in our possession. Our possession, it is true, is a
joint one with Austria; nevertheless, it is a possession for
whose abandonment we should be justified in laying down
our conditions.   One of these—indeed one quite indispensable, without the fulfilment of which we do not intend
to give up this possession—is the future sole proprietorship
of Kiel harbour by Prussia.

' In view of the rights which are in our hands and in
those of Austria, and are unassailable so long as one of
the pretenders does not succeed in satisfying us that he
has a stronger right than that which has passed to us
from King Christian IX of Denmark,—in view of the
rights which are possessed in full sovereignty by us and
Austria, I do not see how the final fulfilment of our conditions could elude us, so long as we do not lose patience,
but wait quietly to see if there is anybody who will
undertake to besiege Düppel when the Prussians are
inside it. . . .

' Nevertheless, if you doubt the possibility of realising
our projects, I have already in committee recommended
an expedient.   Limit your grants so that the amounts
demanded shall only be payable when we actually possess
Kiel, and say if you like, " No Kiel, no money ! "   I believe
that you would not refuse such a condition to any other
ministers than those who now have the honour to enjoy
the confidence of his Majesty the King. . . .

' The confidence of the people in the wisdom of the
King is great enough to make them say, that were the
country in danger by the introduction of the Two Years'
Service system of perishing or taking harm, the King
would never allow it.   It is just in consequence of
earlier traditions that the importance of the constitution

is underrated. I am convinced that you will not deceive their confidence in the wisdom of the King; yet I cannot deny that it makes a painful impression upon me when I see that, in view of a great national question which has occupied public opinion for twenty years, that very assembly which passes in Europe as the concentration of the intelligence and patriotism of Prussia can rise to no higher altitude than an impotent negative. That, gentlemen, is not the weapon with which to wrest the sceptre from the hand of the monarchy; nor is it the means whereby you will succeed in giving our constitutional system that stability and further development which it needs.'

The Naval Budget was rejected.

In looking back upon this situation, we have lamentable proof of the degree of dishonesty and cosmopolitanism to which political parties with us attained when actuated by party hatred. Something similar may have happened elsewhere; but I know of no other country where the universal national feeling and love for the whole Fatherland offered so little resistance to the excesses of party passion as with us. The expression, considered apocryphal, which Plutarch puts into Cæsar's mouth, namely, that he would rather be the first man in a wretched mountain village than the second at Rome, has always struck me as a genuinely German idea. Only too many among us think thus in public life, and look about for the village; and when they cannot find it on the map, look for the group, sub-group, or coterie, as may be, in which they can be first. This state of mind which you may call egotism or independence—whichever you please—has found its realisation throughout German history, from the rebellious dukes of the first imperial period, down to the innumerable princes, imperial cities, imperial villages, abbeys, knights, holding immediately of the Empire, with, as its result to the Empire, feebleness and defencelessness. At the moment it finds more vigorous expression in the party system, splitting up the nation, than in any disintegration by way of laws or dynasties. Parties diverge less in respect of programmes and principles than of the persons who stand as *condottieri* at the head of each, and seek to gain for themselves as large a following as possible of deputies and pushing publicists, who hope to arrive at power along with their leader or leaders. Differences of principle and programme whereby the groups might be forced into conflict and hostility with one another are not forthcoming in sufficient strength to supply a motive for the passionate encounters which the groups think it necessary to wage between themselves, flinging Conservatives and Free Conservatives into separate camps. Even within the Conservative party certainly many felt that they did not agree with the 'Kreuzzeitung' and its hangers-on. But to fix precisely and express convincingly in a programme the line where principles divide would be a difficult task even for the leaders and their henchmen—just as denominational fanatics, and not laymen only, when you ask them to give the distinguishing characteristics of the various confessions and directions of belief, or to explain the harm they fear for their soul's welfare if they do not fiercely assault some divagation of the heterodox, as a rule turn the dilemma, or leave you still thirsting for information. So far as parties are not grouped simply according to economic interests, they fight in the interests of the rival leaders of their groups, and not according to their personal wishes and ambitions; the whole question is one of Cephas or Paul, not a difference of principle.

The following letter from the King is a reminiscence of the Gastein Convention : [1]

'Berlin: September 15, 1865.

' To-day full possession is taken of the Duchy of Lauenburg, an act resulting from the great and admirable insight and circumspection with which you have adhered to my government. During the four years since I called you to the head of the government of the state, Prussia has won a position that is worthy of her history, and promises her, moreover, further fortune and glory yet to come.   In order to express my thanks and bear open testimony to your distinguished services, for which I have so often had occasion to express my thanks, I hereby raise you and your descendants to the rank of Count, a distinction which will, at any rate, prove how high my appreciation was of your services to your country.

' Your affectionate King,

' WILLIAM.'

The negotiations between Berlin and Vienna and between Prussia and the other German states, which occupied the time from the Gastein Convention to the outbreak of the war, are known from the public records. In South Germany strife and conflict with Prussia partly gave way before a 'Germano-patriotic' feeling; in Schleswig-Holstein, those whose wishes had not been gratified began to reconcile themselves to the new order of things ; only the Guelfs were never weary of carrying on a paper war over the events of 1866.

The disadvantageous shape in which, as a reward for her exertions and achievements, the Vienna Congress left Prussia could only be maintained if we were sure of those

[1] *Bismarck-Jahrbuch*, vi. 203.

states of the old confederacy that had been thrust in between the two parts of the monarchy as a result of the Seven Years' war. I had actively laboured to win over Hanover and my friend Count Platen to this end, and there was every prospect that at least a treaty of neutrality would be brought about when Count Platen was negotiating with me in Berlin on January 21, 1866, about the marriage of Princess Frederica of Hanover with our young Prince Albrecht. We had brought both Courts so far towards an understanding that the only thing still to be done was to bring about a meeting between the young lady and gentleman, in order to make sure of their impression of each other.

But as early as March or April they began in Hanover to call up their reserves under threadbare pretexts. Influences had been brought to bear upon King George, especially by his half-brother, the Austrian general, Prince Solms, who had come to Hanover and won the King over by an exaggerated description of the Austrian forces—800,000 men were said to be in readiness—and, as I learnt from confidential Hanoverian sources, also by an offer of territorial aggrandisement, to the extent of the district of Minden at least. My official inquiries with respect to the armaments of Hanover were answered with the information, which sounded almost like banter, that for economic reasons the autumn manœuvres must be held in the spring.[1]

As late as June 14 I had a conversation[2] at Berlin with the heir to the throne of Electoral Hesse, Prince Frederick William, in the course of which I recommended him to take a special train to Cassel and secure the

[1] Cf. *Politische Reden*, iv. 137.
[2] Cf. Sybel, iv. 439, note 1.

neutrality of Electoral Hesse, or at least of the troops there, either by using his influence with the Elector or independently of him. The Prince refused to go any sooner than by the train in the time-table. I represented to him that in that case he would get there too late to prevent a war between Prussia and Hesse, and secure a continued existence for the Electorate. If the Austrians were victorious, he could always plead ' vis major ; ' his neutral attitude might even win some bits of Prussian territory for him; but if we were victorious after his refusal to remain neutral, the Electorate would cease to exist. The Hessian throne was surely worth a special train. The Prince put an end to the interview with these words : ' I suppose we shall meet once again in this life, and 800,000 good Austrian troops have still a word to say in the matter.' And indeed the demand, addressed in the most friendly tone by the King to the Elector from Horsitz on the 6th, and from Pardubitz on July 8, that he should conclude an alliance with Prussia and withdraw his troops from the hostile camp, met with no response.

The hereditary Prince of Augustenburg, by declining the so-called February conditions, had also neglected the favourable moment. The following version has recently been put about from a Guelf quarter.[1] The author of it maintains that he heard from the Prince how in an audience with King William he had pledged himself to the concessions demanded, and how the King had assured him of his installation in his dukedom, promising him that the matter should be formally settled the next day by the minister-president. I am said to have presented

[1] *Recollections and Experiences of Major-General Dammer* (Hanover, 1890), p. 94 &c.

myself to the Prince on the following day, but to have told him that my carriage was standing at the door, that I was obliged to go off that moment to the Emperor Napoleon at Biarritz. The Prince is said to have been required to leave a plenipotentiary at Berlin, and to have been not a little astonished to read in the Berlin newspapers on the following day that he had declined the Prussian propositions.

This is a clumsy invention, both in the main point and in all its particulars. The negotiations with the Hereditary Prince have been described by Sybel[1] from the documents; I have some particulars to add thereto from my own recollections and notes. The King never came to an agreement with the Hereditary Prince; I was never in the latter's house, and never mentioned the name of Biarritz or Napoleon to him. In 1864 I went to Baden on October 1, from thence on the 5th to Biarritz. In 1865 I went to the latter place direct on September 30, and in 1863 I was not at Biarritz at all. I twice had conversations with him, and the following letter[2] from him refers to the former of these, which took place on November 18, 1863.

'Gotha: December 11, 1863.

'Your Excellency will allow me to address a few lines to you, occasioned by an article contained in No. 282 of the "Kreuzzeitung" [of December 3], of which I have only lately been informed. In this article I am reported to have said to a deputation, amongst other things, "Herr von Bismarck is no friend of mine." I am unable to quote my exact words on the occasion, as the reference is to an expression that fell from me in conversation.

[1] Vol. iii. p. 337.
[2] *Bismarck-Jahrbuch*, v. 256.

It is quite possible I may have expressed my regret that your political views on the present position of the Schleswig-Holstein affair did not coincide with my own— an opinion I had no hesitation in expressing openly to yourself during my last visit to Berlin. I am nevertheless absolutely certain that I never used the expression attributed to me in the newspaper ; as I have always made it a fixed rule to keep political and personal matters apart. I therefore most genuinely regret that such a report should have found its way into the papers.

'I have considered it so much the more my duty not to withhold this explanation, as I am bound to recognise the handsome manner in which you openly said to me at Berlin that personally you were quite convinced of the justice of my claim and approved of it ; but that if I tried to get it recognised you could, in view of the engagements entered into by Prussia, as well as of the general situation, make me no promises.

' FREDERICK.'

On January 16, 1864, his Majesty wrote to me [1] as follows :

' My son came to me again yesterday evening to present to me the request of the Hereditary Prince of Augustenburg, that I would receive a letter from him by the hand of Herr Samwer, and to ask if in order to do this I would not attend his *soirée*, where I could meet S. in a private apartment quite unobserved. I declined to do so till I had read the Prince's letter, and so bade my son send it to me. This was done, and I enclose it.[2] It

[1] *Bismarck-Jahrbuch*, v. 254.
[2] Published in Jansen-Samwer's *Schleswig-Holstein's Befreiung*, p. 695, appendix 11.

contains nothing objectionable, except at the end, where he asks me if I can not give S. any hope. Perhaps you can get an answer ready by to-morrow for me to give to S.[1] If I chose to see him *incognito* at my son's, I could still give him no other hope than what is indicated in the stipulation,[2] i.e. that when we have won the victory we will see what new bases can be established for the future, and await the verdict of Frankfort-on-Main as to the succession.

'W.'

Again, on January 18 : [3]

'I inform you that after all I resolved to see Samwer at my son's for about six to ten minutes in his presence.[4] I spoke to him quite in the tenor of the projected answer,[5] but somewhat *more coolly* and *very seriously*. Above all, I said most decidedly that the Prince must in no case make a raid into Schleswig.

'W.'

In a memorandum of Feburary 26, 1864, the Crown Prince indicated, as justified by the circumstances, the following claims of Prussia : [6] Rendsburg to be a federal fortress, Kiel to be a Prussian marine station, accession to the Customs Union, the construction of a canal between the two seas, and a military and naval convention with

---

[1] See this letter of the King of January 18 *composed* by *Bismarck*, in Jansen-Samwer, p. 601, appendix 13.

[2] Signed on January 16 by Rechberg and Werther.

[3] *Bismarck-Jahrbuch*, v. 255.

[4] Samwer's memorandum gives the course of this conversation, *op. cit.* p. 696 &c. appendix 12.

[5] I.e. the answer to the letter of the 18th, which was laid before the King in draft on the 17th.

[6] It is based on the letter of the Hereditary Prince Frederick of February 19, 1864 ; Jansen-Samwer, p. 705 &c.

Prussia.   He cherished a hope that the Hereditary Prince
would be ready to agree to these terms.

After the Prussian plenipotentiaries at the London
Conference had on May 28, 1864, delivered the declaration
that the German Powers desired the constitution of
Schleswig-Holstein as an independent state under the
sovereignty of the Hereditary Prince of Augustenburg, I
had a conversation with the Prince at my residence on the
evening of June 1, 1864, from nine till twelve o'clock,
in order to decide whether I could advise the King to
support his candidature.   The conversation turned principally on the points indicated by the Crown Prince in
the memorandum of February 26.   The expectation of
his Royal Highness, that the Hereditary Prince would be
ready to agree to this, I did not find to be justified.   The
substance of the latter's explanations has been given by
Sybel,[1] from the documents.   What he most vigorously
resisted were the cessions of territory for the purpose of
constructing fortresses; why, they might run to a square
[German] mile, he said.   I was obliged to consider that
our demand was refused, and that no good would come of
any further negotiation, at which the Prince seemed to hint,
for he said, on taking his leave : ' We shall see each other
again, I suppose.'   He did not say it in the threatening
sense in which Prince Frederick of Hesse said the same
words to me two years later, but as an expression of a mind
not made up.   I never saw the Hereditary Prince again till
the day after the battle of Sedan, when he was wearing
the uniform of a Bavarian general.   After peace was

[1] Sybel, iii. 337 &c.   Cf. Bismarck's account of this conversation in
the *Staats-Anzeiger* of July 2, 1865; also the expressions in the speeches
of June 13, 1865, and December 20, 1866, *Politische Reden*, iii. 387, 389 ;
iv. 102 &c. ; the Duke's statement in Jansen-Samwer, p. 731 (cf. p. 336
&c.).

concluded with Denmark on October 30, 1864, the
conditions were formulated under which we would regard
the formation of a new Schleswig-Holstein state as not
endangering the interests of Prussia and Germany. On
February 22, 1865, they were communicated to Vienna.
They coincided with those recommended by the Crown
Prince.

One of the enterprises, the possibility of which I had
advanced, is now [1] after long delay being carried into execution : the North Sea and Baltic Canal. In the interest
of German sea power, which was then capable of development only under the name of Prussia, I (and not I
alone) had attached great importance to the building of
the canal and the possession and fortification of both its
mouths. The desire to make a concentration of our
naval forces possible, by cutting through the stretch of
land separating the two seas, was still very vigorous as
an after-effect of the almost morbid enthusiasm for the
fleet in 1848 ; it slumbered, however, for a time when
we had the territory in question at our free disposal. In my
endeavours to revive this interest I met with opposition in
the Committee for National Defence, of which the Crown
Prince was President, but Count Moltke the real head.

The latter, as a member of the Reichstag, gave it as
his opinion on June 23, 1873,[2] that the canal would only
be navigable in summer, and was of doubtful military
value ; with the forty to fifty million thalers which it
would cost, it would be better to build a second fleet. The
reasons advanced against me in the suit for the royal

[1] That is at the date of the writing of these Reminiscences, 1891-92.
[2] Moltke's speeches. *Werke*, vii. 25.

decision weighed more with the King because of the great regard his Majesty had for the military authorities than because of their intrinsic value. They culminated in the argument that so costly a public work as the canal would require for its protection in time of war a number of troops which could not be withdrawn from the army without weakening it. The number of men we should require to have at our disposal for the protection of the canal in the event of the Danes co-operating with a landing of the enemy was estimated at 60,000 men. I objected that we should always need to protect Kiel (with its suburbs), Hamburg, and the road from the latter to Berlin, even if there were no canal in existence. Owing to the excessive pressure of other business and the manifold struggles of the 'seventies, I could not apply the time and energy necessary to overcome the resistance offered by these authorities to my project in the imperial councils, and the matter was pigeon-holed. I ascribe the resistance I experienced principally to that military jealousy with which in 1866, 1870, and also later, I had to maintain struggles that were more painful to my feelings than most others.

In my endeavours to win the Emperor's consent I rather gave prominence to the military considerations likely to appeal to him than to any political advantages on commercial grounds. The Dutch navy had the advantage of being able to use inland canals which allowed a passage for the largest vessels. Our corresponding need of a communication by canals is essentially increased by the existence of the Danish peninsula and the division of our fleet between two separate seas. If our united fleet can issue from the harbour of Kiel, from the mouth of the Elbe, and even, if the canal is lengthened, from the Jahde also, without a blockading foe being aware of it beforehand, the latter would be compelled to maintain a squadron equivalent to our whole fleet in each of the seas. On this and other grounds I was of opinion that the making of the canal would be more advantageous for the defence of our coasts than if we applied the cost of it to building fortresses and enlarging our fleet, especially as we had not unlimited resources for manning our fleet. My wish was to continue the canal from the lower Elbe so far in a westerly direction that the mouths of the Weser, the Jahde, and eventually also of the Ems, could be made into *sortie* ports which the blockading enemy would have to observe. The western continuation of the canal would be comparatively less costly than the cutting through of the backbone of the Holstein peninsula ; inasmuch as there are lines of uniform elevation, by means of which we could turn the high ground of the Geest on the promontory between the Weser and the mouth of the Elbe.

In view of a blockade, presumably by the French, the protection of Heligoland by the neutrality of England has till now been to our advantage ; a French squadron could have no coal depôt there, but would be obliged, in order to get supplies, to return to a French port at regular and not too long intervals, or would have to maintain a large number of tenders constantly going backwards and forwards. Now we should have to defend the rock with our own forces if we wished to hinder the French from gaining a firm footing there in case of war. What the reasons were that relaxed the resistance of the Committee of National Defence in the year 1885, I do not know. Perhaps Count Moltke had in the meantime convinced himself that the idea of an alliance between Germany and Denmark, which he had formerly entertained, was impracticable.

CHAPTER XX

NIKOLSBURG

ON the evening of June 30, 1866, his Majesty, together with the headquarters, entered Reichenberg. The town, with a population of 28,000, contained 1,800 Austrian prisoners, and was occupied by no more than 500 Prussian artillerymen armed with old carbines. Only a few leagues off lay the Saxon cavalry. They could have reached Reichenberg in a night, and carried off the whole of our headquarters, his Majesty included. Thanks to the telegraph, it was generally known that we had our quarters at Reichenberg. I took the liberty of calling the King's attention to the fact, and in consequence the command was given for the artillerymen to repair singly, and without attracting attention, to the castle, where the King had his quarters. The military set were offended at this interference of mine; and in order to prove to them that my concern was not for *my own* security, I quitted the castle (whither his Majesty had commanded me) and retained my quarters in the town. This was the germ of a bad feeling towards me on the part of the military authorities on account of my personal position towards the King, which proceeded from departmental jealousy, and was destined to develop still further in the course of this campaign and of the French war.

After the battle of Königgrätz the situation was such that a favourable response on our part to the first advances of Austria with a view to peace negotiations, was not only possible, but seemed demanded by the interference of France. The latter dates from the telegram, addressed to his Majesty, which arrived at Hořicz * between July 4 and 5, in which Louis Napoleon informed the King that the Emperor Francis Joseph had ceded Venetia to him, and had invited his intervention. The brilliant success of the King's arms compelled Napoleon to quit [1] the reserve he had hitherto maintained. This interference was evoked by our victory ; up to this time Napoleon had calculated on our being defeated and in need of assistance. If on our part the victory of Königgrätz had been utilised to the utmost by the attack of General von Etzel, and by the energetic pursuit of the defeated foe by means of our cavalry, which was still intact, in all probability the mission of General von Gablenz to the Prussian headquarters would even then have led to the conclusion not merely of an armistice, but also to the bases of the future peace, considering the moderation which prevailed on our part, and was at that time still shared by the King, in respect to the conditions of peace—a moderation which, however, even then claimed more from Austria than was of any use, and which would have left us as our future associates all the states which had hitherto been members of the Confederation, but with their territories diminished and their feelings offended. At my suggestion his Majesty sent to the Emperor a reply which was dilatory, but yet rejected any armistice which did not contain guarantees for peace.

Subsequently, at Nikolsburg, I asked General von Moltke what he would do if France actively intervened.

---

* So written by the general staff. It is pronounced Horsitz.

[1] See the text of the telegram in L. Schneider, i. 253 &c.

His reply was: 'I should adopt a defensive attitude towards Austria, confining myself to the line of the Elbe, and in the meantime prosecuting the war actively against France.'

This opinion confirmed me still more in my resolution to advise his Majesty to make peace on the basis of the territorial integrity of Austria. I was of opinion that, in case of French interference, we must either make peace with Austria, imposing moderate conditions, and at the same time if possible contract an alliance with her with a view to an attack on France, or else we must quickly and completely cripple Austria by a sharp onslaught, and also by furthering disaffection in Hungary, and perhaps in Bohemia as well; until then we must maintain a defen- sive attitude towards France instead of towards Austria, as Moltke wished. I believed that the war against France, which Moltke said he would conduct first of all, and that rapidly, would not be so easy; that France had, indeed, but little strength left to take the offensive, but, judging from historical experience, would soon be strong enough to act on the defensive in the country itself, and so spin the war out. Then, perhaps, we should not be able victoriously to maintain our defensive against Austria on the Elbe if we had to carry on a war of invasion in France, with Austria and South Germany as hostile elements in our rear. I was moved by this prospect to still livelier exertions in the cause of peace.

A participation on France's part in the war would have brought, at the moment, perhaps only 60,000 French troops (perhaps still less) into the struggle in Germany. Nevertheless, this accession of strength to the South German federal army would have sufficed to restore energy and unity of command, probably under a

French commander-in-chief. The Bavarian army alone, at the time of the suspension of hostilities, was said to be 100,000 strong, and, with the other available German troops, all of them good and brave soldiers, and 60,000 Frenchmen, we should have been brought face to face with an army of 200,000 men from the south-west, under united and vigorous French leadership, instead of the former timid and disunited troops ; and we should have had no equivalent forces with which to meet them in front of Berlin without weakening ourselves in the direction of Vienna. Mainz was occupied by federal troops under the command of the Bavarian general, Count Rechberg ; had the French once got into the place it would have taken hard work to get them out again.

Under the pressure of the French intervention, and at a time when it was impossible to see whether we should succeed in making head against them in the field of diplomacy, I resolved to advise the King to make an appeal to the Hungarian nationality. If Napoleon intervened in the war in the manner indicated, if Russia's attitude remained doubtful, and especially if the cholera made further ravages in our ranks, our position might become so difficult that we should be obliged[1] to seize every weapon offered us by the outbreak of the national movement, not only in Germany, but also in Hungary and Bohemia, in order to avoid succumbing.

On July 12, in our quarters at Czernahora, there was held a council of war—or as the military preferred to

[1] Cf. the statement in the speech of January 16, 1874, *Politische Reden*, vi. 140.

call it, a meeting to hear the reports of the generals; for the sake of brevity, however, and in order to be more intelligible, I make use of the former expression, which von Roon * also uses, although Field-Marshal Moltke, in a paper sent to Professor von Treitschke on May 9, 1881, has observed that no ' council of war ' was held in either of the wars.[1]

In 1866, whenever I was within reach, I was included in these deliberations, which were held under the presidency of the King, at first regularly and afterwards at longer intervals. On this particular occasion we discussed the direction of our further advance upon Vienna. I arrived late at the discussion, and the King explained to me that the point before them was how to capture the fortifications of the Floridsdorf lines in order to reach Vienna; that to do this the nature of the works demanded that heavy artillery should be brought up from Magdeburg,[†] and that for this a fortnight's time would be necessary. After breaches had been made, the works would have to be stormed, and for this the probable loss was reckoned at 2,000 men. The King asked for my opinion on the question. My first impression was that we could not lose a fortnight without bringing at least the danger of *French* interference very much nearer than it otherwise

* In his letter to his wife of February 7, 1871. *Denkwürdigkeiten*, iii.[4] 297.

[1] See Moltke, *Gesammelte Schriften*, iii. 415 &c.

† In the work by the general staff we read under the date July 14 (p. 484): Colonel Mertens was telegraphed to at Dresden to have in readiness fifty heavy guns that were on their way thither [and consequently, it is to be presumed, had not yet arrived], so that they could be sent off without loss of time by the railroad as soon as the order for them came. The railway on the other side of Lundenburg was destroyed. General von Hindersin was therefore ordered to bring together a park of transport material at the place indicated.

would be.* I laid stress on my apprehension, and said :
' We cannot spend fourteen days in waiting without considerably increasing the dead-weight of the French *arbi-*
trium. I asked whether we were obliged to storm the
Floridsdorf fortifications at all, or if we could not take them
in flank—by making a quarter wheel to the left we could
make for Pressburg and there the Danube could be crossed
with less trouble. The Austrians would then either accept
battle in an unfavourable position south of the Danube
with their front to the east, or would retreat upon Hungary,
and then Vienna could be taken without drawing a sword.
The King asked for a map, and gave his decision in
favour of this proposal. The execution of the plan was
adopted, unwillingly as it appeared to me, but it was
nevertheless carried out.

According to the work of the general staff (p. 522) the
following order from the general headquarters was issued
on July 19 : ' It is the intention of his Majesty the
King to concentrate the army in a position behind the
Russbach. In this situation the army will first of all be
in a position to resist an attack which the enemy might
undertake with about 150,000 men from Floridsdorf.
Afterwards, it can, from this position, either reconnoitre
and attack the Floridsdorf entrenchments, or, leaving
behind a corps of observation before Vienna, march off
as quickly as possible to Pressburg. Both armies will push
forward their advance-guards and reconnoitring parties to
the Russbach in the direction of Wolkersdorf and Deutsch-
Wagram. Simultaneously with this advance, an attempt
will be made to take Pressburg by surprise, and there to
secure if necessary the passage of the troops across the
Danube.'

* The situation was similar to what it was in 1870 before Paris.

It was my object, in view of our subsequent relations with Austria, as far as possible to avoid cause for mortifying reminiscences, if it could be managed without prejudice to our German policy. A triumphant entry of the Prussian army into the hostile capital would naturally have been a gratifying recollection for our soldiers, but it was not necessary to our policy. It would have left behind it, as also any surrender of ancient possessions to us must have done, a wound to the pride of Austria, which, without being a pressing necessity for us, would have unnecessarily increased the difficulty of our future mutual relations. It was already quite clear to me that we should have to defend the conquests of the campaign in further wars, just as Frederick the Great had to defend the results of his two first Silesian wars in the fiercer fire of the Seven Years' war. That a war with France would succeed that with Austria, lay in the logic of history, even had we been able to allow the Emperor Napoleon the petty expenses which he looked for from us as a reward for his neutrality. As regards Russia, too, it is doubtful what would happen if it were then made clear to her what accession of strength the national development of Germany would bring to us. We could not foresee how far the later wars would make for the maintenance of what had already been won; but in any case it would be of great importance whether the feeling we left behind in our opponents were implacable or the wounds we had inflicted upon them and their self-respect were incurable. Moved by this consideration, I had a political motive for avoiding, rather than bringing about, a triumphal entry into Vienna in the Napoleonic style. In positions such as ours was then, it is a political maxim after a victory not to enquire how much you can squeeze out of your opponent,

but only to consider what is politically necessary. The
ill-feeling which my attitude earned for me in military
circles I considered was the result of a military departmental policy to which I could not concede a decisive
influence on the policy of the state and its future.

When it came to the point of dealing with Napoleon's
telegram of July 4, the King had sketched out the conditions of peace as follows : a reform of the Federation
under the headship of Prussia ; the acquisition of
Schleswig-Holstein, Austrian Silesia, a strip on the
frontier of Bohemia, and East Friesland ; the substitution
of the respective heirs-apparent for the hostile sovereigns
of Hanover, Electoral Hesse, Meiningen, and Nassau.
Subsequently other demands were advanced, which partly
originated with the King himself, and were partly due
to external influences. The King wished to annex parts
of Saxony, Hanover, Hesse, and especially to bring Anspach and Baireuth again into the possession of his house.
The reacquisition of the Franconian principalities touched
his strong and justifiable family sentiment very nearly.

At one of the first Court entertainments at which I
was present in the 'thirties, a fancy ball at the residence
of Prince William, as he then was, I recollect seeing him
in the costume of the Elector Frederick I. The choice
of this dress, so different in character from the others,
was the expression of family sentiment, of the pride of
descent—and seldom can this costume have appeared
more natural and becoming than it was when worn by
Prince William, then in his thirty-seventh year ; and I
have always had a lively recollection of his appearance in
it. This strong dynastic family feeling was perhaps still
more sharply marked in the Emperor Frederick III, but
it is certain that in 1866 the King felt it harder to

renounce his claims upon Anspach and Baireuth than to
give up Austria and Silesia, German Bohemia, and parts
of Saxony.   I gauged the proposed acquisitions from
Austria and Bavaria by the question, whether the inhabitants, in case of future war, would remain faithful to the
King of Prussia in the event of the withdrawal of the
Prussian officials and troops, and continue to accept
commands from him ; and I had not the impression that
the population of these districts, which had become habi-
tuated to Bavarian and Austrian conditions, would be
disposed to meet Hohenzollern predilections.

The old original seat of the Brandenburg Margraves to
the south and east of Nuremberg, if formed, let us say,
into a Prussian province with Nuremberg as its capital,
would scarcely be a part of the country which Prussia in
case of war could denude of troops and leave under the
protection of its devotion to the ruling house.   During
the short period of the Prussian occupation dynastic
feeling had taken no very deep root in the province
despite the skilful administration of Hardenberg, and
had since then been completely forgotten during the subsequent Bavarian period, except where it was kept in
remembrance by religious agencies ; this occurred but
seldom and never lasted long.   Even if occasionally the
feelings of the Bavarian Protestants were offended, their
sensibility on the point had never expressed itself in the
shape of a recollection of Prussia.   Moreover, after such
an excision, the Bavarian stock, from the Alps to the
Upper Palatinate, in the exasperation caused by such a
mutilation of the kingdom, would always have to be regarded as an element difficult to appease and dangerous
to future unity in proportion to its indwelling strength.
Nevertheless I did not succeed at Nikolsburg in getting

the King to accept my views as to the peace we were to conclude. I was therefore obliged to let Herr von der Pfordten, who had arrived there on July 24, travel back empty-handed, and had to content myself with a criticism of his attitude before the war. He was nervous about giving up Austrian support altogether, although he would very readily have withdrawn himself from the influence of Vienna if it could have been done without danger; but the old tendencies of the Confederation of the Rhine, or reminiscences of the position which the minor German states had occupied under French protection from 1806 to 1814, had no place in his mind—in short, an honest and erudite, but politically by no means adroit, German professor. These considerations, which influenced me as regards the Franconian principalities, I insisted upon to his Majesty with regard to Austrian Silesia as well, which was one of the most loyal provinces of the Austrian Empire, and had, moreover, a preponderance of the Slavonic element in its population. I also insisted upon it with regard to the Bohemian districts, Reichenberg, the Eger valley, and Carlsbad, which the King, at the instance of Prince Frederick Charles, wanted to retain as a *glacis* in front of the Saxon mountains. To this was to be added that Karolyi later categorically refused every cession of territory, even down to the tiny district of Braunau which I had mentioned to him, and the possession of which had some importance in the interest of our railways. I preferred to renounce our claim even to that, if insistence upon it threatened to delay a conclusion of preliminaries and accentuate the danger of French interference.

The King's wish to retain West Saxony, Leipzig, Zwickau, and Chemnitz, in order to establish communica-

tion with Baireuth, collided with Karolyi's declaration
that he must insist upon the integrity of Saxony as a
conditio sine qua non of the conditions of peace. This
difference in Austria's treatment of her allies was due to
the personal relations of the Emperor of Austria and the
King of Saxony; and also to the behaviour of the Saxon
troops after the battle of Königgrätz, for during the retreat
they had been the steadiest and least broken body of
troops in the army. The other German troops had fought
bravely, when they were actually engaged, but this happened too late, and without practical result, and there prevailed in Vienna an impression, which was not justified by
circumstances, that Austria had not been sufficiently supported by her allies, especially Bavaria and Wurtemberg.

The work of the general staff says (under the date
July 21): 'At Nikolsburg negotiations had been going on
for several days, the immediate object of which was a five
days' truce. The point was, above all else, to gain time
for diplomacy.* Now, when the Prussian army occupied
the Marchfeld, a fresh catastrophe was immediately impending.'

I asked Moltke if he considered our enterprise at
Pressburg as dangerous, or whether we might be free of
all concern about it. So far we had not a spot upon our
white waistcoat. If we were sure of a happy issue to it,
we must allow the battle to be fought out, and the truce
postponed by half a day; victory would naturally strengthen
our position in negotiating; otherwise it would be better
to abandon the enterprise altogether. He replied that he
considered the issue as doubtful and the operations as
risky; but in war everything was hazardous. This decided

---

* In view of the French interference, diplomacy had less time to lose
than the army.

me to recommend to the King the following arrangement
as to the truce: to suspend hostilities at midday on the
22nd and not resume them till midday on the 27th.   At
half-past seven on the morning of the 22nd, General von
Fransecky received news of the truce that was to commence
on the same day, with instructions to make his dispositions
accordingly.   The battle in which he was engaged at
Blumenau had therefore to be suspended at twelve
o'clock.

Meanwhile in my conferences with Karolyi and with
Benedetti, who, thanks to the clumsiness of our military
police in the rear of the army, had succeeded in reaching
Zwittau on the night of July 11 to 12, and there suddenly
appeared beside my bed, I had found out the conditions
on which we could procure peace.   Benedetti declared as
the basis of Napoleon's policy, that an augmentation of
Prussia to the extent of four million souls in North
Germany at the utmost, with the retention of the line of
the Main as the frontier on the south, would not entail
French intervention.   He hoped, I suppose, to form a
South German confederation affiliated to France.   Austria
withdrew from the German confederation, and was ready
to recognise all the arrangements that the King might
make in North Germany, reserving however the integrity
of Saxony.   These conditions contained all we wanted ;
that is to say, a free hand in Germany.

I was firmly resolved, in consequence of the above considerations, to make a cabinet question of the acceptance
of the peace offered by Austria.   The position was difficult.   All the generals shared the disinclination to break

off the uninterrupted course of victory; and during these days the King was more often and more readily accessible to military influences than to mine. I was the only person at headquarters who was politically responsible as a minister and forced by the exigencies of the situation to form an opinion and come to a decision without being able to lay the responsibility for the result upon any other authority, either in the shape of the decision of my colleagues or superior commands. I was just as little able as any one to foresee what shape future events would take, and the consequent judgement of the world; but I was the only one present who was under a legal obligation to hold, to utter, and to defend an opinion. This opinion I had formed after careful consideration of the future of our position in Germany and our relations to Austria; and was ready to be responsible for it and to defend it before the King. I was well aware that the general staff nicknamed me the ' Questenberg in the camp '—an identification with the *Hofkriegsrath* in ' Wallenstein,' which was not flattering to me.

On July 23, under the presidency of the King, a council of war was held, in which the question to be decided was whether we should make peace under the conditions offered or continue the war. A painful illness from which I was suffering made it necessary that the council should be held in my room. On this occasion I was the only civilian in uniform. I declared it to be my conviction that peace must be concluded on the Austrian terms, but remained alone in my opinion; the King supported the military majority. My nerves could not stand the strain which had been put upon them day and night; I got up in silence, walked into my adjoining bed-chamber and was there overcome by a violent paroxysm of tears. Meanwhile, I heard the council dispersing in the next room. I thereupon set to work to commit to paper the reasons which in my opinion spoke for the conclusion of peace; and begged the King, in the event of his not accepting the advice for which I was responsible, to relieve me of my functions as minister if the war were continued. With this document[1] I set out on the following day to explain it by word of mouth. In the antechamber I found two colonels with a report on the spread of cholera among their troops, barely half of whom were fit for service.[*] The alarming figures confirmed my resolve to make the acceptance of the Austrian terms a cabinet question. Besides my political anxieties, I feared that by transferring the operations to Hungary, the nature of that country, which was well known to me, would soon make the disease overwhelming. The climate, especially in August, is dangerous; there is great lack of water; the country villages are widely distributed, each with many square miles of open field attached; and, finally, plums and melons grow there in abundance. Our campaign of 1792 in Champagne was in my mind as a warning example; on that occasion it was not the French but dysentery that caused our retreat. Armed with my document I unfolded to the King the political and military reasons which opposed the continuation of the war.

We had to avoid wounding Austria too severely; we had to avoid leaving behind in her any unnecessary bitterness of feeling or desire for revenge; we ought rather to reserve the possibility of becoming friends again with our adversary of the moment, and in any case to regard the

---

[1] Partly printed in Sybel, v. 294.

[*] During the campaign 6,427 men succumbed to this disease.

Austrian state as a piece on the European chessboard and the renewal of friendly relations with her as a move open to us. If Austria were severely injured, she would become the ally of France and of every other opponent of ours ; she would even sacrifice her anti-Russian interests for the sake of revenge on Prussia.

On the other hand, I could see no future acceptable to us for the countries constituting the Austrian monarchy, in case the latter were split up by risings of the Hungarians and Slavs or made permanently dependent on those peoples. What would be put in that portion of Europe which the Austrian state from Tyrol to the Bukowina had hitherto occupied ? Fresh formations on this surface could only be of a permanently revolutionary nature. German Austria we could neither wholly nor partly make use of. The acquisition of provinces like Austrian Silesia and portions of Bohemia could not strengthen the Prussian state ; it would not lead to an amalgamation of German Austria with Prussia, and Vienna could not be governed from Berlin as a mere dependency.

If the war were continued, the probable theatre would be Hungary. The Austrian army which, if we crossed the Danube at Pressburg, would not be able to hold Vienna, would scarcely retreat southwards, where it would be caught between the Prussian and Italian armies, and, by its approach to Italy, once more revive the military ardour of the Italians which, already depressed, had been restricted by Louis Napoleon ; it would retreat towards the east, and continue its defence in Hungary—if only in the expectation of the prospective intervention of France and the weakening of Italy's interest in the matter, through France's agency. Moreover I held, even from

a purely military standpoint, and according to my knowledge of Hungarian territory, that a prosecution of the
war there would not repay us, and that the successes to
be won there would be out of all proportion to the
victories we had hitherto gained, and consequently be
calculated to diminish our *prestige*—quite apart from the
fact that the prolongation of the war would pave the way
for a French intervention. We must finish off rapidly ;
before France won time to bring further diplomatic action
to bear upon Austria.

To all this the King raised no objection, but declared
the actual terms inadequate, without, however, definitely
formulating his own demands. Only so much was clear,
that his claims had grown considerably since July 4.
He said that the chief culprit could not be allowed to
escape unpunished, and that justice once satisfied, we
could let the misguided partners off more easily, and he
insisted on the cessions of territory from Austria which
I have already mentioned. I replied that we were not
there to sit in judgement, but to pursue the German
policy. Austria's conflict in rivalry with us was no more
culpable than ours with her ; *our task was the establishment or initiation of German national unity under the
leadership of the King of Prussia.*

Passing on to the German states, he spoke of various
acquisitions by cutting down the territories of all our
opponents. I repeated that we were there not to administer
retributive justice, but to pursue a policy ; that I wished
to avoid, in the German federation of the future, the
sight of mutilated territories, whose princes and peoples
might very easily (such is human weakness) retain a lively
wish to recover their former possessions by means of
foreign help ; such allies would be very unreliable. The

same would be the case if, for the purpose of compensating
Saxony, Würzburg or Nuremberg were demanded of
Bavaria, a plan, moreover, which would interfere with the
dynastic predilection of his Majesty for Anspach.   I
had also to resist plans which were aimed at an enlargement of the Grand Duchy of Baden, the annexation of
the Bavarian Palatinate, and an extension in the region
of the lower Main. The Aschaffenburg district of Bavaria
was at the same time regarded as a fit compensation to
Hesse-Darmstadt for the loss of Upper Hesse, which
would result from the projected Main frontier.   Later, at
Berlin, the only part of this plan still under negotiation
was the cession of that portion of Bavarian territory which
lay on the right bank of the Main, inclusive of the town
of Baireuth, to Prussia ; the question then arose whether
the boundary should run on the Northern or Red Main
or the Southern or White Main.   What seemed to me to
be paramount with his Majesty was the aversion of the
military party to interrupt the victorious course of the
army.   The resistance which I was obliged, in accordance
with my convictions, to offer to the King's views with
regard to following up the military successes, and to his
inclination to continue the victorious advance, excited
him to such a degree that a prolongation of the discussion became impossible ; and, under the impression
that my opinion was rejected, I left the room with
the idea of begging the King to allow me, in my capacity
of officer, to join my regiment. On returning to my room
I was in the mood that the thought occurred to me
whether it would not be better to fall out of the open
window, which was four storeys high ; and I did not look
round when I heard the door open, although I suspected
that the person entering was the Crown Prince, whose room

in the same corridor I had just passed. I felt his hand on
my shoulder, while he said : 'You know that I was
against this war. You considered it necessary, and the
responsibility for it lies on you. If you are now persuaded that our end is attained, and peace must now be
concluded, I am ready to support you and defend your
opinion with my father.' He then repaired to the King,
and came back after a short half-hour, in the same calm,
friendly mood, but with the words : 'It has been a very
difficult business, but my father has consented.' This
consent found expression in a note written with lead
pencil on the margin of one of my last memoranda,
something to this effect : 'Inasmuch as my Minister-
President has left me in the lurch in the face of the enemy,
and here I am not in a position to supply his place, I have
discussed the question with my son ; and as he has associated himself with the Minister-President's opinion, I find
myself reluctantly compelled, after such brilliant victories
on the part of the army, to bite this sour apple and accept
so disgraceful a peace.' I do not think I am mistaken as
to the exact words, although the document is not accessible
to me at present. In any case I have given the sense of
it ; and, despite its bitterness of expression, it was to me
a joyful release from a tension that was becoming un-
bearable. I gladly accepted the royal assent to what
I regarded as politically necessary without taking offence
at its ungracious form. At this time military impressions
were dominant in the King's mind ; and the strong need
he felt of pursuing the hitherto dazzling course of victory
perhaps influenced him more than political and diplomatic considerations.

The only residuum that the above note of the King's,
which the Crown Prince brought me, left in my mind

was the recollection of the violent agitation into which
I had been obliged to put my old master, in order to
obtain what I considered essential to the interests of the
country if I were to remain responsible. To this day
these and similar occurrences have left no other impression upon me than the painful recollection that I had
been obliged to vex a master whom personally I loved
as I did him.

After the preliminaries with Austria had been signed,
the plenipotentiaries of Wurtemberg, Baden, and Darm-
stadt appeared. I refused for the present to receive the
Wurtemberg minister, Varnbüler, because our irritation
against him was much stronger than it was against
Pfordten. Politically he was more skilful than the latter,
but, on the other hand, less fettered by German national
scruples. His temper at the outbreak of the war had
expressed itself in a ' Væ victis ! ' and was to be explained
by the relations between Stuttgart and France, which
were chiefly maintained by the partiality of the Queen of
Holland, a Wurtemberg princess.

As long as I remained at Frankfort she took much
interest in me, encouraging me in my opposition to
Austrian policy, and further evincing her anti-Austrian
sentiments by singling me out with an obvious purpose
for marked favour at the house of her envoy Herr von
Scherff, and not without discourtesy towards the Austrian
envoy-president, Baron Prokesch, at a time when Louis
Napoleon still cherished the hope of a Prussian alliance
against Austria, and already had the Italian war in his
mind. I leave it undecided whether even at that time

the predilection for Napoleonic France alone dictated the policy of the Queen of Holland, or if it were only the restless desire to meddle in politics at any price that led her to take sides in the struggle between Prussia and Austria, and moved her to a conspicuously bad treatment of my Austrian colleague and to a marked preference of me. Anyhow, after 1866 I found the Princess, who in former days had been so gracious to me, among the keenest opponents of the policy which I was following in anticipation of the breach of 1870. It was in the year 1867 that suspicion was first thrown upon us in French official statements of having designs on Holland, especially in the expression of the Minister Rouher in a speech against Thiers, March 16, 1867, to the effect that France would not tolerate our advance to the Zuider Zee. It is not probable that the Zuider Zee had been discovered by the French themselves, or even that the orthography of the name was correctly given in the French press without foreign help. It is allowable to conjecture that the thought of this piece of water was suggested to French suspicion from Holland. Even the Netherland descent of M. Drouyn de Lhuys does not entitle me to presume in his colleague so exact a local knowledge of geography outside the French frontier.

As I assigned the policy of Wurtemberg to the Rhine-confederation category, I determined for the time to decline to receive Herr von Varnbüler at Nikolsburg. Moreover, a conversation between us which was brought about by the intervention of Prince Frederick of Wurtemberg—brother of the commander of our Guards— and the Grand Princess Helene who was very kindly disposed towards us, was barren of political result. I did not negotiate with Herr von Varnbüler till a later date at Berlin; and his mobile susceptibility to the political impressions of every situation showed itself in the fact that he was the first of the South German ministers with whom I could conclude the well-known treaty of alliance.

CHAPTER XXI

THE NORTH GERMAN *BUND*

AT Berlin I was ostensibly occupied with Prussia's relations to the newly acquired provinces and the other North
German states, but in reality with the humour of the
foreign Powers and in pondering upon their probable
attitude.   To me, and perhaps to every one, our internal
affairs had a provisional and immature aspect.   The
reaction of the aggrandisement of Prussia, of the impending negotiations concerning the North German Confederation and its constitution, made our internal development
appear to be carried along by the current as much as our
relations to foreign states, whether in or outside Germany,
in consequence of the European situation prevailing when
the war had been interrupted.   I took it as assured that war
with France would necessarily have to be waged on the
road to our further national development, for our development at home as well as the extension beyond the Main,
and that we must keep this eventuality in sight in all our
domestic as well as in our foreign relations.   In some
aggrandisement of Prussia in North Germany Louis Napoleon saw not only no danger to France, but a means against
the unification and national development of Germany; he
believed that the non-Prussian portions of Germany would
then feel a greater need of French support.   He cherished
reminiscences of the confederation of the Rhine, and
wished to hinder development in the direction of a United

Germany. He believed that he could do this because he did not realise the national drift of the time, and judged the situation in accordance with his schoolboy reminiscences of South Germany, and from diplomatic reports which were only based on ministerial moods and sporadic dynastic feeling. I was convinced that their importance would vanish; I assumed that a United Germany was only a question of time, that the North German Confederation was only the first step in its solution; but that the enmity of France and perhaps of Russia, Austria's need of revenge for 1866, and the King's Prussian and dynastic particularism must not be called too soon into the lists. I did not doubt that a Franco-German war must take place before the construction of a United Germany could be realised. I was at that time preoccupied with the idea of delaying the outbreak of this war until our fighting strength should be increased by the application of the Prussian military legislation not only to Hanover, Hesse, and Holstein, but, as I could hope even at that time from the observation I had made, to the South Germans. I considered a war with France, having regard to the success of the French in the Crimean war and in Italy, as a danger which I at that time over-estimated; inasmuch as I imagined the attainable number of troops in France, their order and organisation, and the tactical skill, to be higher and better than proved to be the case in 1870. The courage of the French soldiers, the high pitch of national sentiment and of injured vanity, were verified to the full extent, as I had estimated them in the eventuality of a German invasion in France, based on a remembrance of the experiences of 1814, of 1792, and of the Spanish War of Succession at the beginning of last century, when the invasion of foreign armies always produced phenomena like putting a stick into an ant-heap.

I at no time regarded a war with France as a simple matter, considered quite apart from the possible allies that France might find in Austria's thirst for revenge, or in Russia's desire for a balance of power. My strenuous efforts to postpone the outbreak of war until the effect of our military legislation and our military training could be thoroughly developed in all portions of the country which had been newly joined to Prussia, were therefore quite reasonable ; and this aim of mine was not even approximately reached in the Luxemburg question in 1867. Each year's postponement of the war would add 100,000 trained soldiers to our army. In the attitude I took up towards the King on the question of the bill of indemnity, and in dealing with the question of the constitution in the Prussian Diet, I felt the urgent necessity of letting other countries see no trace of actual or prospective obstacles consequent on our internal condition ; I wished to offer them the spectacle of a united national sentiment ; and the more so inasmuch as it was impossible to judge what allies France would have on her side in a war against us. The negotiations and *rapprochements* between France and Austria soon after 1866, at Salzburg and elsewhere, under the direction of Herr von Beust, might prove successful ; and the very appointment of that Saxon minister in a bad temper to the control of Viennese policy already pointed to the probability that it would take the direction of revenge.

Italy's attitude was not to be reckoned upon as soon as French pressure was applied, as we discovered by her submissiveness to Napoleon in 1866. During a conference I had with General Govone in Berlin, in the early part of

1866, he was horrified when I expressed the wish that
he should enquire at home if we could rely on Italy's
loyalty to her engagements even against Napoleonic ill-
humour. He replied that a question of this kind would
be telegraphed to Paris the very same day with the question : 'What answer shall be given?' To judge by the
attitude of Italian policy during the war, I could not
place any definite reliance on public opinion in Italy, not
only on the ground of Victor Emmanuel's personal friendship to Louis Napoleon, but also by the standard of the
partisanship announced by Garibaldi in the name of Italian
public opinion. Not only my apprehensions, but the
public opinion of Europe considered that a league of Italy
with France and Russia was not outside the bounds of
probability.

From Russia active support of such a coalition
was scarcely to be expected. By the influence which
during the time of the Crimean war I had been able to
exercise in favour of Russia on the resolutions of King
Frederick William IV, I had gained for myself the good-
will of the Emperor Alexander, and his confidence in
me was strengthened during my residence as ambassador
in St. Petersburg. Meanwhile, in the Russian cabinet,
under the leadership of Gortchakoff, the doubt as to the
advantage for Russia of so important an increase of
Prussian power began to outweigh the Emperor's friendship for King William and his gratitude for our policy
during the Polish question of 1863. If the communication be accurate which was made by Drouyn de Lhuys
to Count Vitzthum von Eckstädt,[1] then in July 1866
Gortchakoff invited France to a common protest against
the overthrow of the German confederation, and experi-

---

[1] *London, Gastein and Sadowa*, Stuttgart, 1890, p. 248.

enced a rebuff. In his first feeling of surprise, immediately upon the dispatch of Manteuffel to St. Petersburg, the Emperor Alexander had acquiesced in the result of the Nikolsburg preliminaries in general and *obiter*. At first the hatred against Austria, which, since the time of the Crimean war, had dominated the public opinion of Russian ' society,' had found satisfaction in her defeat; this feeling, however, was opposed to such Russian interests as were connected with the Czar's influence in Germany and the dangers with which it was threatened by France.

I took it indeed for granted that we could count on Russian support against any coalition that France might form against us ; but that we should not receive it till we had had the misfortune to suffer defeats, by which the question whether Russia could tolerate the proximity of a victorious Franco-Austrian coalition on her Polish frontiers would be brought nearer. The inconvenience of such a neighbour would perhaps be increased if, instead of the anti-papal kingdom of Italy, the Papacy itself were to become a third in the league of the two great Catholic Powers. I considered it, however, probable, that until the nearer approach of a danger such as would result from Prussian defeat, Russia would not be displeased, or at all events would offer no interference, if a numerically superior coalition had poured a little water into our wine of 1866.

From England we certainly could rely on no active support against the Emperor Napoleon, although English policy required a strong and friendly continental Power with many battalions, and this necessity had been attended to under the Pitts, father and son, to the advantage of Prussia, later to that of Austria, then under Palmerston, until the Spanish marriages, and afterwards again under Clarendon, in favour of France. The requirement of England's policy was either an *entente cordiale* with France, or the possession of a strong ally against the enmity of France. England is, indeed, ready to accept the stronger German-Prussia in place of Austria; and during the situation of the autumn of 1866 we could in any case count upon platonic goodwill and didactic newspaper articles from over there; but this theoretical sympathy would scarcely have condensed itself into an active support by land and by sea. The occurrences of 1870 have shown my estimation of England to have been correct. The representation of France in North Germany was undertaken in London with a readiness which was at least mortifying to us; and during the war England never compromised herself so far in our favour as thereby to endanger her friendship with France: on the contrary.

It was chiefly under the influence of these reflections in the sphere of our foreign policy that I determined to regulate the movements of our home policy in accordance with the question whether it would support or injure impressions of the power and coherence of the state. I argued to myself that our first great aim must be independence and security in our foreign relations; that to this end not only was actual removal of internal dissensions requisite, but also any appearance of such a thing must be avoided in the sight of the foreign Powers and of Germany; that, if we first gained independence of foreign influence, we should then be able to move freely in our internal development, and to organise our institutions in as liberal or reactionary a manner as should seem right and fitting; that we might adjourn all domestic questions until we had secured our national aims abroad. I never doubted the possibility of giving to the royal power the strength necessary in order that our clock should be correctly set at home, provided that we first secured the necessary freedom from without to live as an independent great nation. Until that should be accomplished I was ready, if necessary, to pay ' black-mail ' to the Opposition, in order to be in a position in the first place to throw into the scale our full power, and diplomatically to use the appearance of this united power and, in case of need, even to have the possibility of letting loose national revolutionary movements against our enemies.

At a meeting of one of the committees of the Prussian Diet a question was asked by the Progressist party, and, I suspect, not without knowledge of the efforts of the Extreme Right, whether the government was prepared to introduce the Prussian Constitution in the New Provinces. An evasive answer would have aroused, or would have animated, the distrust of the constitutional parties. I was firmly convinced that it was imperative not to obstruct the development of the German question by any doubts as to the loyalty of the government to the Constitution; that every fresh dissension between the government and the Opposition would have strengthened the resistance to our new national structure which we had to expect from abroad. Thereupon I strove to convince the Opposition and its speakers that they would do well for the present to allow all domestic constitutional questions to remain in the background; that the German nation, when once united, would be in a position to settle her internal affairs as she thought best; that it was our present task to place the nation in this position; but all these considerations were useless in face of the narrow-minded provincial party politics of the Opposition leaders, while the discussions raised by them placed the national aim too much in the front not only in the sight of foreign countries, but also in that of the King, who at that time still looked more to the power and greatness of Prussia than to the constitutional union of Germany. He was wholly free from any ambitious calculations in the direction of Germany. Even in 1870 he described the title of Emperor contemptuously as a ' fancy-dress major,' whereupon I answered, that his Majesty certainly already by the Constitution held the full prerogatives of the position, and that the title of Emperor merely implied the outward sanction; to some extent, as if an officer, who was commissioned to take charge of a regiment, were definitely appointed to the command. It was more flattering to his dynastic feeling to exercise this power simply as the born King of Prussia, than as an Emperor who had been elected and set up by a constitution—just as a prince who commands a regiment prefers to be addressed as your Royal Highness, and not as Colonel; and a lieutenant who is a count as Count and not as Lieutenant. I had to take these peculiarities of my master into account if I wished to retain his confidence; and without him and his confidence my way in German politics would have been impassable.

Looking to the necessity, in a fight against an overwhelming foreign Power, of being able, in extreme need, to use even revolutionary means, I had had no hesitation whatever in throwing into the frying-pan, by

means of the circular dispatch of June 10, 1866, the most
powerful ingredient known at that time to liberty-
mongers, namely, universal suffrage, so as to frighten
off foreign monarchies from trying to stick a finger into
our national omelette. I never doubted that the German
people would be strong and clever enough to free themselves from the existing suffrage as soon as they realised
that it was a harmful institution. If it cannot, then
my saying that Germany can ride when once she has
got into the saddle [1] was erroneous. The acceptance of
universal suffrage was a weapon in the war against Austria
and other foreign countries, in the war for German Unity,
as well as a threat to use the last weapons in a struggle
against coalitions. In a war of this sort, when it becomes
a matter of life and death, one does not look at the weapons
that one seizes, nor the value of what one destroys in
using them : one is guided at the moment by no other
thought than the issue of the war, and the preservation
of one's external independence ; the settling of affairs and
reparation of the damage has to take place after the
peace. Moreover, I still hold that the principle of universal suffrage is a just one, not only in theory but also
in practice, provided always that voting be not secret,
for secrecy is a quality that is indeed incompatible with
the best characteristics of German blood.

The influence and the dependence on others that the
practical life of man brings in its train are God-given
realities which we cannot and must not ignore. If we
refuse to transfer them to political life, and base that
life on a faith in the secret insight of everybody, we
fall into a contradiction between public law and the
realities of human life which practically leads to con-

[1] Speech on March 11, 1867. *Political Speeches*, iii. 184.

stant frictions, and finally to an explosion, and to which there is no theoretical solution except by way of the insanities of social-democracy, the support given to which rests on the fact that the judgement of the masses is sufficiently stultified and undeveloped to allow them, with the assistance of their own greed, to be continually caught by the rhetoric of clever and ambitious leaders.

The counterpoise to this lies in the influence of the educated classes, which would be greatly strengthened if voting were public,* as for the Prussian Diet. It may be that the greater discretion of the more intelligent classes rests on the material basis of the preservation of their possessions. The other motive, the struggle for gain, is equally justifiable ; but a preponderance of those who represent property is more serviceable for the security and development of the state. A state, the control of which lies in the hands of the greedy, of the *novarum rerum cupidi*, and of orators who have in a higher degree than others the capacity for deceiving the unreasoning masses, will constantly be doomed to a restlessness of development, which so ponderous a mass as the commonwealth of the state cannot follow without injury to its organism. Ponderous masses, and among these the life and development of great nations must be reckoned, can only move with caution, since the road on which they travel to an unknown future has no smooth iron rails. Every great state-commonwealth that loses the prudent and restraining influence of the propertied class, whether that influence rests on material or moral grounds, will always end by being rushed along at a speed which must shatter the coach of state, as happened in the

* Secret voting was, of course, first brought into the law through Fries's motion, while the proposals of the government advocated public voting.

development of the French Revolution. The element
of greed has the preponderance arising from large masses
which in the long run must make its way. It is in
the interests of the great mass itself to wish decision
to take place without dangerous acceleration of the
speed of the coach of state, and without its destruction.
If this should happen, however, the wheel of history
will revolve again, and always in a proportionately shorter
time, to dictatorship, to despotism, to absolutism, because in the end the masses yield to the need of order;
if they do not recognise this need *a priori*, they always
realise it eventually after manifold arguments *ad hominem*;
and in order to purchase order from a dictatorship and
Cæsarism they cheerfully sacrifice that justifiable amount
of freedom which ought to be maintained, and which the
political society of Europe can endure without ill-health.

I should regard it as a serious misfortune, and as an
essential weakening of our security in the future, if we
in Germany are driven into the vortex of this French
cycle. Absolutism would be the ideal form of government
for an European political structure were not the King
and his officials ever as other men are to whom it is not
given to reign with superhuman wisdom, insight and
justice. The most experienced and well-meaning absolute
rulers are subject to human imperfections, such as over-
estimation of their own wisdom, the influence and eloquence of favourites, not to mention petticoat influence,
legitimate and illegitimate. Monarchy and the most
ideal monarch, if in his idealism he is not to be a common
danger, stand in need of criticism; the thorns of criticism
set him right when he runs the risk of losing his way.
Joseph II is a warning example of this.

Criticism can only be exercised through the medium

of a free press and parliaments in the modern sense of the term. Both correctives may easily weaken and finally lose their efficacy if they abuse their powers. To avert this is one of the tasks of a conservative policy, which cannot be accomplished without a struggle with parliament and press. The measurement of the limits within which such a struggle must be confined, if the control of the government, which is indispensable to the country, is neither to be checked nor allowed to gain a complete power, is a question of political tact and judgement.

It is a piece of good fortune for his country if a monarch possess the judgement requisite for this—a good fortune that is temporary, it is true, like all human fortune. The possibility of establishing ministers in power who possess adequate qualifications must always be granted in the constitutional organism; but also the possibility of maintaining in office ministers who satisfy these requirements in face of occasional votes of an adverse majority and of the influence of courts and camarillas. This aim, so far as human imperfections in general allow its attainment, was approximately reached under the government of William I.

The opening of the Prussian Parliament was to follow immediately upon our arrival at Berlin, and the speech from the throne was deliberated upon at Prague. Thither came deputies of the Conservative group, whose ranks during the struggle had at times dwindled down to as few as eleven members, but by the election of July 3 had, under the effect produced by the first victories before

Königgrätz, been reinforced to more than a hundred. The result would have been even more favourable to the government if the election had taken place a few days after the decisive battle; but even as it was, taken together with the enthusiastic disposition of the country, it was, at any rate, adapted to inspire hopes of success not only in Conservatives but in reactionaries also. The strengthening of the position of the monarchy that had resulted from the parliamentary situation at the outbreak of the war, and the clumsy and ambitious obstinacy of the opposition, provided those whose aim was a return to absolutism, or at least a restoration on the lines of the Estates General, with a pretext for a suspension and revision of the Prussian constitution. It was not fashioned for an enlarged Prussia, still less for being fitted into the future constitution of Germany. The charter of the constitution itself contained an article (No. 118) which—owing its existence, as it did, to the influence of the national temper at the time of the drawing up of the constitution, and borrowed from the draft of 1848—justified the subordination of the Prussian constitution to a new German constitution that had yet to be devised. An opportunity was thus given of unhinging the constitution and the efforts of the majority during the conflict after parliamentary government, with a formal appearance of legality; and this lay at the root of the exertions of the Extreme Right and the members they sent as deputies to Prague.

Another opportunity of combining the settlement of internal dissensions with that of the German question had fallen into the King's hands, when the Emperor Alexander, in 1863, at the time of the Polish rebellion and the attempt to surprise us at the Frankfort Diet of Princes, had in an autograph letter vigorously recommended an alliance between Prussia and Russia. The letter, written in the Emperor's delicate hand, over many closely-written pages, spun out at great length and in a style more declamatory than his pen possessed suggested Hamlet's words :

> ' Whether 'tis nobler in the mind to suffer
> The slings and arrows of outrageous fortune,
> Or to take arms against a sea of troubles,
> And by opposing end them ? '

but suggested them in an affirmative instead of an interrogative sense.   Its tenor was that the Emperor was tired of the chicaneries of the Western Powers and of Austria and Poland, and had determined to draw the sword and rid himself of them ; appealing to the friendship of the King, and to their common interests, he invited him to joint action, on lines similar to but wider than those of the Alvensleben convention of February of the same year.   It was difficult for the King, on the one hand, to send a refusal as his reply to his near relation and most intimate friend, or, on the other, to familiarise himself with the resolve to expose his country to the horrors of a great war, and force upon the state and the dynasty the risks contingent on such a course of action.   Moreover, that strain in his private feelings which made him inclined to take part in the Frankfort Diet of Princes—I mean his sense of being closely bound up with every old princely house— ran counter in him to the temptation to yield to the appeal of his friend and nephew, and comply with the family traditions of Prussia and Russia, a compliance which must lead to a breach in his relations with the German confederation and the collective body of the German princely houses.   In my report, which occupied

me several days, I avoided laying stress on the aspect of
affairs that would have been important in our internal
policy, because I was not of opinion that a war waged
in alliance with Russia against Austria and all the
adversaries with whom we had to fight in 1866, would
have brought us any nearer the fulfilment of our task as
a nation. It is true that war may be used as a means
of getting the better of internal difficulties—it is a device
much resorted to, especially in French politics; but in
Germany such a means would only have been practicable
if the war in question lay in the line of the national
development. To that end it would above all things
have been necessary that it should not be carried
on with Russian assistance, which public opinion even
to this day condemns in an impolitic manner. German
unity must be realised without any foreign influence,
merely by Germany's own strength. Moreover, the
conflict of mind under which the King laboured at
the time I entered the ministry, even up to the resolve
to abdicate, had considerably lost its influence over his
resolutions since he had found ministers who were ready to
represent his policy openly and without subterfuge. Since
then he had acquired the conviction that the position of the
Crown, if matters had come to the point of revolutionary
outbreak, would have been stronger; the intimidation
of the Queen and the ministers of the new era had lost its
power. On the other hand, in my statement to him I did
not conceal my estimate of the military strength that an
alliance between Germany and Russia would have,
particularly at the outset.

The geographical position of the three great Eastern
Powers is of such a kind that each of them, as soon as it
is attacked by the two others, finds itself strategically at a

disadvantage, even if she have England or France as an ally in Western Europe. The isolated power would be most at a disadvantage if Austria were exposed to a Russo-German attack; least, if it were a case of Russia against Austria and Germany; but even Russia would at the outset of a war be in a serious plight in face of a combined advance of the two German powers upon the Bug. Her geographical position and ethnographical formation set Austria at a great disadvantage in the matter of war with the two neighbouring empires, for French assistance could scarcely arrive in time to restore the balance. But whether Austria succumbed at the outset to a coalition between Russia and Germany, or whether the alliance of her opponents were broken up by some clever treaty of peace between the three Emperors, or even merely weakened in consequence of some defeat of Austria, the preponderance of Russia and Germany would in any case be decisive. Granting equally good generalship and equal bravery in the great armies, a great strength of the German-Russian combination, if it holds firmly together from the outset, lies in the conformation of the individual territories of those Powers. But calculation upon military success and belief in it are in themselves uncertain, and will become still more so if the estimated strength on this side is not homogeneous, but rests upon alliances.

In my draft of the answer, which turned out still longer than the letter of the Emperor Alexander, stress was laid upon the fact that a joint war against the Western Powers must necessarily, in its final development, by reason of the geographical conditions and of France's craving for the Rhine countries, be reduced to a war between France and Prussia; that a Prusso-Russian initiative of the war would render our position worse in

Germany; that Russia, being at a distance from the
theatre of war, would suffer less of its miseries, while
Prussia, on the other hand, would have to maintain not
only her own but likewise the Russian forces; and that
Russian policy would then—for, if my memory does not
deceive me, this is the expression I used—be sitting on
the longer arm of the lever, and, just as in the congress
of Vienna, and with still greater weight, would be able,
if we were victorious, to dictate even to us what form
our peace should take, exactly as Austria could have
done in 1859, in respect to our conditions of peace with
France, if we had then entered into the war against
France and Italy. I do not recall the text of my argument, although I had it again before me a few years ago
with reference to our explanation with Russia on policy,
and was happy to find that I then possessed sufficient
energy to draw up with my own hand so long a minute
in writing which the King could read—a manual labour
which could not have been conducive to the success of
my Gastein course. Although the King did not view the
question from the German national point of view to the
same degree as I did, he did not succumb to the temptation to ally himself with Russia in order to put a forcible
end to the arrogance of Austrian policy, and of the
majority in the Diet, and to the contempt which both
showed for the Prussian Crown. If he agreed to the
Russian demand we should probably, considering the
rapidity of our mobilisation, the strength of the Russian
army in Poland, and the military weakness of Austria at
that time, have overrun Austria, with or without the help
of Italy, whose covetousness was still unsatisfied, and
before France could afford her effective help. If one could
have been certain that the result of this overrunning

would be an imperial triple alliance, on condition of letting Austria off easily, then possibly my judgement of the situation could not appropriately have been called accurate. But this certainty, in view of the divergent interests of Russia and Austria in the East, did not exist; it was hardly probable, and by no means in conformity with Russian policy, that a victorious Prusso-Russian coalition should act towards Austria with even the measure of forbearance which was contemplated on the Prussian side in 1866, in the interest of a possible future *rapprochement.* For this reason I was afraid that, in the event of our victory, we should not agree with Russia respecting the future of Austria, and that Russia herself, after further successes against France, would not be willing to resign the chance of keeping Prussia in a dependent position on her western boundary. Least of all could any help towards a national policy in the sense of Prussian hegemony have been expected from Russia. Tilsit, Erfurt, Olmütz and other historic memories said: *Vestigia terrent.* In short, I had not confidence enough in Gortchakoff's policy, to let us reckon on the same security that Alexander I afforded in 1813, until the questions of the future came to discussion at Vienna, as to what was to become of Poland and Saxony, whether Germany had sufficient protection against French invasions independently of Russian decisions, and whether Strasburg should become a fortress of the Confederation. Such were the varied considerations I had to bear in mind in order to decide upon the proposals I wished to lay before the King and the form in which they were to be drafted. I do not doubt that the time will come when our archives will be acccessible to the public, even in respect to these transactions, whether or not in the meantime the proposal is carried out to destroy those documents which testify to my political activity.

The temptation had certainly been great for a monarch whose position was exposed to the extravagant attacks of the Radical party and to the pressure of Austrian diplomacy, not only in the national domain of the Frankfort Congress of Princes, but also in that of Poland, from the three great confederate Powers, England, France, and Austria.

That the King, in 1863, did not allow his deeply mortified feelings as monarch and as Prussian to over-master political considerations shows how strong in him were the sentiment of national honour and sound common-sense in politics.

In 1866 the King could not easily make up his mind upon the question whether he should arbitrarily break down parliamentary resistance and prevent its recurrence, so weighty were the reasons against doing so. By the suspension and revision of the Constitution, by the humiliation of the Opposition in the Diet, an effectual weapon against Prussia in the struggles looming in the future would have been placed in the hands of all those who were discontented with the events of 1866 in Germany and Austria. One would have had to be prepared meanwhile to carry out, in opposition to the parliament and the press, a system of government in Prussia which would be combated by all the rest of Germany. Measures which we should have had to take against the press would have had no validity in Dessau ; and Austria and South Germany would, meanwhile, have taken their revenge by assuming, on Liberal and National lines, the leadership which Prussia had forsaken. The National party in Prussia itself would have sympathised with the adversaries of the government. We could, indeed, have constitutionally gained an increase of strength for the monarchy within the amended boundaries of Prussia, but it would have been in the presence of fiercely dissentient domestic elements, to which the Opposition in the new provinces would have united itself. We should then have carried on a Prussian war of conquest, but the sinews of the national policy of Prussia would have been severed. In the struggle to create for the German nation, by means of unity, the possibility of an existence corresponding to its historical importance, lay the weightiest argument in justification of waging the German ' Bruderkrieg ; ' the renewal of such a war would be unavoidable if the struggle between the German stocks was simply for the sake of strengthening the separate State of Prussia.

I do not consider absolutism by any means a form of government that is desirable or successful in Germany in the long run. The Prussian Constitution, disregarding a few meaningless articles translated from that of Belgium, is in the main reasonable. It has three factors, the King and two Chambers, each of which by its vote can prevent arbitrary alterations of the legal *status quo*. This is a just apportionment of legislative power, but if the latter is emancipated from the public criticism of the press and from parliamentary control, there is increased danger of its going astray. The absolutism of the Crown is just as little tenable as the absolutism of parliamentary majorities ; the necessity for the agreement of both in every alteration of the legal *status quo* is just, and we did not need to make any important improvement in the Prussian Constitution. Government can be carried on with it, and the course of German policy would have been littered up if we had altered it in 1866. Before the victory I would never have mentioned the word 'Indemnity ; ' * but after the victory the King was in a position to make the concession magnanimously, and to conclude peace, not with his people— for it was never interrupted, as the course of the war showed—but with the section of the Opposition which had got out of harmony with the government, more from national than from party grounds.

Such were pretty nearly the thoughts and arguments with which, during the many hours' journey from Prague to Berlin, on August 4, I tried to combat the difficulties which his own views, but still more external influences, and especially the influence of the Conservative deputation, had left on the King's mind. To this was added a view of political affairs which made his Majesty regard a request for a bill of indemnity as an admission of a wrong committed.† I sought in vain to demolish this verbal and legal error by showing that in granting the indemnity there was nothing more than the recognition of the fact that the government and its royal chief, *rebus sic stantibus*, had acted correctly ; the demand for the bill of indemnity was a desire for this recognition. In all constitutional life, in the scope it allows to governments, it is a necessary condition that they cannot always find indicated in the Constitution a compulsory

* [That is, indemnity for unconstitutional action on the part of ministers during the ' Conflict ' period.]

† The statement in Roon's *Denkwürdigkeiten* (*Deutsche Revue*, 1891, vol. i. p. 133 ; edition in book form, ii. 482): ' To secure Bismarck's adhesion it was in any case decisive that he knew accurately the placable views of his King,' is erroneous.

course for every situation. The King adhered to his dislike to indemnity; while, for our parliamentary opponents, of whom at most only those who afterwards formed the party of Freethought were malevolent, while the others were merely mistaken, it appeared to me necessary to build a golden bridge, either in policy or in words, in order to restore the internal peace of Prussia, and from this solid Prussian basis to continue the German policy of the King. This interview, which lasted several hours, was very trying to me, because I had to be on my guard all the time. It took place in a railway *coupé* for three, with the King and the Crown Prince. But the latter did not support me, although by the mobile expression of his features he, at all events, strengthened me in regard to his father by the manifestation of his full agreement.

I had been in correspondence from Nikolsburg with the other ministers, so that the draft of the speech from the throne had been drawn up, and had been accepted by his Majesty, with the exception of the clause relating to the indemnity. At last, however, the King reluctantly assented to that also, and thus it was possible to open the Diet on August 5 with a speech from the throne which announced that the representatives of the country were to proceed to an *ex post facto* approval of the administration carried on without an Appropriation Act. *In verbis simus faciles!*

The next business was the regulation of our relations to the various German states with whom we had been at war. We might have done without annexations for Prussia and have sought compensation for them in the Constitution of the Confederation. But his Majesty had no stronger faith in the practical effects of clauses of the Constitution than in the old Federal Diet, and

insisted on the enlargement of Prussia in order to fill
up the gap between the east and west provinces, and
make Prussia a tenable territory in a ring-fence in case of
the failure, sooner or later, of the national reconstruction.
In the annexation of Hanover and the Electorate of
Hesse, therefore, the question was one of the establishment of a connexion effective in all eventualities between
the two divisions of the monarchy. The difficulties of
the customs connexion between our two territories, and
the attitude of Hanover in the last war, had again made
evident the need of absolute territorial cohesion in the
north, under one hand. In future wars, with Austria or
other countries, we ought not to be again exposed to the
possibility of having one or two hostile bodies of good
troops in our rear. The apprehension that matters might
some day take this shape was heightened by the excessive idea which King George V entertained of his
own mission and that of his dynasty. One is not every
day in a position to remedy a perilous situation of the
kind, and the statesman who is placed by circumstances
in a position to do so, and does not avail himself of it,
takes a great responsibility upon himself; for international policy and the right of the German nation to live
and breathe as a nation undivided cannot be judged
according to principles of private right. The King of
Hanover sent to Nikolsburg, by an aide-de-camp, a letter to
the King, which I begged his Majesty not to receive, for
we had to keep in our eye the point of view, not of good
fellowship, but of politics; and the independence of
Hanover, with the power of leading its troops into the
field for or against Prussia according to the judgement
of the Sovereign of the day, placed at its disposal by
international law, was incompatible with carrying out

German unity. The durability of treaties alone, without the guarantee of adequate power at home under the lead of the Prince, never sufficed to secure for the German nation peace and unity in the Empire.

I succeeded in getting the King away from the idea of treating with Hanover and Hesse on the basis of the dismemberment of these lands, and of confederation with their former sovereigns as partial princes of a residue. If the Elector had retained Fulda and Hanau, and George V Kalenburg and Lüneburg with the prospect of succession in Brunswick, neither the Hanoverians and Hessians, nor the two Princes themselves, would have been contented members of the North German Confederation. This plan would have given us discontented confederation, with a tendency to 'Rheinbündelei' for the sake of winning back their lost territory.

Likewise such unconditional devotion to Austria as Nassau had shown was a dangerous phenomenon in the immediate neighbourhood of Coblenz, especially in the event of alliances between France and Austria, such as had come into menacing prospect during the Crimean war and the Polish complications of 1863. His Majesty had inherited his dislike of Nassau from his father. Frederick William III used to travel through the Duchy without seeing the Duke. The Duke's contingent had made itself particularly disagreeable in Prussia during the time of the Confederation of the Rhine, and King William I was prejudiced against concessions to the Duke by the vehement opposition made by deputations of previous subjects of Nassau, whose standing cry was: 'Save us from the Prince and his huntsmen!'

There remained treaties of peace to be concluded with Saxony and the South German states. Herr von

Varnbüler showed the same vivacity of temperament as
in the preparations for war, and was the first with whom
a conclusion was arrived at.[1] It was a question among
other things whether, as Wurtemberg had taken possession of Prussian Hohenzollern, we should now, as the
King desired, turn the tables and demand an enlargement
of Hohenzollern at the expense of Wurtemberg. I could
not see any advantage either for Prussia or for our
national future in doing this, and, in general, regarded
the principle of retaliation as no sound basis for our
policy,[2] since even where our feelings had been injured,
it ought to be guided, not by our own irritation, but by
consideration of its object. Just because Varnbüler had
some diplomatic sins towards us to his account, he was
a useful intermediary for me; and by agreeing to forget
the past, through the example of Wurtemberg in concluding its treaty (August 13), I gained the way to the
others.

I do not know whether Roggenbach was acting under
the orders of the Grand Duke of Baden in the conclusion
of peace, when he represented to me that Bavaria was a
hindrance to German unification owing to its size, and
would more easily fit into a future reconstruction of
Germany if it were reduced, and that it was therefore
advisable to restore a better balance of power in South
Germany by increasing Baden, and bringing it into immediate juxtaposition with Prussia by the incorporation
with it of the Palatinate; in which connexion further
changes, in accordance with the desire of Prussia to recover the dynastic family domains of Anspach-Baireuth,
including the absorption of Wurtemberg, were kept in
view. I did not accept this suggestion, but declined it

[1] See above, p. 53.   [2] See above, p. 50.

a limine. Even if I had been willing to consider it exclusively on the ground of expediency, it still betrayed a want of a just eye for the future and an obscuration of the political view by the domestic policy of Baden. The difficulty of compelling Bavaria, against her will, to enter a constitution of the Empire which did not suit her would have remained the same even if the Palatinate had been handed over to Baden ; and it is a question whether the Palatinate people would willingly have accepted this connexion in exchange for that with Bavaria. When there was some talk in passing about compensating Hesse for its territory north of the Main by Bavarian territory in the direction of Aschaffenburg, protests reached me from the latter district which, although they came from a strictly Catholic population, amounted to this, that if the undersigned could not remain Bavarians they would rather become Prussians, but disliked being transferred from Bavaria to Hesse. They appeared to be governed by a consideration of the rank of the sovereigns, and by the order of voting in the Federal Diet, in which Bavaria ranked before Hesse. In the same line of ideas I remember from my Frankfort time a saying of a Prussian soldier to one from a small state : ' You shut up ; why, you have not even got a King.' I regarded alterations of state boundaries in South Germany as no step towards unification of the whole.

A reduction of Bavaria in the north would have been against the King's wish at that time, which was to recover Anspach and Baireuth in their old extent. But this plan, however dear to my honoured and beloved master, was as little in accordance with my political views as the Baden one, and I successfully resisted it. In the autumn of 1866 it was not yet possible to forecast the future attitude of Austria. The jealousy of France towards us was admitted, and no one knew better than I the disappointment of Napoleon at our successes in Bohemia. He had reckoned with certainty that Austria would beat us, and that we should be reduced to purchase his mediation. Now, if the efforts of France to make up for this error and its consequences had succeeded by means of the irritation necessarily caused in Vienna by our victory, the question would have come to the fore in many German courts whether, in conjunction with Austria, and as it were in a second Silesian war, they wished to renew the struggle against us or not. That Bavaria and Saxony would succumb to this temptation was possible, but that a Bavaria mutilated as Roggenbach wanted would have sought revenge against us in a junction with Austria was probable.

Such a junction would perhaps have embraced a wider area than the Guelf legion, which under French protection took up a position against us shortly afterwards. That with the exception of a few individuals who had passed out of mind it had ceased to appear on the scene in 1870 is largely due to the circumstance that certain confidential persons acquainted with the agreement drawn up in Hanover kept us informed of the preparations that went on, even down to minute details, and offered to frustrate the entire combination if the emoluments of their former posts in Hanover were secured to them. I felt apprehensive at that time, from correspondence intercepted by order of the courts, that we might find it necessary, in view of Guelfic enterprises, to proceed to reprisals which, looking to the risk of war, could not prove other than severe. It must be remembered that we did not then feel sure enough of victory over France, considering what the French army had done in the past, to neglect anything that might prevent our position from being made more difficult. I therefore agreed with the intermediaries, who approached me closer, that their wishes should be fulfilled if they carried out their promises ; and indicated as a note of this condition the question whether we should not be compelled to shoot a Hanoverian for fighting against German forces. No disturbances therefore occurred in the country, and after the outbreak of the war the departure of Guelfs to France, by land and water, was confined to a few who were already compromised. From the behaviour of the Hanoverian troops in the war, it is not probable that a Guelf insurrection at home would have been able to gain many adherents, at least so long as our progress in France was victorious. What would have happened if we had returned beaten and pursued through Hanover I leave untouched. But a prophylactic policy must take even such possibilities into consideration ; at all events I was resolved, under stress of war, to advise the King to adopt every measure of active defence which the instinct of political self-preservation can suggest. And even if only a few severe and apparently cruel punishments had become necessary, such acts of violence against German fellow-countrymen, however much they might be justified by the risks of war, would for generations afterwards have been a hindrance in the way of reconciliation and a pretext for persecutions. It therefore seemed to me important to prevent such possibilities in good time.

The struggles during the previous winter with the
King, who did not want war, and during the campaign,
with the military men, who saw only Austria, not the
other Powers of Europe, before them, and again with
the King respecting the conclusion of peace, and then
again respecting the bill of indemnity, had so exhausted
me that I needed rest and recreation. I went first of all
on September 26 to my cousin, Count Bismarck-Bohlen
at Karlsburg, and then on October 6 to Putbus, where
I fell very ill at the inn. Prince and Princess Putbus
showed me most kind hospitality in a cottage that had
remained standing close to the castle, which had been
burnt down. After the first severe attack had passed
away I was able to take affairs again in hand by correspondence with Savigny. As the last Prussian envoy to
the Federal Diet he naturally inherited the special branch
of the work dealing with the German policy then in the
foreground. He brought the negotiations with Saxony to
a conclusion, which had not been reached before my departure. Their result is *publici juris*, and I can abstain from
criticising them. The military independence of Saxony
was afterwards, through the mediation of General von
Stosch, further developed by his Majesty's personal decisions beyond what was arranged in the treaty.

The prudent and honourable policy of the last two
Saxon kings has justified these concessions—that is to
say, as long as the existing Prusso-Austrian friendship
can be maintained. It is upon grounds due to the
records of past history and religion, on human nature,
and especially on the traditions of the sovereigns, that
the close league between Prussia and Austria, made in
1879, exercises a concentrating pressure on Bavaria and
Saxony, which is stronger in proportion as the German

element in Austria, high and low, is careful to foster its relations with the Hapsburg dynasty. The parliamentary excesses of the German element in Austria, and their ultimate influence on the policy of the dynasty, threatened to weaken the force of the German national element in this direction, and not alone in Austria. The doctrinaire blunders of parliamentary groups are as a rule favourable to the efforts of women and priests who dabble in politics.

CHAPTER XXII

On July 2, 1870, the Spanish ministry decided in favour of the accession to that throne of Leopold, Hereditary Prince of Hohenzollern. This gave the first stimulus in the field of international law to the subsequent military question, but still only in the form of a specifically Spanish matter. It was hard to find in the law of nations a pretext for France to interfere with the freedom of Spain to choose a King; after people in Paris had made up their minds to war with Prussia, this was sought for artificially in the name Hohenzollern, which in itself had nothing more menacing to France than any other German name. On the contrary, it might have been assumed, in Spain as well as in Germany, that Prince Hohenzollern, on account of his personal and family connexions in Paris, would be a *persona grata* beyond many another German Prince. I remember that on the night after the battle of Sedan I was riding along the road to Donchéry, in thick darkness, with a number of our officers, following the King in his journey round Sedan. In reply to a question from some one in the company I talked about the preliminaries to the war, and mentioned at the same time that I had thought Prince Leopold would be no unwelcome neighbour in Spain to the Emperor Napoleon, and would travel to Madrid *via* Paris, in order to get into touch with the imperial French policy, forming as it did a part of the conditions under which he would have had to govern Spain. I said: 'We should have been much more justified in dreading a close understanding between the Spanish and French crowns than in hoping for the restoration of a Spanish-German anti-French constellation after the analogy of Charles V; a king of Spain can only carry out Spanish policy, and the Prince by assuming the crown of the country would become a Spaniard.' To my surprise there came from the darkness behind me a vigorous rejoinder from the Prince of Hohenzollern, of whose presence I had not the least idea; he protested strongly against the possibility of presuming any French sympathies in him. This protest in the midst of the battlefield of Sedan was natural for a German officer and a Hohenzollern Prince, and I could only answer that the Prince, as King of Spain, could have allowed himself to be guided by Spanish interests only, and prominent among these, in view of strengthening his new kingdom, would have been a soothing treatment of his powerful neighbour on the Pyrenees. I made my apology to the Prince for the expression I had uttered while unaware of his presence.

This episode, introduced before its time, affords evidence as to the conception I had formed of the whole question. I regarded it as a Spanish and not as a German one, even though I was delighted at seeing the German name of Hohenzollern active in representing monarchy in Spain, and did not fail to calculate all the possible consequences from the point of view of our interests—a duty which is incumbent on a foreign minister when anything of similar importance occurs in another state. My immediate thought was more of the economic than of the political relations in which a Spanish King of German extraction

could be serviceable. For Spain I anticipated from the
personal character of the Prince, and from his family relations, tranquillising and consolidating results, which I
had no reason to grudge the Spaniards. Spain is among
the few countries which, by their geographical position
and political necessities, have no reason to pursue an anti-
German policy; besides which, she is well adapted, by
the economic relations of supply and demand, for an extensive trade with Germany. An element friendly to us
in the Spanish government would have been an advantage
which in the course of German policy there appeared no
reason to reject *a limine*, unless the apprehension that
France might be dissatisfied was to be allowed to rank as
one. If Spain had developed again more vigorously than
hitherto has been the case, the fact that Spanish diplomacy was friendly towards us might have been useful to
us in time of peace; but it did not seem to me probable
that the King of Spain, on the outbreak of the war between Germany and France, which was evidently coming
sooner or later, would, with the best will in the world,
be in a position to prove his sympathy with Germany by
an attack on France or a demonstration against her ; and
the conduct of Spain after the outbreak of the war which
we had drawn upon us by the complaisance of German
princes showed the accuracy of my doubt. The chivalrous Cid would have called France to account for interference in Spain's free choice of a king, and not have
left the vindication of Spanish independence to foreigners.
The nation, formerly so powerful by land and sea, cannot
at the present day hold the cognate population of Cuba
in check; and how could one expect her to attack a
Power like France from affection towards us ? No Spanish
government, and least of all an alien king, would possess

power enough in the country to send even a regiment to the
Pyrenees out of affection towards Germany. Politically
I was tolerably indifferent to the entire question. Prince
Anthony was more inclined than myself to carry it
peacefully to the desired goal. The memoirs of his
Majesty the King of Roumania are not accurately informed as regards details of the ministerial co-operation
in the question. The ministerial council in the palace
which he mentions did not take place. Prince Anthony
was living as the King's guest in the palace, and had
invited him and some of the ministers to dinner. I
scarcely think that the Spanish question was discussed at
table. If the Duke of Gramont [1] labours to adduce proof
that I did not stand aloof from and averse to the Spanish
proposal, I find no reason to contradict him. I can no
longer recall the text of my letter to Marshal Prim,
which the Duke has heard mentioned; if I drew it up
myself, about which I am equally uncertain, I should
hardly have called the Hohenzollern candidature 'une
excellente chose:' the expression is not natural to me.
That I regarded it as 'opportune,' not 'à un moment
donné,' but in principle and in time of peace is correct.
I had not the slightest doubt in the matter that the
grandson of the Murats, a favourite at the French Court,
would secure the goodwill of France towards his country.

The intervention of France at its beginning concerned
Spanish and not Prussian affairs; the garbling of the
matter in the Napoleonic policy, by virtue of which the
question was to become a Prussian one, was internation-
ally unjustifiable and exasperating, and proved to me that
the moment had arrived when France sought a quarrel

[1] Gramont, *La France et la Prusse avant la guerre.* Paris, 1872,
p. 21.

against us and was ready to seize any pretext that seemed available. I regarded the French intervention in the first instance as an injury, and consequently as an insult to Spain, and expected that the Spanish sense of honour would resist this encroachment. Later on, when the turn of affairs showed that, by her encroachment on Spanish independence, France intended to threaten us with war, I waited for some days expecting that the Spanish declaration of war against France would follow that of the French against us. I was not prepared to see a self-assertive nation like Spain stand quiet behind the Pyrenees with ordered arms, while the Germans were engaged in a deadly struggle against France on behalf of Spain's independence and freedom to choose her king. The Spanish sense of honour which proved so sensitive in the Carlist question simply left us in the lurch in 1870. Probably in both cases the sympathies and international ties of the Republican parties were decisive.

The first demands of France respecting the candidature for the Spanish throne, and they were unjustifiable, had been presented on July 4, and answered by our Foreign Office evasively, though in accordance with truth, that the *ministry* knew nothing about the matter. This was correct so far, that the question of Prince Leopold's acceptance of his election had been treated by his Majesty simply as a family matter, which in no way concerned either Prussia or the North German Confederation, and which affected solely the personal relations between the Commander-in-Chief and a German officer, and those between the head of the family and, not the royal family of Prussia but, the entire family of Hohenzollern, or all the bearers of that name.

In France, however, a *casus belli* was being sought

against Prussia which should be as free as possible from German national colouring ; and it was thought one had been discovered in the dynastic sphere by the accession to the Spanish throne of a candidate bearing the name of Hohenzollern. In this the overrating of the military superiority of France and the underrating of the national feeling in Germany was clearly the chief reason why the tenability of this pretext was not examined either with honesty or judgement. The German national outburst which followed the French declaration, and resembled a stream bursting its sluices, was a surprise to French politicians. They lived, calculated, and acted on recollections of the Confederation of the Rhine, supported by the attitude of certain West German ministers ; also by Ultramontane influences, in the hope that the conquests of France, ' gesta Dei per Francos,' would make it easier in Germany to draw further consequences from the Vatican council, with the support of an alliance with Catholic Austria. The Ultramontane tendencies of French policy were favourable to it in Germany and disadvantageous in Italy ; the alliance with the latter being finally wrecked by the refusal of France to evacuate Rome. In the belief that the French army was superior the pretext for war was lugged out, as one may say, by the hair ; and instead of making Spain responsible for its reputed anti-French election of a king, they attacked the German Prince who had not refused to relieve the need of the Spaniards, in the way they themselves wished, by the appointment of a useful king, and one who would presumably be regarded as *persona grata* in Paris ; and the King of Prussia, whom nothing beyond his family name and his position as a German fellow-countryman had brought into connexion with this Spanish affair. In the very fact that the French cabinet

ventured to call Prussian policy to account respecting the
acceptance of the election, and to do so in a form which,
in the interpretation put upon it by the French papers,
became a public threat, lay a piece of international im-
pudence which, in my opinion, rendered it impossible for
us to draw back one single inch.   The insulting character
of the French demand was enhanced, not only by the
threatening challenges of the French press, but also by
the discussions in parliament and the attitude taken by
the ministry of Gramont and Ollivier upon these manifestations.   The utterance of Gramont in the session of
the ' Corps Législatif ' of July 6 :—

'We do not believe that respect for the rights of a
neighbouring people binds us to suffer a foreign Power
to set one of its Princes on the throne of Charles V. . . .
This event will not come to pass, of that we are quite
certain. . . . Should it prove otherwise we shall know
how to fulfil our duty without shrinking and without
weakness '—
this utterance was itself an official international threat,
with the hand on the sword hilt.   The phrase, *La
Prusse cane* (Prussia climbs down), served in the press to
illustrate the range of the parliamentary proceedings of
July 6 and 7; which, in my feeling, rendered all compliance incompatible with our sense of national honour.

On July 12 I decided to hurry off from Varzin to
Ems to discuss with his Majesty about summoning the
Reichstag for the purpose of the mobilisation.   As I
passed through Wussow my friend Mulert, the old clergyman, stood before the parsonage door and warmly greeted
me ; my answer from the open carriage was a thrust in
carte and tierce in the air, and he clearly understood
that I believed I was going to war.   As I entered the

courtyard of my house at Berlin, and before leaving the
carriage, I received telegrams from which it appeared
that the King was continuing to treat with Benedetti,
even after the French threats and outrages in parliament
and in the press, and not referring him with calm reserve to his ministers. During dinner, at which Moltke
and Roon were present, the announcement arrived from
the embassy in Paris that the Prince of Hohenzollern
had renounced his candidature in order to prevent the
war with which France threatened us. My first idea was
to retire from the service, because, after all the insolent
challenges which had gone before, I perceived in this
extorted submission a humiliation of Germany for which
I did not desire to be responsible. This impression of a
wound to our sense of national honour by the compulsory
withdrawal so dominated me that I had already decided
to announce my retirement at Ems. I considered this
humiliation before France and her swaggering demonstrations as worse than that of Olmütz, for which the previous
history on both sides, and our want of preparation for
war at the time, will always be a valid excuse. I took it
for granted that France would lay the Prince's renunciation to her account as a satisfactory success, with the feeling that a threat of war, even though it had taken the form
of international insult and mockery, and though the pretext
for war against Prussia had been dragged in by the head
and shoulders, was enough to compel her to draw back,
even in a just cause; and that even the North German
Confederation did not feel strong enough to protect the
national honour and independence against French arrogance. I was very much depressed, for I saw no means
of repairing the corroding injury I dreaded to our national
position from a timorous policy, unless by picking quarrels

clumsily and seeking them artificially. I saw by that time that war was a necessity, which we could no longer avoid with honour. I telegraphed to my people at Varzin not to pack up or start, for I should be back again in a few days. I now believed in peace ; but as I would not represent the attitude by which this peace had been purchased, I gave up the journey to Ems and asked Count Eulenburg to go thither and represent my opinion to his Majesty. In the same sense I conversed with the Minister of War, von Roon : we had got our slap in the face from France, and had been reduced, by our complaisance, to look like seekers of a quarrel if we entered upon war, the only way in which we could wipe away the stain. My position was now untenable, solely because, during his course at the baths, the King, under pressure of threats, had given audience to the French ambassador for four consecutive days, and had exposed his royal person to insolent treatment from this foreign agent without ministerial assistance. Through this inclination to take state business upon himself in person and alone, the King had been forced into a position which I could not defend ; in my judgement his Majesty while at Ems ought to have refused every business communication from the French negotiator, who was not on the same footing with him, and to have referred him to the department in Berlin. The department would then have had to obtain his Majesty's decision by a representation at Ems, or, if dilatory treatment were considered useful, by a report in writing. But his Majesty, however careful in his usual respect for departmental relations, was too fond not indeed of deciding important questions personally, but, at all events, of discussing them, to make a proper use of the shelter with which the Sovereign is purposely surrounded against

importunities and inconvenient questionings and demands.
That the King, considering the consciousness of his
supreme dignity which he possessed in so high a degree,
did not withdraw at the very beginning from Benedetti's
importunity was to be attributed for the most part to the
influence exercised upon him by the Queen, who was at
Coblenz close by. He was seventy-three years old, a
lover of peace, and disinclined to risk the laurels of 1866
in a fresh struggle ; but when he was free from the
feminine influence, the sense of honour of the heir of
Frederick the Great and of a Prussian officer always
remained paramount. Against the opposition of his
consort, due to her natural feminine timidity and lack of
national feeling, the King's power of resistance was
weakened by his knightly regard for the lady and his
kingly consideration for a Queen, and especially for his
own Queen. I have been told that Queen Augusta
implored her husband with tears, before his departure
from Ems to Berlin, to bear in mind Jena and Tilsit and
avert war. I consider the statement authentic, even to
the tears.

Having decided to resign, in spite of the remonstrances
which Roon made against it, I invited him and Moltke
to dine with me alone on the 13th, and communicated to
them at table my views and projects for doing so. Both
were greatly depressed, and reproached me indirectly
with selfishly availing myself of my greater facility for
withdrawing from service. I maintained the position that
I could not offer up my sense of honour to politics, that
both of them, being professional soldiers and consequently
without freedom of choice, need not take the same point
of view as a responsible Foreign Minister. During our
conversation I was informed that a telegram from Ems,

in cipher, if I recollect rightly, of about 200 'groups,' was
being deciphered. When the copy was handed to me it
showed that Abeken had drawn up and signed the telegram at his Majesty's command, and I read it out to my
guests,* whose dejection was so great that they turned
away from food and drink. On a repeated examination
of the document I lingered upon the authorisation of his
Majesty, which included a command, immediately to
communicate Benedetti's fresh demand and its rejection
both to our ambassadors and to the press. I put a few
questions to Moltke as to the extent of his confidence in
the state of our preparations, especially as to the time
they would still require in order to meet this sudden risk
of war. He answered that if there was to be war he
expected no advantage to us by deferring its outbreak ;
and even if we should not be strong enough at first to
protect all the territories on the left bank of the Rhine

---

* The telegram, handed in at Ems on July 13, 1870, at 3.50 p.m. and
received in Berlin at 6.9, ran as deciphered :

' His Majesty writes to me : " Count Benedetti spoke to me on the
promenade, in order to demand from me, finally in a very importunate
manner, that I should authorise him to telegraph at once that I bound
myself for all future time never again to give my consent if the Hohenzollerns should renew their candidature. I refused at last somewhat sternly,
as it is neither right nor possible to undertake engagements of this kind
à tout jamais. Naturally I told him that I had as yet received no news,
and as he was earlier informed about Paris and Madrid than myself, he
could clearly see that my government once more had no hand in the matter."
His Majesty has since received a letter from the Prince. His Majesty having
told Count Benedetti that he was awaiting news from the Prince, has decided, with reference to the above demand, upon the representation of Count
Eulenburg and myself, not to receive Count Benedetti again, but only to
let him be informed through an aide-de-camp : That his Majesty had now
received from the Prince confirmation of the news which Benedetti had
already received from Paris, and had nothing further to say to the ambassador. His Majesty leaves it to your Excellency whether Benedetti's fresh
demand and its rejection should not be at once communicated both to our
ambassadors and to the press.'

against French invasion, our preparations would nevertheless soon overtake those of the French, while at a later period this advantage would be diminished; he regarded a rapid outbreak as, on the whole, more favourable to us than delay.

In view of the attitude of France, our national sense of honour compelled us, in my opinion, to go to war; and if we did not act according to the demands of this feeling, we should lose, when on the way to its completion, the entire impetus towards our national development won in 1866, while the German national feeling south of the Main, aroused by our military successes in 1866, and shown by the readiness of the southern states to enter the alliances, would have to grow cold again. The German feeling, which in the southern states lived along with the individual and dynastic state feeling, had, up to 1866, silenced its political conscience to a certain degree with the fiction of a collective Germany under the leadership of Austria, partly from South German preference for the old imperial state, partly in the belief of her military superiority to Prussia. After events had shown the incorrectness of that calculation, the very helplessness in which the South German states had been left by Austria at the conclusion of peace was a motive for the political Damascus that lay between Varnbüler's 'Væ victis' and the willing conclusion of the offensive and defensive alliance with Prussia. It was confidence in the Germanic power developed by means of Prussia, and the attraction which is inherent in a brave and resolute policy if it is successful, and then proceeds within reasonable and honourable limits. This nimbus had been won by Prussia; it would have been lost irrevocably, or at all events for a long time, if in a question of national honour the opinion gained ground among the people that the French insult, *La Prusse cane*, had a foundation in fact.

In the same psychological train of thought in which during the Danish war in 1864 I desired, for political reasons, that precedence should be given not to the old Prussian, but to the Westphalian battalions, who so far had had no opportunity of proving their courage under Prussian leadership, and regretted that Prince Frederick Charles had acted contrary to my wish, did I feel convinced that the gulf, which diverse dynastic and family influences and different habits of life had in the course of history created between the south and north of the Fatherland, could not be more effectually bridged over than by a joint national war against the neighbour who had been aggressive for many centuries. I remembered that even in the short period from 1813 to 1815, from Leipzig and Hanau to Belle-Alliance, the joint victorious struggle against France had rendered it possible to put an end to the opposition between a yielding Rhine-Confederation policy and the German national impetus of the days between the Vienna congress and the Mainz commission of enquiry, days marked by the names of Stein, Görres, Jahn, Wartburg, up to the crime of Sand. The blood shed in common, from the day when the Saxons came over at Leipzig down to their participation at Belle-Alliance under English command, had fostered a consciousness before which the recollections of the Rhine-Confederation were blotted out. The historical development in this direction was interrupted by the anxiety aroused by the over-haste of the national craving for the stability of state-institutions.

This retrospect strengthened me in my conviction, and

the political considerations in respect to the South German states proved applicable likewise, *mutatis mutandis*, to our relations with the populations of Hanover, Hesse, and Schleswig-Holstein. That this view was correct is shown by the satisfaction with which, at the present day, after a lapse of twenty years, not only the Holsteiners, but likewise the people of the Hanse towns remember the heroic deeds of their sons in 1870. All these considerations, conscious and unconscious, strengthened my opinion that war could be avoided only at the cost of the honour of Prussia and of the national confidence in it. Under this conviction I made use of the royal authorisation communicated to me through Abeken, to publish the contents of the telegram; and in the presence of my two guests I reduced the telegram by striking out words, but without adding or altering, to the following form: 'After the news of the renunciation of the hereditary Prince of Hohenzollern had been officially communicated to the imperial government of France by the royal government of Spain, the French ambassador at Ems further demanded of his Majesty the King that he would authorise him to telegraph to Paris that his Majesty the King bound himself for all future time never again to give his consent if the Hohenzollerns should renew their candidature. His Majesty the King thereupon decided not to receive the French ambassador again, and sent to tell him through the aide-de-camp on duty that his Majesty had nothing further to communicate to the ambassador.' The difference in the effect of the abbreviated text of the Ems telegram as compared with that produced by the original was not the result of stronger words but of the form, which made this announcement appear decisive, while Abeken's version would only have been regarded as a fragment of a negotiation still pending, and to be continued at Berlin.

After I had read out the concentrated edition to my two guests, Moltke remarked : ' Now it has a different ring ; it sounded before like a parley ; now it is like a flourish in answer to a challenge.' I went on to explain : ' If in execution of his Majesty's order I at once communicate this text, which contains no alteration in or addition to the telegram, not only to the newspapers, but also by telegraph to all our embassies, it will be known in Paris before midnight, and not only on account of its contents, but also on account of the manner of its distribution, will have the effect of a red rag upon the Gallic bull. Fight we must if we do not want to act the part of the vanquished without a battle. Success, however, essentially depends upon the impression which the origination of the war makes upon us and others ; it is important that we should be the party attacked, and this Gallic overweening and touchiness will make us if we announce in the face of Europe, so far as we can without the speaking-trumpet of the Reichstag, that we fearlessly meet the public threats of France.'

This explanation brought about in the two generals a revulsion to a more joyous mood, the liveliness of which surprised me. They had suddenly recovered their pleasure in eating and drinking and spoke in a more cheerful vein. Roon said : ' Our God of old lives still and will not let us perish in disgrace.' Moltke so far relinquished his passive equanimity that, glancing up joyously towards the ceiling and abandoning his usual punctiliousness of speech, he smote his hand upon his breast and said : ' If I may but live to lead our armies in such a war, then the devil may come directly afterwards and fetch away the " old carcass." '

He was less robust at that time than afterwards, and doubted whether he would survive the hardships of the campaign.

How keenly he wanted to put in practice his military and strategic tastes and ability I observed not only on this occasion, but also in the days before the outbreak of the Bohemian war. In both cases I found my military colleague in the King's service changed from his usual dry and silent habit, cheerful, lively, I might even say merry. In the June night of 1866, when I had invited him for the purpose of ascertaining whether the march of the army could not be begun twenty-four hours sooner, he answered in the affirmative and was pleasantly excited by the hastening of the struggle. As he left my wife's drawing-room with elastic step, he turned round at the door and asked me in a serious tone : ' Do you know that the Saxons have blown up * the bridge at Dresden ? ' Upon my expression of amazement and regret he replied : ' Yes, with water, for the dust.' An inclination to innocent jokes very seldom, in official relations like ours, broke through his reserve. In both cases his love of combat and delight in battles were a great support to me in carrying out the policy I regarded as necessary, in opposition to the intelligible and justifiable aversion in a most influential quarter. It proved inconvenient to me in 1867, in the Luxemburg question, and in 1875 and afterwards on the question whether it was desirable, as regards a war which we should probably have to face sooner or later, to bring it on *anticipando* before the adversary could improve his preparations. I have always opposed the theory which says ' Yes ; ' not only at the Luxemburg period, but likewise subsequently

* [Play on the word *gesprengt*.]

for twenty years, in the conviction that even victorious wars cannot be justified unless they are forced upon one, and that one cannot see the cards of Providence far enough ahead to anticipate historical development according to one's own calculation. It is natural that in the staff of the army not only younger active officers, but likewise experienced strategists, should feel the need of turning to account the efficiency of the troops led by them, and their own capacity to lead, and of making them prominent in history. It would be a matter of regret if this effect of the military spirit did not exist in the army; the task of keeping its results within such limits as the nations' need of peace can justly claim is the duty of the political, not the military, heads of the state. That at the time of the Luxemburg question, during the crisis of 1875, invented by Gortchakoff and France, and even down to the most recent times, the staff and its leaders have allowed themselves to be led astray and to endanger peace, lies in the very spirit of the institution, which I would not forgo. It only becomes dangerous under a monarch whose policy lacks sense of proportion and power to resist one-sided and constitutionally unjustifiable influences.

CHAPTER XXIII

VERSAILLES

THE ill-feeling towards me, which had survived in the higher military circles from the Austrian war, lasted throughout the French war; fostered not indeed by Moltke and Roon, but by the 'demigods,' as the higher staff officers were then called. It made itself perceptible to me and my staff during the campaign even down to the matter of rations and quartering.[1] It would have gone still further if it had not found a corrective in the unvarying tactful courtesy of Count Moltke. Roon was not in a position in the field to support me as a friend and colleague; on the contrary, he needed my support at last at Versailles to make good his military convictions in the King's circle.

As early as the journey to Cologne I learnt by accident that at the outbreak of war the plan of excluding me from the military consultations had been settled. Thus much I was able to gather from a conversation between General von Podbielski and Roon, which I unwillingly overheard as it took place in an adjoining compartment with a broad opening in the partition just over me. The former expressed his satisfaction loudly somewhat in this strain: 'So arrangements have been made this time that the same thing does not happen

[1] Cf. Bismarck's official letter to Roon of August 10, 1870, in Poschinger, *Bismarck-Portefeuille*, ii. 189 &c.

to us again.' Before the train started I heard enough
to understand what 'then' as opposed to this time the
General had in his mind, namely, my participation in the
military councils during the Bohemian campaign, and
especially the alteration of the line of march to Pressburg
instead of to Vienna.

The arrangement indicated by these speeches became
practically evident to me; I was not only not admitted to
the military consultations, as was the case in 1866, but
strict secrecy about all military measures and intentions was generally observed towards me. This result of
the departmental rivalry, which is natural to our official
circles, was such an evident injury to the conduct of
business, that Count Eberhard Stolberg, a patriot who,
alas, perished all too soon, and who was then at headquarters upon Red Cross business, was led by the intimate friendship between us to call the King's attention to the disadvantages of the exclusion of his responsible political adviser. To the Count's statement his
Majesty made reply: 'I had been generally admitted to
the military council during the Bohemian war, and it
had happened that, in opposition to the majority, I had
hit the nail on the head; and that if this had irritated
the other generals and they wished to consult only their
own department, it was not to be wondered at'—*ipsissima
verba regis*, according to the testimony of Count Stolberg,
not only to me but to others. The weight of influence
which the King allowed me in 1866 was certainly contrary to military traditions, if once the Minister-President
was ranked only according to the character of the uniform he wore in the field, that of a field-officer in a cavalry
regiment; and so the military boycott, as one would now
say, was maintained against me in 1870.

If the theory which the staff urged against me, and which is said to be taught as part of military science, can be expressed by saying that the Minister of Foreign Affairs comes again to the fore only when the commanders of the army find that the time has arrived for closing the temple of Janus, surely the double face of Janus conveys the warning that the government of a state engaged in war must look in more directions than towards the scene of the struggle only. The task of the commanders of the army is to annihilate the hostile forces; the object of war is to conquer peace under conditions which are conformable to the policy pursued by the state. To fix and limit the objects to be attained by the war, and to advise the monarch in respect to them, is and remains during the war just as before it a political function, and the manner in which these questions are solved cannot be without influence on the method of conducting the war. The ways and means of the latter will always depend upon whether the result finally obtained is the one desired, or more or less; whether cessions of territory are to be demanded or forborne, and whether temporary occupation is required, and for how long.

Still more difficult in the same line is it to judge whether and with what motives other Powers might be inclined to assist the adversary, in the first instance diplomatically, and eventually by armed force; what prospect the representatives of such a combination have of obtaining their object in foreign courts; how the parties would group themselves if it came to conferences or to a congress; and whether there is danger of further wars being developed from the intervention of neutrals. But above all is the difficulty of deciding when the right moment has come for introducing the transition from war to peace; for

this purpose are needed knowledge of the European conditions, which is not apt to be familiar to the military
element, and information which cannot be accessible to it.
The negotiations at Nikolsburg in 1866 show that the
question of war or peace always belongs, even in war, to
the responsible political minister, and cannot be decided
by the technical military leaders. But the minister concerned can only give the King expert advice, if he possesses a knowledge of the actual position at any moment
and of the views of those who conduct the war.

In the fifth chapter of the first volume mention has been
made of the plan of the dismemberment of Russia which
the 'Wochenblatt' party favoured, and which Bunsen developed in all its innocent nakedness, in a memorandum
handed to the Minister von Manteuffel.[1] Assuming the
case, which was then impossible, that the King had been
gained over to this Utopia—assuming further that the
Prussian armies and any allies they might have were
making victorious advances, even then a fine set of questions would have forced themselves up : whether the
further acquisition of Polish territories and populations
were desirable ; whether it was necessary to draw the
projecting frontier of the Poland created by the congress,
the point of egress for Russian armies, further towards
the East and further from Berlin, just as in the West it
was requisite to remove the pressure which Strasburg
and the lines of Weissenburg exercised on South Germany ; and whether Warsaw in Polish hands might be
more inconvenient for us than in Russian. All these are
purely political questions, and who will wish to deny
that their decision must have exercised a fully justifiable influence on the direction, method, and scope of

[1] See above, vol. i. p. 122.

the conduct of the war, and that a reciprocal action in advising the Crown would have had to exist between diplomacy and strategy?

If I acquiesced even at Versailles in not being summoned to vote on military matters, I was nevertheless, as leading minister, responsible for the proper political utilisation of the military, as well as of the foreign situation; and I was constitutionally the responsible adviser of the King in the question whether the military situation rendered advisable any particular political steps, or the refusal of any particular demand from other Powers. At that time I sought as far as possible to procure such intelligence about the military situation as I required for forming an opinion on the political, by keeping up confidential relations with some of the unemployed royalties who formed the 'second step' at the headquarters, and met at the Hôtel des Réservoirs; for these princely gentlemen learnt considerably more about the military transactions and views than the responsible Minister for Foreign Affairs, and gave me many a very valuable piece of information which they assumed was of course no secret for me. Russell, too, the English correspondent at headquarters, was usually better informed than myself as to the views and occurrences there, and was a useful source of intelligence.

In the Council of War Roon was the only supporter of my opinion that we should lose no time about ending the war if we wanted to make sure of stopping interference from the neutrals and their congress; he advocated the necessity of pressing forward the attack against

Paris with heavy guns, in opposition to the method of
famine, which in the circles where exalted ladies met was
regarded as more humane. The time which the latter
would demand could not be ascertained, owing to our
ignorance of the commissariat of Paris.[1] Territorially the
siege gained no ground; sometimes it even receded, and
events in the provinces could not be reckoned on with
certainty, especially as long as news was lacking as
to the whereabouts of the army of the South and of
Bourbaki. It was not known for a considerable time
whether it would operate against our line of communication with Germany, or would appear by the sea
route on the Lower Seine. We lost about two thousand
men before Paris every month, conquered no ground
from the besieged, and lengthened quite incalculably
the period during which our troops remained exposed to
the caprices of fortune, which might occur by unforeseen accidents in battle and by sickness, like the cholera
in 1866 before Vienna. The delay in the decision caused
me more serious disquietude in the political sphere from
my anxiety respecting the intervention of neutrals. The
longer the struggle lasted, so much the more would one
have to reckon with the possibility that latent ill-will and
wavering sympathies would admit of one of the other
Powers, alarmed at our success, being found ready to take
the initiative in a diplomatic intervention, and this would
then bring about the accession of others or of all the
others. Even though at the time of the circular tour of
M. Thiers in October, 'Europe was not to be found,'
the discovery of this factor at any of the neutral

---

[1] On September 22, Moltke had written to his brother Adolf that he
privately cherished the hope of shooting hares at Creisau by the end of
October. (Moltke, *Gesammelte Werke*, iv. 198.)

courts, and even in America, by the road of republican sympathies, might nevertheless be brought about through the slightest impulse which one cabinet might give to the other, while adopting as the basis of its initiative fishing questions as to the future of the European balance of power or the philanthropic hypocrisy by which the fortress of Paris was protected against serious siege. If in the course of the months, and in view of the fluctuating prospects before Paris, during the time which bore the label 'No news from before Paris,' the hostile elements and the jealous dishonest friends, who were not wanting to us in any of the Courts, had succeeded in bringing about an understanding between the other Powers, or even between any two of them, to address to us a warning or a question, ostensibly suggested by philanthropic feelings, no one could know how quickly a first movement of this kind might develop to a collective and in the first instance diplomatic attitude of the Neutrals. National Liberal parliamentarians wrote to one another in August 1870 'that every foreign mediation for peace was to be unconditionally rejected,' but they did not tell me how it was to be prevented except by the rapid capture of Paris.

Count Beust has been solicitous in his endeavour to show how 'uprightly, even if unsuccessfully,' he laboured to bring about a collective mediation of the Neutrals.[1] He mentions that as early as September 28 he had given instructions to the Austrian ambassador in London, and on October 12 to the ambassador at St. Petersburg, to represent the view that a collective step alone would have a prospect of success; that two months later he sent word to Prince

[1] *Aus drei Viertel-Jahrhunderten.* Stuttgart, 1887. Part ii. pp. 361, 395 &c.

Gortchakoff: 'Le moment d'intervenir est peut-être venu.' He reproduces a dispatch of October 13, during a critical time for us, fourteen days before the capitulation of Metz, sent by him to Count Wimpffen at Berlin, who there misread it.* In it he alludes to a memorandum in which at the beginning of October I had called attention to the consequences which must follow if Paris, with its two millions of inhabitants, continued its resistance even to the commencement of failure in provisions; and he indicates it, quite justly, as my object to remove the responsibility for this from the Prussian government.

'Premising this,' he continues, 'I cannot help expressing my fear that some day before the judgement of history a portion of this responsibility will fall upon the Neutrals if in silent indifference they allow the danger of an unheard-of disaster to be placed before their eyes. I must therefore request your Excellency, if the matter is brought before you, to express openly our regret that in a situation in which the Royal Prussian government foresees catastrophes such as are alluded to in that memorandum, there is yet manifested the most decided effort to keep off every personal intervention of a third Power. . . . It is not considerations of private interest which lead the government of Austria-Hungary to complain that at the point at which things have arrived every peaceful influence of the Neutral Powers is lacking. But they cannot, in the manner recently shown by the Saint Petersburg cabinet, approve and recommend entire abstinence on the part of uninterested Europe. They much more consider it a duty to state that they still believe in European common interests, and

* It is curious that Count Wimpffen should have misread the instruction. It merely enjoins him to express himself in this sense in certain contingencies.

that they would prefer peace obtained by the impartial influence of the Neutrals to the destruction of further hundreds of thousands.'

As to what 'impartial intervention' would have been Count Beust leaves no doubt: 'moderate the demands of the conqueror, soften the bitterness of the sentiments which must crush the vanquished.'[1] That the feelings of the French respecting the humiliation they suffered would at the present day be less bitter towards us if the Neutrals had compelled us to be satisfied with less can hardly have been believed by one so well acquainted with French history and the French national character as Count Beust.

An intervention could only tend to deprive us Germans of the prize of victory by means of a congress. This danger, which troubled me day and night, made me feel the necessity of hastening the conclusion of peace, in order to be able to establish it without the intervention of Neutrals. That this would not be practicable before the capture of Paris was evident from the traditional pre-eminence of the capital in France. As long as Paris held out, as long as we could not expect that the leading circles in Tours and Bordeaux, or the provinces, would give up the hope of any such change as might be looked for, whether from new *levées en masse*, as they made themselves felt in the battle on the Lisaine, or from the ultimate 'Discovery of Europe,' or from the halo which, in German natures, especially those of ladies at great Courts, surrounded the English catchwords : 'Humanity, civilisation,' so long did the foreign Courts, who got their information about the situation in France much more from French than from German sources, have in view the possibility of assisting the French in their

[1] Dispatch to Count Chotek of October 12, Beust, *op. cit.* ii. 397.

conclusion of peace. So far as I was concerned, my task was therefore directed to a settlement with France before the Neutral Powers arrived at an understanding as to the influence they should exert on the peace, exactly as in 1866 our need was to conclude with Austria before French intervention could become active in South Germany.

It could not be said for certain what conclusions would have been arrived at if at Wörth, Spichern, and Mars la Tour the success had been on the side of the French or less brilliant on ours. I received at the time of those battles visits from Italian republicans, who were convinced that King Victor Emanuel entertained the intention of supporting the Emperor Napoleon, and were inclined to oppose this view because they feared that the result of carrying out the intentions ascribed to the King would be to strengthen the dependence of Italy upon France, which offended their national feeling. Even in the years 1868 and 1869 similar anti-French suggestions were made to me from the Italian, and not merely from the republican side, in which discontent at the supremacy of France over Italy was sharply conspicuous. At that time, as subsequently at Homburg (Palatinate), on the march towards France, I answered the Italians: We had so far no proofs that the King of Italy would prove his friendship for Napoleon to the point of attacking Prussia; it was contrary to my political conscience to seize an initiative for a rupture which would have given Italy a pretext and justification for a hostile attitude. If Victor Emanuel seized the initiative for a rupture, then the republican tendency of those Italians who disapproved of such a policy would not prevent me from advising the King my master to support the malcontents in Italy by such money and weapons as they wanted.

I found the position of the war too serious and too dangerous to consider myself justified, during a conflict in which not only our national future, but even our existence as a state, was at stake, in refusing any support whatever in critical turns of affairs. Just as in 1866, after and in consequence of the intervention involved in Napoleon's telegram of July 4, I had not shrunk from the idea of assistance by a Hungarian insurrection, so I should also have considered that of the Italian republicans as acceptable, if it had been a question of averting defeat and of defending our national independence. The aspirations of the King of Italy and Count Beust, which were thrust back by our first brilliant successes, might revive again in the stagnation before Paris, and all the more easily that in the influential circles of so weighty a factor as England we could by no means count upon trustworthy sympathies, especially such as would have been ready to realise themselves, if only diplomatically.

In Russia the personal feelings of Alexander II, not only those of friendship for his uncle but also those against France, afforded us a security which might certainly be weakened by the French sympathies and vanity of Prince Gortchakoff and by his rivalry towards myself. It was consequently a fortunate thing that the situation offered a possibility of doing Russia a service in respect to the Black Sea. Just as the sensibilities of the Russian Court, which, owing to the Russian relationship of Queen Mary were enlisted by the loss of the Hanoverian crown, found their counterpoise in the concessions which were made to the Oldenburg connexions of the Russian dynasty in territorial and financial directions in 1866; so did the possibility occur in 1870 of doing a service not only to the dynasty, but also to the Russian kingdom, in respect to the politically absurd, and therefore in the long run impossible, stipulations which circumscribed the independence of its Black Sea coasts. They were the most inept conclusions of the peace of Paris ; one cannot permanently deny the exercise of the natural rights of sovereignty on its own coasts to a nation of a hundred millions of inhabitants. A charge of the kind which was allowed on Russian territory to foreign Powers was a humiliation which a great nation could not endure for long. We had in this an opportunity of improving our relations with Russia.

Prince Gortchakoff entered only reluctantly upon the initiative with which I sounded him in this direction. His personal ill-will was stronger than his Russian sense of duty. He did not want any obligation from us, but estrangement from Germany and gratitude in France. In order to make our offer effectual in St. Petersburg, I needed the thoroughly honourable and always friendly co-operation of the then Russian Military Plenipotentiary, Count Kutusoff. I shall hardly do injustice to Prince Gortchakoff if, after my relations to him, which lasted for several years, I assume that personal rivalry towards me weighed heavier with him than the interests of Russia ; his vanity and his jealousy of me were greater than his patriotism.

Indicative of the morbid vanity of Gortchakoff were some expressions which he used to me on the occasion of his residence at Berlin in May 1876. He spoke of his weariness and his wish to retire and added : 'Je ne puis, cependant, me présenter devant Saint-Pierre au ciel sans avoir présidé la moindre chose en Europe.' I therefore begged him to undertake the presidency of the diplomatic conference held at the time, which however was only semi-official, and he did so. While idly listening to his long presidential address I wrote in pencil: 'Pompous, pompo, pomp, pom, po.' My neighbour, Lord Odo Russell, snatched the paper from me and kept it.

Another expression on this occasion ran thus: 'Si je me retire, je ne veux pas m'éteindre comme une lampe qui file, je veux me coucher comme un astre.' With these ideas it is not to be wondered at that his last appearance at the Berlin congress in 1878 did not satisfy him, for the Emperor had not appointed him but Count Shuvaloff as chief plenipotentiary, so that only the latter, and not Gortchakoff, controlled the Russian vote. Gortchakoff had, to a certain degree, extorted his membership of the congress from the Emperor, owing his success, perhaps, to the considerate treatment which is traditional in the higher service of Russia towards meritorious statesmen. He sought even at the congress to keep his Russian popularity, as understood by the 'Moscow Journal,' free as far as possible from the effects of Russian concessions, and under pretext of illness stayed away from sittings of the congress in which they were in view, but took care to show himself as in good health at the ground-floor window of his residence, Unter den Linden. He wanted to reserve the power of maintaining afterwards in Russian society that he was innocent as regarded the Russian concessions—an unworthy egotism at the cost of his country.

However, the result for Russia, even after the congress, remained one of the most favourable, if not the most favourable which she has ever obtained since the Turkish wars. The direct gains to Russia were those in Asia Minor, Batoum, Kars, &c. But if Russia had really found

it to her interest to emancipate the Balkan states of the
Greek confession from Turkish rule, the result would then
have been, in this direction also, a very important advance
of the Greek Christian element, and still more a considerable retreat of Turkish domination. Between the
original conditions of the peace of San Stefano under
Ignatieff and the results of the congress the difference
was politically unimportant, as was clearly proved by the
facility with which Southern Bulgaria revolted and became annexed to Northern Bulgaria. And even if it had
not taken place, the net gain to Russia after the war, and
in consequence of the decisions of the congress, remained
more brilliant than those of earlier times.

The indignation of Russia at the result of the Berlin
That Russia, by bestowing Bulgaria on the nephew of
the then Russian Empress, the Prince of Battenberg, gave
it into insecure hands, was a development which could not
be foreseen at the Berlin congress. The Prince of Battenberg was the Russian candidate for Bulgaria, and from his
near relationship to the imperial house it was also to be
expected that these connexions would be firm and lasting.
The Emperor Alexander III accounted for the revolt of
his cousin simply by his Polish descent : 'Polskaja mat'
was his first exclamation in his disappointment as to his
cousin's behaviour.

The indignation of Russia at the result of the Berlin
congress was one of the manifestations which become
possible, though contrary to all truth and reason, in a
press so little intelligible to the people as that of Russia
in its foreign relations, and with the coercion which
is easily exercised upon it. The whole influence which
Gortchakoff, spurred on by chagrin and envy at his
former colleague, the German Chancellor, exercised in
Russia with the support of French sympathisers and their

French connexions (Vannovski, Obrucheff), was strong
enough to represent in the press, with the Moscow
'Viedomosti' at its head, an appearance of indignation at
the injury which Russia through German perfidy suffered
at the Berlin conference. But the fact is that no wish
was expressed by Russia at the Berlin congress which
Germany would not have proposed for acceptance if
circumstances required, by energetic representation to the
English Prime Minister, notwithstanding that the latter
was ill and kept his bed a good deal. Instead of being
thankful for this, it was found conducive to Russian
policy, under the leadership of the worn-out but nevertheless still morbidly vain Prince Gortchakoff and of
the Moscow newspapers, to work on towards a further
estrangement between Russia and Germany, for which
there is not the slightest necessity in the interest of either
one or the other of these great adjoining empires.
We envy one another nothing, and have nothing to win
from one another which we could turn to account. Our
reciprocal relations are only endangered by personal
feelings, such as those of Gortchakoff were, and those of
high Russian military men are, owing to their French
connexions ; or by royal losses of temper such as those
which came about before the Seven Years' war owing to
the sarcastic remarks of Frederick the Great about the
Empress of Russia. For this reason the personal relations
of the monarchs of the two countries to one another are
of great importance for the peace of the two neighbour-
empires ; which no divergence of interests, only the
personal sensibilities of influential statesmen could afford
occasion for interrupting.

His subordinates in the ministry said of Gortchakoff :
'Il se mire dans son encrier,' just as Bettina used to say

about her brother-in-law, the celebrated Savigny: 'He
cannot cross a gutter without looking at himself in it.'
A great portion of Gortchakoff's dispatches, and especially
the most important, are not his, but Jomini's, a very
clever editor: the son of a Swiss general, whom the
Emperor Alexander induced to join the Russian service.
When Gortchakoff dictated, there was more rhetorical
effect in the dispatches, but those of Jomini were more
practical. When he dictated he used to take a regular
pose, which he introduced with the word 'écrivez!' and
if the secretary thoroughly appreciated his position he
turned at particularly well-rounded phrases an admiring
glance on his chief, who was very sensible to it. Gortchakoff was equally perfect master of the Russian, German,
and French languages.

Count Kutusoff was an honourable soldier without
personal vanity. He was originally, as his name would
signify, in a prominent position at St. Petersburg, as
officer of the cavalry guard, but did not possess the favour
of the Emperor Nicholas. When the latter, as I was
told in St. Petersburg, called out to him in front of the
regiment: 'Kutusoff, you cannot ride, I will transfer you to
the infantry,' he sent in his resignation, and it was only in
the Crimean war that he again entered the service in a
subordinate rank. He remained in the army under Alexander II, and finally became Military Plenipotentiary
at Berlin, where his honest *bonhomie* won him many
friends. He accompanied us as Russian aide-de-camp
to the Prussian King in the French war, and it was
perhaps a result of the unjust opinion of his horsemanship
formed by the Emperor Nicholas that he traversed on
horseback all the tracts over which the King and his
suite were driven, frequently from fifty to seventy versts

in the day. To give an idea of his *bonhomie* and of the tone at the hunting-parties at Wusterhausen, he on one occasion mentioned in the King's presence that his family came from Prussian Lithuania, and had arrived in Russia under the name of Kutu ; whereupon Count Fritz Eulenburg remarked in his witty way : ' Consequently you first appropriated the final " soff " * in Russia '—general amusement, in which Kutusoff heartily joined.

Besides the conscientious reports of this old soldier, the regular autograph correspondence of the Grand Duke of Saxony with the Emperor Alexander offered a way of sending ungarbled communications direct to the latter. The Grand Duke, who is and always has been favourable towards me, was an advocate at St. Petersburg for friendly relations between the two cabinets.

The possibility of an European intervention was a cause of disquietude and impatience to me in view of the slow progress of the siege. In situations such as ours before Paris the vicissitudes of war are not excluded even with the best generalship and the utmost bravery ; they can be produced by chances of every kind, and to these our position, between the army of the besieged, numerically very strong, and the forces from the provinces so difficult to calculate upon as regards number and locality, offered a rich field, even if our troops before Paris and in the west, north, and east of France remained free from disease. The question how the standard of health of the German army would be maintained in the hardships of such an unusually severe winter was beyond all calculation. Under these circumstances it was no sign of excessive anxiety if I was tormented during sleepless nights by the apprehension that our political interests, after such

* [*Soff* = guzzle.]

great successes, might be severely injured through the
hesitation and delay in taking further steps against
Paris. A decision, memorable in the world's history,
of the secular struggle between the two neighbouring
peoples was at stake, and in danger of being ruined,
through personal and predominantly female influences
with no historical justification, influences which owed
their efficacy, not to political considerations but to
feelings which the terms humanity and civilisation,
imported to us from England, still rouse in German
natures. Even during the Crimean war it was preached
to us from England, and not without effect on our
mood, that we ought to take up arms for the Turks
'for the saving of civilisation.' The decisive questions
could, if it were considered desirable, be treated as exclusively military, and that might have been adopted as
a pretext for refusing me the right of taking part in the
decision. They were such, however, that on their solution
depended the possibility of diplomacy in the last resort ;
and if the conclusion of the French war had been a little
less favourable to Germany, then would this mighty war,
with its victories and its enthusiasm, have remained without the effect it produced on our national unification. I
never doubted that the victory over France must precede
the restoration of the German kingdom, and if we did not
succeed in bringing it this time to a perfect conclusion,
further wars without the preliminary security of our
perfect unification were full in view.

It must not be assumed that the other generals
could, *from a purely military standpoint*, have been of
a different opinion from Roon ; our position, between the
besieged army, which numerically was stronger than ourselves, and the French forces in the provinces, was

strategically an exposed one, and its maintenance without promise of success, unless it were utilised as the basis of a forward movement in the shape of an assault. The anxiety to put an end to it in military circles in Versailles was as great as the uneasiness at home concerning the slow progress. Even without taking into account the possibility of sickness and unforeseen defeats, in consequence of mishaps or blunders, one could not fail to hit upon the line of thought that disturbed me, and to ask oneself whether the prestige gained and the political impression made upon the neutral Courts by our first rapid and great victories would not be enfeebled by the apparent inactivity and weakness of our position before Paris, and whether the enthusiasm, in the fire of which a lasting unity might be forged, would hold out.

The fighting in the provinces near Orleans and Dijon continued to bring us fresh victories, thanks to the heroic courage of the troops, which, indeed, far exceeded the measure that can be relied upon as a basis for strategical calculations. But the moral impetus, by which our inferior forces there had, notwithstanding frost, snow, and a dearth both of victuals and war material, beaten the numerically stronger masses of the French, might be destroyed at any moment by some accident or other; a thought sufficient to force every commander, unless he calculated exclusively in optimistic conjectures, to the conviction that we should have to put an end to our uncertain position as speedily as possible by expediting our assault on Paris.

To put this assault into effect, however, we had no orders, and were, as was the case before the lines of Floridsdorf in July 1866, without heavy siege guns. The transport of the latter had not kept pace with the progress of our army; in order to effect it, our railway resources fell short at the points where the lines were interrupted or where they stopped altogether, as at Lagny.

The speedy conveyance of siege ordnance and of the mass of heavy ammunition, without which the bombardment could not begin, might, however, with the rolling stock at hand have been effected more rapidly than was the case. But as some of the officials informed me, about 1,500 trucks were laden with provisions for the Parisians, in order to assist them at once, if they surrendered, and these 1,500 trucks were therefore not available for the transport of ammunition. The bacon stored in them was afterwards refused by the Parisians; and after my departure from France, in consequence of the changes made at his Majesty's instance by General von Stosch at Ferrières in our treaty concerning the maintenance of the German troops, was assigned to them and consumed with great reluctance, as it had been kept in stock too long.

As the bombardment could not begin before a sufficient quantity of ammunition was at hand to enable the firing to be proceeded with effectively and without intermission, large numbers of horses were required in the absence of railway material, and for these an outlay of millions was necessary. I am unable to comprehend how any doubts could be entertained as to these millions being available so soon as their necessity for military purposes was proved. It appeared to me to be a considerable step in advance when Roon, who was already nervously excited and exhausted, informed me one day that the responsibility had now been shifted upon him personally by the question whether he was ready to bring up the guns within some limited time; he said that he was in doubt whether it was possible. I begged him to immediately undertake the task set him, and declared myself ready to give him an order on the federal Treasury for any sum that might be necessary if he would purchase 4,000 horses—that being his approximate estimate of the number required—and use them for the transport of the guns. He gave the requisite orders, and the bombardment of Mont Avron, which had long been awaited in our camp with painful impatience and was hailed with shouts of joy, was the result of this turn in events for which thanks were really due to Roon. He found in Prince Krafft Hohenlohe a willing supporter in getting the guns brought up and distributed.

In putting to oneself the question as to what can have induced other generals to oppose Roon's view, it is difficult to discover any technical reasons for the delay in the measures taken towards the close of the year. The hesitating course adopted appears senseless and dangerous viewed either from a military or a political standpoint, and, from the rapid and determined conduct of the war right up to the siege, it may be concluded that the reasons are not to be looked for in the indecision of our army leaders. The notion that Paris, although fortified and the strongest bulwark of our opponents, might not be attacked in the same way as any other fortress, had been imported into our camp from England by the roundabout route of Berlin, together with the phrase about the ' Mecca of civilisation,' and other expressions of humanitarian feeling rife and effective in the *cant* of English public opinion—a feeling which England expects other Powers to respect, though she does not always allow her opponents to have the benefit of it. From London representations were received in our most influential circles, to the effect that the capitulation of Paris ought not to be brought about by bombardment, but only by hunger. Whether the latter method was the more humane is a debatable point, as is also the question whether the horrors of the Commune would have broken out, had not the famine prepared the way for the liberation of anarchist savagery. Another question that may be left unanswered is whether sentiment alone, unaccompanied by political calculation, played a part in the propagation by England of the humanitarian idea of starving out the city. England was under no practical necessity, either economical or political, of protecting either France or ourselves from loss or weakness caused by the war. But in any case, the delays in overpowering Paris, and in putting an end to the military operations, increased the danger that the fruits of our victories would be spoilt. Trustworthy information from Berlin apprised me that the cessation of our activity gave rise to anxiety and dissatisfaction in expert circles, and that Queen Augusta was said to be influencing her royal husband by letter, in the interests of humanity. An allusion to information of this kind which I made to the King occasioned a violent outburst of anger, taking the form not of denial that the rumours were true, but of a sharp reprimand against the utterance of any such dissatisfaction respecting the Queen.

The initiative for any change in the conduct of the war did not as a rule emanate from the King, but from the staff of the Army or from that of the Crown Prince, who was the general in command. That this circle was open to English views if presented in a friendly manner was only natural; the Crown Princess, Moltke's late wife, the wife of Count Blumenthal, chief of the staff, and afterwards field-marshal, and the wife of von Gottberg, the staff officer next in influence, were all Englishwomen.

The reasons of the delay in the attack upon Paris, concerning which those behind the scenes had observed silence, became the subject of discussion in the press in consequence of the appearance of extracts from Count Roon's papers in the 'Deutsche Revue' of 1891.[1] All attempts to refute Roon's statements avoid mention of the Berlin and English influences, as well as of the fact that 800, and according to others 1,500, trucks stood for weeks laden with provisions for the Parisians ; and all, with the exception of one anonymous newspaper article, likewise shirk the question whether the leaders of the army paid timely attention to the transport of siege ordnance. I have found nothing to induce me to make any alteration in the above notes on the matter, which were written before the appearance of the numbers of the 'Deutsche Revue' in question.

The assumption of the Imperial title by the King upon the extension of the North German Confederation was a political necessity, since, by reminding us of days when it meant legally more but practically less than now, it constituted an element making for unity and centralisation. I was convinced, too, that the steadying pressure upon the institutions of our Empire could not but be more lasting in proportion as the Prussian upholder of them avoided the attempt, dangerous but a vital feature of the old German history, to inculcate upon the other dynasties the superiority of our own. King William I was not free from an inclination to do this, and his reluctance to take the title was not unconnected with

[1] Edition in book form, iii.[4] 243 sqq.

the desire to obtain an acknowledgement rather of the superior respectability of the hereditary Prussian Crown than of the Imperial title. He regarded the Imperial crown in the light of a modern office that might be conferred on any one, the authority of which had been disputed by Frederick the Great and had oppressed the Great Elector. At the first mention of it he said, ' What have I to do with the fancy-ball Major* ? ' To this I replied among other things, ' Your Majesty surely does not desire always to remain neuter—*das Präsidium* ? In the expression " presidency " lies an abstraction, in the word " Emperor " a great power.'

When at the first favourable turn in the war I approached the Crown Prince, he also did not always evince sympathy for my endeavours to restore the Imperial title, though they did not spring from Prussian and dynastic vanity, but solely from the belief in its utility for the furtherance of national union. From some one or other of the political dreamers to whom he gave ear his Royal Highness had imbibed the idea that the heritage of the Roman Empire revived by Charlemagne had been the misfortune of Germany, a foreign idea harmful to the nation. Historically true though this may be, the guarantee against analogous dangers which the Prince's advisers saw in the title of ' King ' of the Germans was equally unreal. There was not in these days any danger that the title, which lives only in the memory of the nation, would aid in alienating Germany's strength from her own interests and in rendering it subservient to trans-Alpine ambition all the way to Apulia. The desire, emanating from his erroneous conception, that the Prince unfolded to me gave me the impression of being a busi-

* [*Charakter-Major.* Or, possibly, ' brevet-major.']

ness proposal seriously meant, which he wished me to put into execution. My objection, which was based on the co-existence of the Kings of Bavaria, Saxony, and Wurtemburg with the proposed King in Germany or King of the Germans, to my surprise led to the further conclusion that those dynasties would have to cease bearing the regal title and reassume the ducal. I expressed my conviction that they would not do this of their own free will. Were it desired, on the other hand, to use force, this procedure would not be forgotten for centuries, and would sow the seeds of distrust and hate.

In the Diary published by Geffcken there is a suggestion that we did not know our own strength. The employment of our strength in the state of affairs at that time would have become the weakness of Germany's future. The Diary was probably not written at the time day by day, but subsequently completed with turns of phrase, by which courtly aspirants sought to render the contents more credible. In the personal statement which I published [1] I expressed my conviction that it was doctored, as well as my indignation at the plotters and sycophants who obtruded themselves upon so unsuspecting and noble a nature as that of the Emperor Frederick. When I wrote those words I had no idea that the forger was to be looked for in the direction of Geffcken, the Hanseatic Guelf, whose enmity to Prussia had not prevented him from aspiring for years past to gain the favour of the Prussian Crown Prince in order more successfully to injure him, his family and state, while playing an important part himself. Geffcken belonged to the pushing lot who had been embittered since 1866 on account of the disregard in which they and their importance were held.

[1] Sep. 23, 1888.

In addition to the Bavarian commissioners there was present at Versailles, as the especial confidant of King Lewis, Count Holnstein, who stood in close relations to the monarch as his Master of the Horse. It was he who, at a moment when the question of the title had become critical and seemed in danger of breaking down on account of Bavaria's silence and the disinclination of King William, undertook at my request to hand his master a letter from me which, in order not to delay its delivery, I wrote on a dinner-table after the cloth had been removed, upon flimsy paper, and with refractory ink.[1] In this I set forth my idea that the Bavarian Crown would not, without wounding Bavarian self-esteem, be able to concede the presidential rights to the King of Prussia, though the consent of Bavaria had already as a matter of business been given ; that the King of Prussia was a neighbour of the King of Bavaria, and that criticism of the concessions which Bavaria was making and had made would, in view of the diversity of racial relations, become keener and more easily affected by the rivalries of the German races. The exercise of Prussian authority within the frontiers of Bavaria was a novelty and would wound Bavarian susceptibilities, while a German Emperor was not a neighbour of Bavaria of different stock, but a compatriot ; in my opinion, King Lewis could fittingly grant only to a German Emperor, and not to a King of Prussia, the concessions he had already made to the authority of the presidency. To these main points in my case I also added personal arguments recalling the particular goodwill which the Bavarian dynasty had, at the time that it ruled in the March of Brandenburg (in the person of the Emperor Lewis), borne for more than a generation to my forefathers. I considered this *argumentum*

---

[1] Cf. *supra*, vol. i. p. 383.

ad hominem useful in addressing a monarch with such leanings as the King, though I believe that the political and dynastic estimate of the difference between the presidential rights of a German Emperor and a Prussian King was what turned the scale. The Count started upon his journey to Hohenschwangau within two hours, on November 27, and completed it under great difficulties and with frequent interruptions in four days. The King was confined to his bed with the toothache, and at first refused to see him, but had him admitted when he heard that the Count had come with a commission and a letter from me. He carefully read my letter twice over in bed in the Count's presence, asked for writing materials, and committed to paper the desired communication to King William of which I had made out a draft. In this the main argument for the imperial title was reproduced, with the more stringent suggestion that Bavaria could make *only* to the German Emperor, but not to the King of Prussia, the concession already agreed to but not yet ratified. I had especially chosen this form of expression in order to overcome the aversion of my royal master to the imperial title. Count Holnstein returned to Versailles bearing this letter from the King on the seventh day after his departure, that is, on December 3 ; it was officially handed to our King on the same day by Prince Leopold, the present regent, and constituted an important factor in the success of the difficult labours the result of which, owing to King William's resistance and the absence of any definite statement of the Bavarian views, had often been doubtful. By this double journey, performed in one sleepless week, and by the able execution of his commission at Hohenschwangau, Count Holnstein rendered important service in the establishment of our national unity, through the removal of external obstacles in the question of the imperial title.

His Majesty raised a fresh difficulty when we were fixing the form of the imperial title, it being his wish to be called Emperor of Germany if emperor it had to be. In this phase both the Crown Prince, who had long given up his idea of a King of the Germans, and the Grand Duke of Baden lent me their support, each in his own way, though neither openly attempted to overcome the old monarch's violent dislike to the 'fancy-dress major.'[1] The Crown Prince supported me passively with his company in the presence of his father and by occasional brief expressions of his views. These, however, did not strengthen me in my stand against the King, but tended rather to excite further the irritability of my august master. For the King, in conscientious remembrance of his oath to the Constitution and the ministerial responsibility, was more inclined to make concession to the minister than to his son. Differences of opinion between himself and the Crown Prince he regarded from the point of view of the *pater familias*.

In the final conference on January 17, 1871, he declined the designation of German Emperor, and declared that he would be Emperor of Germany or no emperor at all. I pointed out that the adjectival form German Emperor and the genitival Emperor of Germany differed in point both of language and period. People had said Roman Emperor and not Emperor of Rome; and the Czar did not call himself Emperor of Russia, but Russian, as well as 'united-Russian' (*wserossiski*) Emperor. The King disputed the latter statement warmly,

[1] See above, p. 126.

appealing to the fact that the reports of his Russian Kaluga regiment were always addressed *pruskomu*, which he translated wrongly. He would not believe my assurance that the form in question was the dative of the adjective, and only allowed himself to be subsequently convinced by Hofrath Schneider, his usual authority for the Russian language. I further urged that under Frederick the Great and Frederick William II the thalers were inscribed *Borussorum* not *Borussiae rex;* that the title Emperor of Germany involved a sovereign claim to the non-Prussian dominions, which the princes were not inclined to allow; that it was suggested in the letter from the King of Bavaria that 'the exercise of the presidential rights should be associated with the assumption of the title of German Emperor,' and finally, that the said title had, on the proposition of the federal council, been adopted in the new draft of Article 11 of the Constitution.

The discussion then turned upon the difference in rank between emperors and kings, between arch-dukes, grand dukes, and Prussian princes. My exposition that in principle emperors do not rank above kings found no acceptance, although I was able to show that Frederick William I, at a meeting with Charles VI, who, in point of fact, stood in the position of feudal lord to the Elector of Brandenburg, claimed and enforced his rights to equality as King of Prussia by causing a pavilion to be erected which was entered by both monarchs simultaneously from opposite sides, so that they might meet each other in the centre.

The agreement which the Crown Prince showed to my argument irritated the old gentleman still more, and striking the table he cried : 'And even if it had been so,

K 2

I now command how it is to be. Arch-dukes and grand
dukes have always had precedence of Prussian princes,
and so it shall continue.' With that he got up and went
to the window, turning his back upon those seated at the
table. The discussion on the question of title came to no
clear conclusion ; nevertheless, we considered ourselves
justified in preparing the ceremony for the proclamation of
the Emperor, but the King had commanded that there
should be no mention of the German Emperor but of the
Emperor of Germany.

This position of affairs induced me to call upon the
Grand Duke of Baden on the following morning, before
the solemnity in the *Galerie des Glaces,* and to ask him how
he, as the first of the princes present, who would presumably
be the first to speak after the reading of the proclamation,
intended to designate the new Emperor. The Grand
Duke replied, 'As Emperor of Germany, according to his
Majesty's orders.' Among the arguments with which I
urged upon the Grand Duke that the concluding cheers
for the Emperor could not be given under this form, the
most effective was my appeal to the fact that the forthcoming text of the Constitution of the empire was already
forestalled by a decree of the Reichstag in Berlin. The
reference to the resolution of the Reichstag, appealing, as
it did, to his constitutional train of ideas, induced him to
go and see the King once more. I was left ignorant of
what passed between the two sovereigns, and during the
reading of the proclamation I was in a state of suspense.
The Grand Duke avoided the difficulty by raising a cheer,
neither for the German Emperor nor for the Emperor of
Germany, but for the *Emperor William.* His Majesty
was so offended at the course I had adopted, that on de-
scending from the raised daïs of the princes he ignored me

as I stood alone upon the free space before it, and passed me by in order to shake hands with the generals standing behind me. He maintained that attitude for several days, until gradually our mutual relations returned to their old form.

CHAPTER XXIV

THE *CULTURKAMPF*

WHILE at Versailles I had, from November 5 to 9, carried on negotiations with Count Ledochowski, Archbishop of Posen and Gnesen, mainly referring to the territorial interests of the Pope.   In accordance with the proverb 'One hand washes the other,' I proposed that reciprocity in the relations between the Pope and ourselves should be effected by bringing Papal influence to bear upon the French clergy in the interests of peace, being always afraid, as I was, that the interference of the neutral powers might spoil the results of our victories. Ledochowski, and, within narrower limits, Bonnechose, Cardinal Archbishop of Rouen, tried to induce several members of the higher clergy to exercise their influence in the direction indicated, but could only report that their advances had been coldly met and declined; from this I concluded that the Papacy must lack either the power or the will to afford us any assistance in obtaining peace of sufficient value to pay the price for the displeasure felt by German Protestants and the Italian National party at the result of an open championship of Papal interests in regard to Rome; as well as for the reaction of the latter sentiment on the future relations of the two nations.

During the vicissitudes of the war, the King at first appeared to be the possibly dangerous opponent for us among the conflicting Italian elements. Subsequently the Republican party under Garibaldi, who had, at the outbreak of the war, led us to look forward to their support against any Napoleonic fancies of the King's, opposed us on the battlefield with an enthusiasm more dramatic than practical, and with military performances that shocked our soldierly notions. Between these two elements there lay the sympathy which the public opinion of educated Italians openly expressed, and ever cherished, towards a people whose struggles in the past and the present were parallel to their own ; there lay also the national instinct which eventually proved strong and real enough to enter into the triple alliance with their former opponent, Austria. By openly espousing the cause of the Pope and his territorial claims we should have broken with this national tendency manifested by Italy. Whether and how far we should in return have received the assistance of the Pope in our internal affairs is doubtful. Gallicanism came to seem to me stronger in regard to infallibility than I could estimate it in 1870, and the Pope weaker than I had believed him to be on account of his surprising victories over all the German, French, and Hungarian bishops. In our own country the Jesuitic ' Centrum ' was, at the moment, stronger than the Pope, or, at least, independent of him ; the Germanic group and party-spirit of our Catholic compatriots is an element against which even the Papal will cannot make its way.

In the same way I leave it an open question whether the elections for the Prussian Parliament which were held on the 16th of the same month were influenced by the failure of Ledochowski's negotiations. The latter were renewed in a somewhat different form by the Bishop of Mainz, Baron von Ketteler, who called upon me for that purpose on several occasions at the beginning of the parliamentary session of 1871. I had been in communication with him in 1865, when I asked him whether he would accept the archbishopric of Posen, being led to this by a desire to show him that we were not anti-Catholic, but only anti-Polish. Ketteler had, probably after communicating with Rome, declined on the ground of his ignorance of the Polish language. In 1871 he made representations to me amounting to a demand that the Imperial Constitution should include the articles in that of Prussia dealing with the position of the Catholic church in the state, three of which (15, 16, and 18) were annulled by the law of June 18, 1875. So far as I was concerned, the course of our policy was not determined by religious considerations, but purely by the desire to establish as firmly as possible the unity won on the battlefield.

In religious matters, my toleration has at all times been restricted only by the boundaries which the necessity of various denominations co-existing in the same body politic imposes on the claims of each particular creed. The therapeutic treatment of the Catholic Church in a temporal state is, however, rendered difficult by the fact that the Catholic clergy, if they desire properly to discharge what is theoretically their duty, must claim a share in the secular government extending beyond the ecclesiastical domain ; they constitute a political institution under clerical forms, and transmit to their collaborators their own conviction that for them *freedom* lies in *dominion*, and that the Church, wherever she does not rule, is justified in complaining of Diocletian-like persecution.

It was in this sense that I had some discussion with Herr von Ketteler respecting his more precisely asserted claim to the constitutional right of his Church—that is, of the clergy—to direct the movements of the secular arm. Among his political arguments he used this one, appealing more *ad hominem* : that with regard to our fate after death, the Catholics had stronger guarantees than others, since, presuming the Catholic dogmas to be mistaken, the fate of the Catholic soul could not be worse even if the Evangelical faith turned out to be the right one, but that, assuming the contrary to be the case, the future of the heretic soul was terrible. To this he added the question : ' Do you perchance believe that a Catholic cannot attain salvation ? ' I replied : ' A Catholic layman most certainly can, but I am doubtful about a priest, for in the latter is found "the sin against the Holy Ghost," and the text of the Scriptures is against him.' The Bishop smilingly replied to this rejoinder, which I had made in a bantering tone, by a courteous ironical bow.

After our negotiations had ended without results, the reconstruction of the Catholic party founded in 1860, but now known as the ' Centrum,' was pushed on with increasing zeal, especially by Savigny and Mallinckrodt. This party afforded me an opportunity of observing that in Germany as well as in France the Pope is weaker than he seems, or at any rate not so strong as to make it needful for us to buy his assistance in our affairs by a rupture with the sympathies of other more powerful elements. From the *désaveu* contained in Cardinal Antonelli's letter of June 5, 1871, to Bishop Ketteler, from the mission entrusted to Prince Löwenstein-Wertheim by the Centrum, and from the insubordination of the latter party on the occasion of the Septennate, I received the impression that the party spirit with which Providence has endowed the Centrum in the place of the national feeling of other peoples is stronger

than the Pope, not in a council without laymen, but on
the battlefield of parliamentary and literary struggles
inside Germany. Whether this would also be the case if
the Papal influence attempted to impose itself without
regard to competing forces, such as that of the Jesuits, is a
question which I leave unanswered, without entering into
the subject of the State-Secretary Cardinal Franchi's
sudden death. It has been said of Russia : *gouvernement
absolu tempéré par le régicide.* Would a Pope who went
too far in his disregard of the competing forces in Church
politics be safer from ecclesiastical ' Nihilists ' than the
Czar ? Opposed to bishops assembled in the Vatican, the
Pope is strong, and when he marches *with* the Jesuits
stronger than when he seeks beyond the bounds of his own
capital to break down the opposition of the lay Jesuits,
who are wont to be the supporters of parliamentary
Catholicism.

The beginning of the *Culturkampf* was decided for me
preponderantly by its Polish side. Since the abandonment of the policy of the Flottwells and Grolmanns, since
the solidification of the Radziwill influence upon the King
and the establishment of the ' Catholic section ' in the
Ministry of Public Worship, statistical data proved beyond
doubt the rapid progress of the Polish nationality at the
expense of the Germans in Posen and West Prussia, and
in Upper Silesia the so far sturdy Prussian element of the
' Wasserpolacken ' became Polonised; Schaffranek was
elected there to the Diet, and it was he who, speaking
in parliament, confronted us in the Polish language with
the proverb of the impossibility of the fraternisation of

Germans and Poles. Such things could only happen in Silesia by reason of the official authority of the Catholic section. Upon complaints being made to the Prince-Bishop, Schaffranek was forbidden on his re-election to 'sit' on the Left; as a consequence of this order, the powerfully-built priest stood as upright as a sentinel before the benches of the Left for five or six hours, and when sittings were long ten hours a day, and was thus spared the trouble of rising when he wished to make one of his anti-German speeches.[1] According to official reports, there were whole villages in Posen and West Prussia containing thousands of Germans who through the influence of the Catholic section had been educated according to Polish ideas, and were officially described as 'Poles,' although in the previous generation they were officially Germans. By the powers that had been granted to the section, there was no remedy except the abolition of the latter. This abolition was therefore in my opinion the next object to be striven for. It was *naturally* opposed by the Radziwill influence at Court, and *unnaturally* by my colleague of Public Worship, his wife, and her Majesty the Queen. The chief of the Catholic section at that time was Krätzig, who had formerly been in the private employment of Radziwill and had probably continued so while in the public service. The representative of the Radziwill influence was Prince Boguslaw, the younger of the two brothers, who was also an influential member of the Berlin common council. William, the elder, and his son Anthony, were soldiers too honest to take part in Polish plots against the King and his state. The Catholic section in the Ministry of Public Worship—originally intended to

---

[1] Cf. the expression in the speech of Jan. 28, 1886. *Politische Reden*, xi. 438.

be an institution by means of which Prussian Catholics might defend the rights of their state in their relations with Rome—had, owing to the change of members, gradually become a body in the heart of Prussian bureaucracy defending Roman and Polish interests against Prussia. More than once did I explain to the King that this section was worse than a nuncio in Berlin; that it acted in accordance with instructions which it received from Rome, not always perhaps from the Pope; and that it had lately become open more particularly to Polish influences. I admitted that the ladies in the Radziwill family were friendly to Germany, that the elder brother William was kept in the same groove by his sense of honour as a Prussian officer, and that this was likewise the case with his son Anthony, who was moreover bound to his Majesty by ties of personal affection. But in the driving element of the family, consisting of the ecclesiastics, Prince Boguslaw, and his son, Polish national sentiment was stronger than any other, and was cultivated on the basis that Polish and Romish-clerical interests were concurrent—the only basis practicable in times of peace, but then very readily practicable. Krätzig again, the head of the Catholic section, was as good as a serf of the Radziwills. A nuncio would regard it as his chief duty to defend the interests of the Catholic Church, but not those of the Poles; would not be in intimate relations to the bureaucracy, as were the members of the Catholic section who, among the garrison which held the ministerial citadel in our system of defence against revolutionary attacks, sat as a faction inimical to the state; a nuncio, finally, would as a member of the diplomatic body be personally interested in maintaining good relations between his sovereign and the Court to which he was accredited.

Although I was unsuccessful in conquering the Emperor's dislike to a nuncio in Berlin—a dislike that was, for the rest, rather outwardly external and formal—his Majesty was persuaded of the danger of the Catholic section, and gave his sanction to its abolition in spite of the opposition of his spouse. Conjugal influence induced Mühler to oppose the abolition, concerning which all the other ministers were agreed. A difference arising from a personal matter concerning the administration of the museums served as the ostensible pretext for his resignation ; in reality his fall was due to Krätzig and Polonism, in spite of the support which he and his wife had procured through their connexion with ladies at Court,

I should never have thought of occupying myself with the legal details of the May Laws ; they were outside my department, and I had neither the intention nor the qualifications to control or to correct Falk as a jurist. I could not, as Minister-President, fulfil the duties of the Minister of Public Worship at the same time, even if I had been in perfect health. It was only by seeing them in practice that I became convinced that the legal details had not been properly conceived for the effect they were wanted to produce. The error in their conception was made evident to me by the picture of dexterous, light-footed priests pursued through back doors and bedrooms by honest but awkward Prussian gendarmes, with spurs and trailing sabres. Whoever supposes that such critical considerations surging up in me would immediately have been embodied in the form of a cabinet crisis between Falk and myself has not the correct judgement, which can only be

gained by experience, of the manner in which the state
machine has to be driven, both as regards itself and its connexion with the monarch and the parliamentary elections.
That machine is unable to perform sudden evolutions, and
ministers of Falk's talents do not grow wild with us. It
was better to have a fellow combatant of such ability and
courage in the ministry than to make myself responsible for
the administration of the Department of Public Worship,
or for a new appointment to it, by encroaching upon the
constitutional independence of his office. I adhered to
this view as long as I could prevail upon Falk to stay.
Only when, contrary to my wishes, he had been so put out
by feminine Court influence and ungracious letters from
the royal hand that it became impossible to keep him, did
I proceed to a revision of what he had left behind—a thing
I was unwilling to do so long as that was only possible by
a rupture with him.

Falk succumbed to the same tactics as had been
brought to bear upon me at Court with similar resources,
but not with similar success ; he succumbed to them
partly because he was more susceptible to Court influences
than I, partly because he was not supported in the same
measure by the sympathy of the Emperor. The anti-
ministerial activity of the Empress originally sprang from
the independence of character which rendered it difficult
for her to side with a government that was not in her
own hands, and which, for a whole generation, attracted
her to the path of opposition against every successive
administration. She was not quick to adopt the opinion
of others. At the time of the *Culturkampf* this propensity
was intensified by the Catholics surrounding her Majesty,
who obtained their information and instructions from the
Ultramontane camp. That party utilised with skill and

discernment the old propensity of the Empress to exercise her influence in the improvement of each successive government. I repeatedly dissuaded Falk from plans of resignation in connexion either with letters of displeasure from the Emperor, which were probably not due to the initiative of the august ruler himself, or with slights offered to his wife at court. I recommended him to maintain a passive attitude towards the ungracious communications of his Majesty, unadorned, as they were, by any counter-signature, and referring less to *Culturkampf* than to the Minister's relations with the High Consistorial Court and the Protestant Church; but in any case to bring his grievances before the State Ministry, whose suggestions, if unanimous, the King was wont to respect. Finally, however, being exposed to mortifications that wounded his sense of honour, he decided to resign. All the accounts which state that I ousted him from the ministry rest upon invention, and I was surprised that he never publicly contradicted them, although he always remained in friendly relations with me. Among the events that decided his retirement I can still remember that it was the disputes with the High Consistorial Court and the clerics connected with it that brought about the rupture with his Majesty, though it was easy to detect, from the manner in which the controversial matters that told against Falk were developed and brought to a head, the collaboration of more dexterous hands and higher skill than was possessed by the official counsellors of the Emperor in his capacity of *summus episcopus.*

After his departure I found myself face to face with the question whether, and how far, in choosing a new

Minister of Public Worship, I was to keep in sight
Falk's rather juristic than political leanings, or follow
exclusively my own views, tending more towards Polonism
than Catholicism.   In the *Culturkampf*, the parliamentary
policy of the government had been crippled by the defection
of the Progressive party and its transition to the Centrum.
Meantime in the Reichstag, without getting any support
from the Conservatives, it was opposed by a majority of
Democrats of all shades, bound together by a common
enmity, and in league with Poles, Guelfs, friends of
France, and Ultramontanes.   The consolidation of our new
imperial unity was retarded by these circumstances, and
would be imperilled were they to continue or to become
aggravated.   The mischief to the nation might be rendered
more serious in this way than by an abandonment of what
was in my opinion the superfluous part of the Falk legislation.   The indispensable part I held to be the removal
of the article from the Constitution, the acquisition of
means for combating Polonism, and, above all, the supremacy of the state over the schools.   If we carried these
points we should still have gained considerably by the
Culturkampf, considering the state in which things were
before the outbreak of the conflict.   I had therefore to
come to an agreement with my colleagues concerning the
extent to which we might go in our compromise with the
Curia.   The resistance of the whole body of ministers
who had taken part in the conflict was more stubborn
than that of my immediate colleagues, and primarily of
Falk's successor, in which capacity I had proposed Herr
von Puttkamer to the King.   But even after this change I
could not immediately effect an alteration in the Church
policy without causing fresh cabinet troubles unwelcome
to the King and undesired by myself.   The memories of

the days when I sought to gain over fresh partisans are among the most unpleasant of my official career. In order to combine with Herr von Puttkamer I should have had to gain the support of the officials of his department with the habit of the *Culturkampf* in them, and that was beyond my powers. The explanation of Falk's Church policy is not to be exclusively sought for in the arena of the conflict with the Catholic Church; it was occasionally traversed and influenced by the Evangelical Church question. In the latter Herr von Puttkamer was in closer agreement than Falk with the views entertained at Court, and my desire to limit the conflict with Rome to a narrower sphere would probably have met with no personal opposition on the part of my new colleague. The difficulties, however, lay partly in the preponderance of the officials, still agitated by the passions of the *Culturkampf*, to whom Herr von Puttkamer further considered himself bound to sacrifice the natural and traditional development of our orthography, partly in the opposition of my other colleagues to any appearance of yielding to the Pope.

My first attempts to introduce peace into ecclesiastical affairs met with no sympathy from his Majesty. The influence of the highest Evangelical clergy was at that time stronger than the Catholicising influence of the Empress, the latter, moreover, receiving no incentive from the Centrum, because that party considered the preliminaries of the compromise unsatisfactory, and because, like the Court, it attached even more importance to fighting me than to seconding any efforts I might put forth. The conflicts that proceeded from the situation repeated themselves, and became gradually more severe.

Many years of labour were still required before it was

possible to enter upon the revision of the May Laws without
occasioning fresh troubles in the cabinet, since a majority
was wanting for the defence of those laws in parliamentary
warfare after the desertion of the Freethought or 'Libera-
list' party to the Ultramontane opposition camp.   I was
satisfied when in opposition to Polonism we succeeded in
maintaining as definite gains the relations between school
and state imposed by the *Culturkampf* and the alteration
made in the articles of the Constitution relating thereto.
Both are, in my opinion, of more value than the injunctions
against clerical activity contained in the May Laws and the
legal apparatus for catching recalcitrant priests, and I ventured to regard as a considerable gain in itself the abolition
of the Catholic section and of the danger to the State arising
from its activity in Silesia, Posen, and Prussia.   After the
Freethought party had not only given up the *Culturkampf*,
prosecuted more by themselves under the leadership of Vir-
chow and his associates than by me, but began to support the
Centrum both in parliament and at the elections, the government was in a minority as against the last-named party.   In
the face of a compact majority consisting of the Centrum,
the Progressives, the Social Democrats, the Poles, the
Alsatians, and the Guelfs, the policy of Falk had no
chance in the Reichstag.   For that reason I considered it
more politic to pave the way for peace provided the
schools remained protected, the Constitution freed from
the abolished articles, and the state rid of the Catholic
section.

When I had at last won the Emperor over, the new
position of the Progressive party and of the Seceders was
a matter of decisive weight in determining what was to be
retained and what given up ; instead of supporting the
government, those sections leagued themselves with the

Centrum at elections and in the divisions, and had conceived hopes which found expression in the so-called 'Gladstone Ministry' (Stosch, Rickert, and others)—that is, in the Liberal-Catholic coalition.

In the year 1886 it was at length possible to terminate the counter-Reformation, partly sought for by me, partly recognised as allowable; and to establish a *modus vivendi* which may still, compared with the *status quo* before 1871, be regarded as a result of the whole *Culturkampf* favourable to the state.

How permanent this will be, and how long the conflict of denominations will now remain quiet, time alone can show. It depends upon ecclesiastical moods and upon the degree of combativeness, not only of the Pope for the time being and his leading counsellors, but also of the German bishops, and of the more or less High Church tendencies governing the Catholic population at different periods. It is impossible to confine within stated limits the claims of Rome upon countries that have religious equality and a Protestant dynasty. It cannot be done even in purely Catholic states. The conflict that has been waged from time immemorial between priests and kings cannot be brought to a conclusion at the present day, and of all places not in Germany. Before 1870 the condition of things caused the position of the Catholic Church in Prussia itself to be recognised by the Curia as a pattern and more favourable than in most of the purely Catholic countries. In our home politics however, and especially in our parliamentary politics, we could trace no effects of this denominational satisfaction. Long before 1871 the group led by the two Reichenspergers was already permanently attached to the opposition against the government of the Protestant dynasty, though its leaders did not on that account incur the personal stigma of being called disturbers of the peace. In any *modus vivendi* Rome will regard a Protestant dynasty and Church as an irregularity and a disease which it is the duty of its Church to cure. The conviction that this is the case is no reason for the state itself to commence the conflict and to abandon its defensive attitude with regard to the Church of Rome, for all treaties of peace in this world are provisional, and only hold good for a time. The political relations between independent powers are the outcome of an unbroken series of events arising either from conflict or from the objection of one or other of the parties to renew the conflict. Any temptation on the part of the Curia to renew the conflict in Germany will always arise from the excitability of the Poles, the desire for power among their nobility, and the superstition of the lower classes fostered by the priests. In the country around Kissingen I have come across German peasants who had had their schooling, and who firmly believed that the priest who stood by the death-bed in the sinful flesh could, by granting or refusing absolution, dispatch the dying man direct to heaven or hell, and that it was therefore necessary to have him for your political friend as well. In Poland I presume it is at least as bad or worse, for the uneducated man is told that German and Lutheran are terms as identical as are Polish and Catholic. Eternal peace with the Roman Curia is in the existing state of affairs as impossible as is peace between France and her neighbours. If human life is nothing but a series of struggles, this is especially so in the mutual relations of independent political bodies, for the adjustment of which no properly-constituted court exists with power to enforce its decrees. The Roman Curia, however, is an independent

political body, possessing among its unalterable qualities
the same propensity to grab all round as is innate in our
French neighbours. In its struggles against Protestantism,
which no concordat can quiet, it has always the aggressive
weapons of proselytism and ambition at its disposal; it
tolerates the presence of no other gods.

While the Culturkampf was raging King Victor
Emanuel paid Berlin a visit lasting from September 22 to
26, 1873. I had heard from Herr von Keudell that the King
had ordered a snuff-box set with diamonds, valued at fifty
or sixty thousand francs—about six or eight times as much
as it is usual to give on such occasions—to be made and
forwarded to Count Launay for presentation to me. At
the same time it came to my knowledge that Launay had
shown the box with an intimation of its value to his
neighbour, Baron Pergler von Perglas, the Bavarian
Ambassador, who was on terms of very close friendship
with our opponents in the *Culturkampf.* The great value
of the present intended for me might therefore cause it
to be regarded as having some connexion with the *rapprochement* with the German empire which the King of
Italy at that time sought and obtained. When I submitted to the Emperor my scruples about taking the
present, he at first supposed that I considered it beneath
my dignity to accept a portrait-box, and saw in this a
departure from traditions to which he was accustomed. I
said : 'I should not have thought of refusing a present
of this kind of the average value. In this case, however,
it is not the royal portrait, but the saleable diamonds
which are of decisive importance in estimating the

matter; out of consideration for the state of the *Culturkampf*, I am obliged to avoid anything that might
serve as a peg for suspicion, since the value of the box,
excessive under the circumstances, has been made known
through those who stand in neighbourly relations to
Perglas, and circulated in society.' The Emperor finally
came over to my way of thinking, and closed the incident with the words: 'You are right—don't accept the
box.' *

On my bringing my views to the knowledge of
Count Launay through Herr von Keudell, the box was
replaced by a very fine and striking portrait of the King
bearing the following autograph inscription alluding to
my order of the Annunciation:

AL PRINCIPE BISMARCK

BERLINO 26 SETTEMBRE, 1873

AFFEZIONATISSIMO CUGINO

VITTORIO EMANUELE.

The King, however, felt a desire to give me a stronger
mark of his goodwill by a gift as valuable as the one
originally intended, but unsaleable, and I received in
addition to the flattering inscription on the portrait an
alabaster vase of unusual size and beauty, the packing

---

* Prince Gortchakoff was of a different opinion concerning the acceptance of a box set with diamonds. During our visit to St. Petersburg in 1872
his Majesty asked me: 'What can I possibly give Prince Gortchakoff?
He has everything already, including my portrait; what do you say to a
bust or a box set with diamonds?' I raised objections to an expensive
box, basing them on Prince Gortchakoff's position and wealth, and the
Emperor said I was right. I thereupon sounded the Prince in confidence,
and at once received this reply: 'Get a good big box given me set with
fine stones (avec de grosses pierres).' I reported this to his Majesty,
feeling somewhat ashamed of my knowledge of human nature; we both
laughed, and Gortchakoff got his box.

and removal of which occasioned me some difficulty when my successor forced me to a precipitate evacuation of my official residence.

The ' Germania' of December 6, 1891, deduces from the correspondence between Count von Roon and Moritz von Blanckenburg, published in the 'Deutsche Revue,' that I had overcome the Emperor's resistance to civil marriages.

Blanckenburg was a comrade in the fight who was above all endeared to me by a friendship dating from our childish days and lasting till his death. This friendship was, however, on his side not identical with confidence or devotion in the field of politics ; here I had to contend with the competition of his political and religious confessors, and these had no intention, nor had Blanckenburg the capacity, to form a broad-minded estimate of the historical progress of German and European politics. He was himself without ambition, and free from the disease of many of his old-Prussian colleagues— jealousy of myself; but it was difficult for his political judgement to tear itself away from the Prussian-Particularistic or even from the Pomeranian-Lutheran standpoint. His thoroughly sound common sense and honesty made him independent of Conservative party movements in which both were wanting ; this independence had, however, to be discounted by the prudence and modesty due to his want of familiarity with the political arena. He was yielding, and not steeled against persuasion, not an immovable pillar upon which I might have leant. The conflict between his goodwill towards me and his inability to

resist other influences finally induced him to retire from
politics altogether. The first time that I put him forward
as Minister of Agriculture, the proposal fell through owing
to the opposition of the very colleagues who had previously
approved of my offer of that post to Blanckenburg. I will
leave it an open question whether my friend's disinclination to be continually exposed to the light of publicity
under the supervision of malevolent spirits may have had
something to do with the failure of my attempt to bring
this Conservative force into the ministry ; but upon his
second and definitive refusal on November 10, 1873, this
was undoubtedly the case.[1] Want of lucidity is shown
in his letter to Roon of April 1874,[2] in which he speaks
at the same time of his refusal and of Falk's abandonment by me. If the Conservative party had shown their
willingness to support me in the persons of their then
spokesmen and leaders, Blanckenburg and Kleist-
Retzow, the composition of the ministry would have been
different, and what is called in the letter the Falk *cul de
sac* would perhaps have been unnecessary. The refusal
to accept office emanated, however, as the letter proves,
from Blanckenburg himself, not, perhaps, without being
influenced by the last battles of the ' poor Lutherans ' or
' old Lutherans ' with whom Blanckenburg was joined
in the 'thirties. When he retired from politics I felt
as though he had left me in the lurch. The statement
that I had overcome the Emperor William's resistance to
civil marriages is one of the inventions of the Democratic Jesuitism which the ' Germania ' represents. The
Emperor's aversion was overcome by the pressure which
the majority of the ministers present at Berlin, assembled

---

[1] *Deutsche Revue*, October 1891.
[2] *Ibid.* December 1891.

without me under Roon's formal presidency, exercised upon his Majesty, and which went so far that the Emperor had to choose between accepting the draft bill and reconstructing the ministry. In my then state of health it would have been beyond my powers to form out of the parties inimical to me and to each other a new cabinet with a view to continuing the contests in all directions. Although the Emperor in his letter of May 8, 1874, says retrospectively that in spite of his having given way he had written against it on two further occasions, those letters were not addressed to me but to the ministry in Berlin, and in his choice between obligatory civil marriages and a change of ministers I only advised him to choose the former. His aversion to civil marriages was undoubtedly stronger even than mine; with Luther I held that marriage was a municipal matter, and my opposition to an acknowledgement of this principle was based rather upon consideration for existing custom and the conviction of the masses than upon any Christian scruples of my own.

CHAPTER XXV

RUPTURE WITH THE CONSERVATIVES

THE rupture between the Conservatives and myself, which occurred amidst much noise in 1872, had been first foreshadowed in 1868 in the debates upon the Hanoverian Provincial Fund. The draft of the bill, submitted to the Diet by the government, in fulfilment of a promise made to the Hanoverians a year before, had already been smartly opposed by the Conservative members in committee, when the deputies von Brauchitsch and von Diest brought forward an amendment in the full house substantially modifying the measure. The former, as spokesman, explained the reasons why the Conservative party could not vote for the bill. I concluded my exhaustive reply with these words: 'Constitutional government is impossible if the government cannot confidently rely upon one of the greater parties even in such exceptional matters as are not entirely to the taste of the party—if that party cannot balance its account in this way: "We support the government throughout; it is true we find that it commits a blunder now and then, but up to the present it has produced fewer blunders than acceptable measures; for that reason we must take the exceptional cases in with the rest." If a government has not at least one party in the country which regards its views and leanings from such a standpoint, then it cannot possibly rule constitutionally, but is compelled to manœuvre and plot against the Constitution ; it must manage to get itself a majority artificially or to recruit a temporary one. It then degenerates into coalition ministries, and its policy betrays fluctuations which have a very prejudicial effect upon the state itself, and more especially upon the Conservative principle.' [1]

Notwithstanding this warning, the bill, with some modifications agreed to by the government, was passed on February 7 by a majority of only thirty-two, most of the Conservatives having voted against it. In the committee of the Upper House, too, the attack was repeated on the part of the Conservatives. What resources were then brought into play is shown by the following incident. Charles von Bodelschwingh, who was Minister of Finance during the Conflict time, and had in 1866 declined to procure the sums required for the war, being for that reason replaced by Baron von der Heydt, had spread a report in the Conservative party that I should really be pleased by the rejection of the measure, and offered to adduce proof of this. When business commenced he came up to me in the House and began a conversation of no importance by asking after my wife ; on leaving me he returned to his colleagues and declared that, after having consulted me, he was sure of the truth of what he had advanced.

From a perusal of the very authentic reports which Roon, who was then at Bordighera, received in February 1868 from members of the Conservative party, and which were reprinted in the ' Deutsche Revue ' of April 1891,[2] it will be seen that the Conservatives desired me to enter their group. I had little leisure time, was pre-occupied by what we had to expect from France ; by the possibility, nay, the probability that Austria, under Beust, would enter into

[1] *Politische Reden*, iii. 456.   [2] Cf. *Denkwürdigkeilen*, iii.[4] 62 sqq.

the French war plans in order to undo the events of 1866 ;
by the question what position Russia, Bavaria and Saxony
would take up at such a juncture ; finally, by the existence
of a Hanoverian legion. These cares, and the labour to
which they forced me, completely exhausted me, and, to
crown all, these gentlemen desired that I should seek out
every single private politician of their group and convert
him. I did even this, as far as I could, but my efforts
were frustrated by Bodelschwingh's intrigues and by the
animosity of Vincke, Diest, Kleist-Retzow and other displeased and jealous members of my own class and former
colleagues in the same group.

What Roon himself thought of the situation reported to
him is evident from his letter to me of February 19, 1868,
written from Bordighera, in which the following passages
occur : [1]

'According to the newspapers, it appears that you and
others have again been quarrelling lustily. This does not
surprise me, but I am sorry that differences of such a serious
nature could not be avoided—differences which cause the
Liberals by profession to shout for joy, and appear to
render the Conservatives by trade still more confused than
they, unfortunately, already are.

'What things, according to Galignani, you are reported
to have said ! I have been promised the shorthand reports
of the matter, but they are, unfortunately, not yet to hand.
I am, nevertheless, perfectly reassured concerning the chief
thing—your threatened resignation—for I consider such
a step to be absolutely impossible, excepting in the event
of physical incapacitation. I am still, however, uneasy
about the ever more threatening dismemberment of the
Conservative party, which, supposing it were to be accom-

[1] *Bismarck-Jahrbuch*, vi. 198, 199.

plished in the manner desired by the Liberals, would
be regarded by me as a very serious and significant
matter, a proceeding which would degrade you and the
government to obedient tools of the Liberal party. Of
course I understand that it is advantageous for our policy
that the Liberals should nourish a hope of being able to
put their hand to the oar as well. But I also realise that it
would be disastrous if the situation were to take such a
turn as to render their participation in the government
an inevitable necessity. You will perhaps object to this,
that the confusion, helplessness, and stupidity of the
Conservatives—apart from the envious and spiteful presumption of individuals—would of itself bring this
about, and that you can do nothing to hinder it. But is
that quite the case? If you had seriously devoted your
considerable resources to indoctrinating and organising
the Conservative party, which unfortunately does not yet
clearly recognise that its task of to-day must differ from
that of 1862 and the following years—ay, if you would
but attempt this to-day, it will be possible not only to avert
the *mésalliance* with the Liberals, but also to convert the
reformed Conservative party into the most enduring and
secure staff for your journey on the difficult but inevitable
road of Conservative progress in internal reforms and
renovation. One man, no matter how excellent the
endowments which God has given him, cannot do everything which has to be done himself. In saying this I desire to exclude any reproach which what I have said above
might seem to cast on you. Rather, I am ready to admit
willingly and repeatedly that you and your aims are not
sufficiently supported by your official colleagues. And if
I spoke of the reform of the Conservative party, I recognise that this task must, in the first instance, devolve on

the Minister of the Interior. But does Count E. possess
the confidence (and sense of duty!) necessary for its performance? Where will you find other colleagues, especially another Minister of the Interior? In the ranks of
the National Liberals? The idea is to me intolerable.
Among the Conservatives? But whom? The organising
and creative spirits in their ranks are unknown magni-
tudes, and much as I dislike our bureaucratic disorder,
I am aware that the person concerned must know it in
order to be able to reform it.'

A few days later, on February 25, Roon wrote to his
eldest son: [1]

'. . . I should prefer to write nothing at all about
politics and conflicts, after writing on the 19th on the
basis of a confidential report sent me on the 9th to express to Count Bismarck my regret that matters should
have turned out thus, &c. The shorthand reports which
have been promised me are not likely to change my view
of things; it is impossible for Bismarck to do everything.
The organisation or re-organisation of the Conservative
party, which has become necessary, is rightfully the
business of the Minister of the Interior, and neither
Bismarck, nor I, nor Blanckenburg, nor any one else is
officially called upon to do it. If the one person whose
business it is, is neither inclined nor fitted for it, he lacks
some indispensable qualification for his office, and we
may draw the necessary conclusion and act accordingly.
The loss of any wholesome influence due to Bismarck's
attitude towards the Conservatives, or to my absence or
Blanckenburg's, scarcely permits us to reproach Bismarck
on good grounds. Those who know, as I do, what enormous duties B. has to, and does, perform, cannot justly

---

[1] *Denkwürdigkeiten*, iii.[4] 70 &c.

blame him for not doing even more, and making up for his colleague's neglect or incapacity. The only possible ground on which we could justly reproach him would be if we could maintain with truth that he has not done all in his power to procure more competent colleagues. Perhaps this might be said, but I, who, in spite of distance, can perhaps judge better and more accurately than any one else of the personal relations in question, feel scarcely able definitely to make any such assertion. However, the breach will be healed, for it must be healed. There is no other party on which we can depend for the main question, but the party *must at last understand* that its ideas and tasks of to-day *must be essentially different* from those of the Conflict time. It must be, and become, a party of *Conservative progress*, and abandon the policy of the drag, however essential and necessary this may have been, and in fact was, at the time of the ascendancy of democratic progress, and the demagogic precipitation which it threatened. These are my ideas *in nuce* about the latest situation; of course they are only suited for communication in the most confidential circles. . . . '

Roon's anticipation was not fulfilled. The Conservative party remained what it was; the contest, which it had begun with me, continued in more or less latent fashion. I can understand that my policy was opposed by that Conservative party which commonly went by the name of ' Kreuzzeitung ; ' by some of its members from honourable motives of principle, which exercised in some individuals a stronger motive power than their national feeling, which was Prussian rather than German. In others, whom I might almost call my second class opponents, the motive was due to place-hunting—*ôte-toi, que je m'y mette*—of these the prototypes were Harry Arnim, Robert Goltz, and others. In the third class I might include those of my own rank among the country nobility, who were annoyed because my exceptional career had caused me to outgrow the conception, more Polish than German, of a traditional equality among the members of that class. They would have pardoned my transformation from a country *Junker* into a minister, but not my emoluments nor perhaps the princely title which had been conferred on me much against my will. 'Your Excellency' was within the limit of customary attainment and appreciation ; 'your serene Highness' challenged criticisms. I can understand this feeling, for this criticism was in correspondence with my own. On the morning of March 21, 1871, when an autograph letter of the Emperor announced my elevation to the rank of prince, I was determined to beg his Majesty to abandon his intention, because this elevation of rank would bring a very uncongenial change in the basis of my fortune and all the conditions of my life. Glad as I was to think of my sons as comfortably situated country nobles, I disliked the idea of princes with an inadequate income, like Hardenberg and Blücher, whose sons did not assume the hereditary title ; in fact the Blücher title was only renewed many decades later (1861) in consequence of a wealthy Catholic marriage. While considering all the reasons against an elevation of rank, which was quite outside the domain of my ambition, I reached the top steps of the palace stairs, and there found, to my surprise, the Emperor at the head of the royal family. He embraced me warmly and with tears, addressing me as Prince, and giving loud expression to his joy at being able to confer this distinction on me. In face of this and the hearty greetings of the royal family, it was impossible for me to express my hesitation. I have never since then lost the feeling that a count may be merely well to do without attracting undue attention, but a prince, if he wishes to avoid this, *must* be actually rich. It would have been easier for me to put up with the ill-will of my former friends and compeers if it had been due to my opinions. It found its expression and its pretext in the condemnatory criticism to which my policy was subjected by the Prussian Conservatives under the leadership of my kinsman, Herr von Kleist-Retzow, at the time of the School Inspection Bill of 1872, and on several other occasions.

The opposition of the Conservatives to the School Inspection Bill, which had been introduced in Mühler's time, was already beginning in the House of Deputies. It aimed at legally vindicating the claims of the local clergy to the inspection of the common schools, even in Poland ; while the proposal gave the office a free hand in the choice of the inspector. In the course of the animated debate which many old members will have recalled in 1892, I spoke thus on February 13, 1872 :

' The previous speaker (Lasker) stated that he and his party could not conceive that on a question which was a matter of principle and had been declared by us important for the safety of the state, on a question of this significance, what had hitherto been the Conservative party should openly declare war against the government. I do not wish to adopt this expression, but I may assuredly declare that I too cannot think that that party is going to leave the government in the lurch on a question which the government is determined for its part to carry by every constitutional means.' [1]

After the Bill had been accepted in the form approved by the government, by 207 votes against 155, the latter given by clericals, Conservatives, and Poles, it was brought on for discussion in the Upper House on March 6. I will quote a passage from my speech :

'The matter has been inflated by the evangelicals to such excessive importance, as though we now desired to depose the clergy in a lump, make a *tabula rasa*, and over-turn the whole evangelical state, with the 20,000 thalers which we are demanding. But for these exaggerations the regrettable disputes and frictions in connexion with this Bill would have been altogether superfluous ; the Bill has only gained its exaggerated importance from the quite unexpected resistance of the evangelical portion of the Conservative party, a resistance into whose origin I will not enter here in detail—I could not do so without becoming personal—but which is a most painful experience for the government and a most discouraging sign for the future. Now that I have declared to you, with an openness to which Conservatives ought never to compel the government, the origin and drift of this Bill, you ought to recognise the necessity of compelling our countrymen, who have hitherto not spoken German, to learn German. That is, in my view, the main point of this Bill.' [2]

In a house of 202, 76 voted against the Bill. On the previous evening I had exerted myself in trying to repre-sent to Herr von Kleist the probable results of the policy into which he was leading his friends, but found myself in face of a *parti pris*, the basis of which I could not con-

[1] *Politische Reden*, v. 283.   [2] *Ibid.* v. 304, 305.

jecture. On that side the breach with me was marked
externally by a distinctness which revealed as much
personal as political animosity. The conviction that that
party-politician, who was on terms of personal intimacy
with me, did grievous mischief to the country and the
Conservative cause, remains with me to this day. If
the Conservative party, instead of breaking with me
and attacking me with a bitterness and fanaticism second
to no party in the Opposition, had assisted the imperial
government in building up the structure of imperial
legislation with honest joint labour, it would not have
failed to show deep traces of this Conservative co-
operation. The completion of the structure was necessary if the political and military attainments were to be
protected from crumbling away and from centrifugal re-
trogression.

I do not know how far I could have gone to meet
Conservative co-operation, certainly further than was the
case under the circumstances to which the rupture gave
rise. At that time, in face of the dangers resulting from
our wars, I regarded the differences between parties as
subordinate, in comparison with the necessity of political
protection from external attack by serrying our ranks as
far as possible as a united nation. The first condition
was, in my view, the independence of Germany, based
upon a unity sufficiently strong for self-protection. I had
then, and still have, sufficient confidence in the sense and
reasonableness of the nation to believe that it will heal
and extirpate excrescences and mistakes in the national
institutions, if only it is not hindered by its dependence
on the rest of Europe and by internal interests of separate
groups, as was the case before 1866. With this view I
regarded, as I do to this day, the question of Liberal or

Conservative as of secondary importance in face of the impending danger of war and coalition, and rather laid stress on the free self-determination of the nation and its princes. I do not yet renounce the hope, although I feel no security, that our political future will not be injured in its future developments by blunders and mishaps.

The more exclusive *rapprochement* with the National Liberal party, to which I was of necessity brought by the desertion of the Conservatives, became a reason or a pretext in the circles of the latter for increased animosity against me. During the time that I was compelled by illness to surrender to Count Roon the chairmanship of the ministry, i.e. from New Year till September 1873, he used every evening to hold large or small meetings at his house, attended by politicians of the Right who were opposed to me. Count Harry Arnim, who was not in the habit of attending gentlemen's parties without some political object, came to these whenever he was at Berlin on leave, playing his part so as to give the company the impression conveyed to me by Roon himself in the words: ' After all he has the making of a capital *Junker* ! ' The context in which he expressed this opinion and its frequent sharply accentuated repetition in the mouth of my friend and colleague, had the effect of reproaching me for my lack of similar qualities, and conveyed a hint that Arnim would manage our domestic policy in a more spirited and Conservative manner if he were in my place. The conversation in which this theme of Arnim's *Junker* tendencies was developed in detail gave me the impression that even my old friend Roon, under the influence of the conventicle meeting at his house, felt his confidence in my policy somewhat shaken.

To these circles belonged also Colonel von Caprivi, at that time chief of a department in the War Ministry. I will not determine to which of the categories of my opponents enumerated on pp. 159, 160 he belonged at that time. I am only acquainted with his personal relations to the staff of the 'Reichsglocke,' e.g. Geheimrath von Lebbin, an official in the Ministry of the Interior, who also exercised in his department an influence hostile to me. Field-Marshal von Manteuffel told me that Caprivi had tried to strain his (Manteuffel's) influence with the Emperor against me, indicating as a ground of complaint and source of danger my 'hostility to the army.' * It is extraordinary that Caprivi did not remember in that connexion how before, and at the time of my taking office in 1862, the army had been attacked, criticised, and curtailed in step-motherly fashion by civilians, and how during my office and under my guidance it had been raised from its common-place garrison existence, and from 1864 to 1871 had passed by way of Düppel, Sadowa, and Sedan, to three triumphal entries into Berlin. I may presume without exaggeration that King William would have abdicated in 1862, that the policy which laid the foundations of the glory of the army would never have come into being, or, at any rate, not in that fashion, if I had not taken over its direction. Would the army have had the opportunity of performing its deeds of heroism and Count Moltke been able to draw his sword if King William I had received other counsels from other persons? Assuredly

---

* Compare with this reproach the letter of the Emperor Frederick, March 25, 1888, *infra*, p. 336.

not, if he had abdicated in 1862 because he could find no
one prepared to share and to face the dangers of his
position.

As early as February 11, 1872, the ' Kreuzzeitung' had
declared a feud against me on the ground that I had pro-
claimed the supremacy of parliament and atheism.   In
1875, under Nathusius Ludom, it opened its campaign of
slander against me, with what were known as the Era
articles of Perrot.*   I then applied by letter to Arnsberg,
one of our highest legal authorities, and to the Minister of
Justice, to ask whether, if I brought a penal action, I
might count with any certainty on the condemnation of
the author ; if not, I should refrain from bringing one, for
a sentence of acquittal might give my enemies a fresh
pretext for calumny.   The answer of both coincided with
that given by my own legal adviser.   The condemnation
was probable, but in view of the cautious wording of the
article, not certain.   At that time, I had not formed any
definite principles on the subject of penal actions, and the
experiences which I had had in the time of conflict were
not exactly encouraging.   I remember that one local
tribunal, I believe at Stendal, in basing its sentence, fully
admitted the grievous character of the insults publicly
directed against me, but explained its reasons for fixing
the minimum penalty of 10 thalers, by saying that I really
was a bad minister.

At the time of the appearance of Perrot's articles,
I could not yet foresee the dimensions which the cam-

* Dr. Perrot, retired captain; born at Trèves, died 1891.   Author of
pamphlets on political economy; ultimately merchant.

paign of slander against me would assume, on the part of my former comrades and particularly among those of my own rank.

No one who has taken part in the political struggles of the present day can fail to have noticed that party politicians, whose courtesy and honour in private life are quite above suspicion, as soon as they enter upon struggles of this nature, regard themselves as exempt from all those rules of honour and decency, whose authority they recognise in other cases. A grotesque exaggeration of the phrase *salus publica suprema lex* causes them to justify a baseness and vulgarity in speech and action, which outside the domain of religious and political conflict would repel them. This renouncing of all that is decent and honourable is dimly connected with a feeling that, in the interest of the party which is substituted for their country, they have to make use of a different standard from that of private life, and that the precepts of honour and good breeding may be interpreted differently and more loosely in party strife than even in war against foreign foes. The irritability which leads to the transgression of the ordinary forms and limits is unconsciously accentuated by the circumstance that in politics and religion no one can give his opponent a conclusive proof for his own conviction, and that no court exists which by its decisions can set at rest differences of opinion.

In politics, as in the domain of religious belief, no other argument can be brought by a Conservative against a Liberal, a Royalist against a Republican, a believer against an infidel, than the tune which is hackneyed by

a thousand variations of eloquence. My political convictions are right and yours are wrong ; my belief is pleasing
to God, your unbelief leads to damnation. This explains
why ecclesiastical differences of opinion bring about
religious wars ; and why political party conflicts, even if not
settled by civil war, still help to overthrow the barriers
which in the intercourse of life outside of politics are
maintained by the honour and decency of well-bred persons.
Would any cultivated and well-bred German attempt in
ordinary intercourse to use the smallest part of the im-
pertinences and insults which he does not hesitate to throw
in the face of his opponent, though as good a citizen as
himself, using, when he speaks from the platform before a
hundred witnesses, an aggressive tone quite inadmissible in
ordinary respectable society ?   Would any one outside the
domain of politics consider it consistent with the position
which he claims to hold as a gentleman of good family, to
make a business in the society with which he associates of
hawking about lies and slanders against other members
of his own society and his own class? Who would
not be ashamed to accuse blameless persons of dishonest actions in this way, without being able to bring
any proofs ? In short, where, except in the region of
political party struggle, would any one be found willingly
to undertake the part of an unconscientious slanderer ?
But as soon as a man can protect himself before his own
conscience and his group, by the plea that he is acting in
the interest of his party, the meanest action is considered
permissible and even excusable.

The slanders against me began in the paper which,
under the Christian symbol of the Cross, and the motto
' With God for King and Fatherland,' had for years
represented, not the Conservative group and still less

Christianity, but only the ambition and spiteful malice of individual editors. On February 9, 1876,[1] I complained in a public speech of the venom of this paper, and was answered by a declaration on the part of the signatories, whose educated contingent consisted of a few hundred evangelical ministers. In this form they opposed me in their official character, making themselves accomplices in the lies of the 'Kreuzzeitung,' and testifying to their mission as servants of a Christian Church and its peace, by publicly countersigning the slanders of this paper. I have always felt a mistrust of politicians in long skirts, whether feminine or ecclesiastic; and this declaration of some hundreds of evangelical pastors in favour of one of the most frivolous slanders directed against the first official in the land was not calculated to strengthen my confidence in politicians who wear the cassock, even though it be the evangelical. The possibility of personal intercourse between me and any of the signatories, many of whom had previously been acquaintances, or even friends of mine, was absolutely at an end after they had associated themselves with the dishonourable insults from Perrot's pen.

It is a hard trial for the nerves of a man of mature age when he is compelled suddenly to break off his former intercourse with all, or almost all, his friends and acquaintances. My health at that time had long been impaired, not by the labour which I had to perform, but by the continuous sense of responsibility for the great events which placed the future of my country at stake. Of course it was impossible during the animated and sometimes stormy development of our politics always to foresee *with certainty* whether the road which I took was the

---

[1] *Politische Reden*, vi. 351.

right one, and yet I was obliged to act as though I could predict with absolute clearness both coming events and the effect which my own decisions would have upon them. The question whether his own estimate, his political instinct, is leading him rightly, is difficult enough for a minister whose doubts are set at rest as soon as he feels himself sheltered under the royal signature or a parliamentary majority : a minister, one might say, of Catholic politics, who has got absolution and is not troubled by the more Protestant question, whether he has got absolution from himself. But for a minister who completely identifies his own honour with that of his country, the uncertainty of the result of each political decision has a most harassing effect. It is just as impossible to foresee with any certainty the political results at the time when a measure has to be carried, as it would be in our climate to predict the weather of the next few days. Yet we have to make our decisions as though we could do so, often enough fighting against all the influences to which we are accustomed to attach weight. Thus, for instance, at Nikolsburg, at the time of the peace negotiations, I was, and remained, the only person who was finally made responsible, and in fact, according to our institutions and customs was responsible, for the events and their results. On that occasion I was obliged to maintain my decision in a hard struggle in opposition not only to all the soldiers, that is to all who were present, but also to the King. The consideration of the question whether a decision is right, and whether it is right to hold fast and carry through what, though upon weak premises, has been recognised as right, has an agitating effect on every conscientious and honourable man. This is strengthened by the circumstance that often many years must elapse before we are able in political matters to convince ourselves whether our wishes and actions were right or wrong. It is not the work which is wearing, but rather the doubts and anxieties; the feeling of honour and responsibility, without being able to support the latter by anything except our own convictions and our own will, and this is more especially the case in the most important crises.

The intercourse with others whom we regard as similarly situated helps us to overcome these crises ; and if this suddenly ceases, from motives which are personal rather than external, envious rather than honest, and in as far as they are honest, of the most illiberal character, and the responsible minister suddenly finds himself boycotted by all his former friends, treated as an enemy, and then left alone with himself and his deliberations, this must increase the ill-effect of all his official anxieties upon his nerves and health.

It was by favouring the National Liberal party that I had brought upon myself the ill-will of my former Conservative colleagues, and it might have been expected that they would have been induced by the vulgar and undignified attacks on my personal honesty to give me some help in repelling them, or, at any rate, to show that they did not approve of the attacks, and did not share my slanderers' views about me. I cannot, however, remember at that time noticing any attempt on the part of the National Liberals to come to my aid, either in the press or by any other public means. There appeared rather to be a certain satisfaction in the National Liberal camp at the attacks made upon me by the Conservative party, and at their rupture with me, as though they were anxious to widen the breach and push the goad a little further in. Liberals and Conservatives were agreed in making use of me, letting me drop, and attacking me, according as the interest of their section dictated. Of course every group professes to be dominated by the interests of the country and the general welfare, and maintains that the party road is the most conducive to the good of the community. But, as a matter of fact, I have retained the impression that each of our groups conducts its politics as though it alone existed, isolated on its own sectional island, without the slightest consideration for the whole or for foreign countries. Nor can it be maintained for a moment that the differences of the group on the political battlefield had been transformed, by the varying political principles and convictions of each individual, into a question of conscience and necessity. Most partisans resemble the adherents of different creeds : they are puzzled when asked to point out the characteristic differences between their own convictions and those of rival creeds. In our parties, the real point of crystallisation is not a programme so much as a person : a parliamentary *condottiere*.

Nor do their conclusions originate in the opinions of the members, but only in the will of the leader or some conspicuous orator, and as a rule these two coincide. The attempt of individual members to make war against the party leader and the fluent orator is combined with so much annoyance, defeat in voting, and interruption of daily customary social intercourse, that it requires a very independent character to represent an opinion differing from the party lead ; nor is even character suffi-cient unless accompanied by a considerable equipment of knowledge and energy. Now this latter increases as we go further to the Left. Conservative parties are, as a rule, composed of contented citizens; those which attack the *status quo* are naturally more largely recruited from the ranks of persons discontented with existing institutions. Among the elements on which contentment depends, a comfortable income does not occupy the smallest place. Now, it is a peculiarity, if not of mankind in general, at any rate of the German nation, that the discontented are more industrious and active than the contented; the needy more energetic than the satisfied. Those Germans who are intellectually and physically satisfied are doubtless sometimes industrious from a sense of duty. But this is not the case with the majority; and among those who fight against the existing system, we seldom find well-to-do people acting from conviction, but often out of ambition, which hopes for speedier satisfaction on this road, unless indeed they have been forced upon it by political or denominational annoyances. The general result is the promotion of superior industry among those forces which attack the existing order of things, and inferior among those who defend it, i.e. the Conservatives. This lack of industry in the majority considerably facilitates the leadership of a Conservative party, and serves to help it more than individual independence and violent obstinacy on the part of individuals can avail to hamper it. According to my experience, the dependence of the Conservative sections on the commands of their leader is at least as strong as, perhaps stronger than, on the Extreme Left. The aversion to rupture is probably greater on the Right than on the Left, and the reproach 'of being ministerial,' which had so strong an effect on every individual, was often a greater hindrance to objective judgement on the Right than on the Left. This reproach imme-

diately ceased to give offence to the Conservative and other
sections when my dismissal rendered the place of ruler
vacant, and every party leader, in the hope of having a
share in filling it, again became servile and ministerial,
to the extent of dishonestly denying and boycotting the
late Chancellor and his policy.

During the period of the 'declarations,' the anti-
ministerial current, i.e. the disfavour with which I was
regarded and treated by many of my compeers, was
greatly furthered by strong influences at Court. The Emperor never refused me his favour and support in matters
of business, but that did not prevent him from reading
the 'Reichsglocke' every day. Of this paper, which only
supported itself by calumniating me, thirteen copies were
provided by the royal Treasury for our and other Courts,
and it sought its collaborators not only among the Catholic
court and country nobility, but even among the evangelicals. The Empress Augusta made me permanently
sensible of her dislike, and her adherents, the highest
officials at the Court, carried their lack of courtesy to such
a pitch that I was forced to make a written complaint to
his Majesty. The result of this was that at least the
outward forms of courtesy were no longer neglected. It
was incivilities of this kind to which he and his wife were
subjected at court, rather than actual difficulties, which
helped to disgust Falk with his position.[1]

[1] See p. 142.

CHAPTER XXVI

INTRIGUES

COUNT HARRY ARNIM carried his wine badly, and one day, after a glass at lunch, he said to me : 'I look upon every front rank man in the profession as a personal enemy, and treat him accordingly. Only he must not be allowed to notice it as long as he is my superior.' This was at the time when he had returned from Rome after the death of his first wife, and his son's Italian nurse was exciting attention on the promenades by her red and gold costume, while Arnim frequently in political discussions quoted Machiavelli and the works of Italian Jesuits and biographers. At that time he posed in the character of an ambitious and unscrupulous man, played the piano fascinatingly, and in consequence of his beauty and versatility was a dangerous character for ladies to whom he paid his court. He had begun very early to develop this versatility, for as a pupil at the Gymnasium of Neustettin, he had served his apprenticeship to the ladies of a company of strolling actors, by replacing the missing orchestra at the piano.

Among the personages who joined with foreign influence, with the ' Reichsglocke ' and its collaborators in aristocratic and court circles and in the ministries of my colleagues, and with the disappointed *Junkers* and their Era articles in the ' Kreuzzeitung,' in the attempt to deprive me of the Emperor's confidence, Count Harry Arnim played a prominent part.

On August 23, 1871, he was appointed ambassador, at my suggestion, and sent in that capacity to Paris, where I hoped that, in spite of all his faults, it would be possible to utilise his distinguished abilities in the service of his Majesty; but he regarded his post there only as a stepping-stone, by help of which he would be able to work more effectively at getting rid of me and becoming my successor. He pointed out, in his private correspondence with the Emperor, that the Prussian Royal House was at that time the oldest in Europe which had maintained itself in unbroken rule; and that this favour of God laid upon the Emperor, as *doyen* of the sovereigns, the duty of watching over and protecting the legitimacy and continuity of other old dynasties. He judged rightly the mental effect of touching this chord in the Emperor's disposition; and had Arnim been our master's only counsellor, he might perhaps have succeeded in obscuring his clear and sober judgement by an artificial and exaggerated sentiment of hereditary and princely duty. But he did not know that his Majesty, in his honest and straightforward fashion, communicated the letters to me, and thus gave me an opportunity of representing to the political understanding, I might almost say the sound common-sense of my master, the risks and dangers of these counsels, which we should encounter if we attempted the restoration of legitimacy in France, on the road recommended by Arnim.

The Emperor afterwards permitted me to publish my written expressions on the subject in answer to Arnim's libels. In one of these I referred to the King's knowledge of the fact that Arnim's sincerity was doubted in authoritative circles, and that he was not desired as ambassador at the English Court ' because no one would believe a word he said.' *

Count Arnim made repeated attempts to obtain from the English cabinet a testimonial contradicting this accusation of mine, and received from the English statesmen, who were more friendly to him than to me, the assurance that they knew nothing whatever of the matter. Still, the anticipatory rejection of Arnim, to which I had referred, had reached the Emperor in a fashion which enabled me to make public reference to his Majesty's testimony about the matter.

When Arnim had convinced himself at Berlin in 1873 that his prospects of taking my place were not yet as mature as he had assumed, he attempted, for the time being, to restore the former friendly relations. He called upon me, regretted that we had drifted apart owing to misunderstandings and the intrigues of other persons, and reminded me of the relations with me that he had once had and valued. Too well acquainted with his mode of procedure and the serious character of his attack on me to be deceived, I spoke quite openly to him, represented to him that he had entered into connexion with all the elements hostile to me with a view to shaking my political position, in the erroneous presumption that he would become my successor, and I declared that I did not believe in his conciliatory attitude. As he left me, the facility to tears which was peculiar to him enabled him to brush one away from his eyes. I had known him from childhood.

My official proceedings against Arnim had been provoked by his refusal to obey official instructions. I said nothing in the legal proceeding about the fact of his having

* Letter to the Emperor, dated April 14, 1873.

used the money which had been given him to represent
our policy in the French press (6,000 to 7,000 thalers)
in attacking our policy and my position in the German
press. His chief organ, in which he attacked me with
ever-increasing confidence of victory, was at that time the
' Spener'sche Zeitung,' which, already moribund, was at
his purchase. In this he let fall hints that he alone was
acquainted with the means of bringing the struggle with
Rome to a victorious issue, and that it was only my
unjustifiable ambition which kept a superior statesman,
like himself, from taking the helm. He never expressed
himself to me on the subject of this secret remedy. It
consisted in the theory endorsed by a few canonists, that
the character of the Roman Catholic Church had been
changed by the Vatican decisions ; it had become a different
personage legally, and thereby lost the rights of property
and treaty, which it had acquired in its former existence.
I had already considered this plan, but do not think it
would have had a stronger effect on the issue of the
quarrel, than the foundation of the Old Catholic Church,
whose legality was clearer and more justifiable, both logically
and juristically, than the suggested renunciation by the
Prussian Government of its relations to the Roman
Church. The number of Old Catholics gives the measure
of the effect which this move would have exercised on the
stability of the Pope's adherents and of Neo-Catholicism.
Still less promising seemed to me the proposal, made
by Count Arnim in one of his public reports, that the
Prussian Government should send *Oratores* to help in
deliberating the dogmatic questions at the Council. I
imagine that this idea was suggested to him by the
frontispiece of Paolo Sarpi's ' History of the Council of
Trent,' which represents the Council, and designates two

persons seated at a table apart as *Oratores Cæsareæ Majestatis.* If my assumption is right, Count Arnim ought to have known that *Orator* in the clerical Latinity of that day is the expression for ambassador.

My only object in the proceedings against him was to obtain the surrender of certain portions, undoubtedly official, of the embassy documents, a demand which Arnim had definitely refused. I only wanted to maintain my official authority as his chief. I never desired a penal sentence against Arnim, nor yet expected it; on the contrary, after it was pronounced, I would have done my best to advocate his pardon, had this been legally admissible in the case of a sentence by default. My motive was not personal revenge, but, if any one desires to find a term of blame for it, rather bureaucratic dogmatism on the part of a superior official, whose authority had been disregarded. In my opinion the sentence of nine months' imprisonment in the first suit was of excessive severity. As for his condemnation in the second trial to five years' imprisonment, this was only rendered possible, as the condemned man himself truly remarked, by the fact that the ordinary judge in a criminal court was not in a position to gauge with full comprehension the sins of diplomacy in international relations. I should only have regarded this sentence as adequate if the suspicion had been proved that the condemned man had utilised his relations to Baron Hirsch in such a way as to render the delay in executing my instructions serviceable in speculations on the Bourse. This was not proved in the legal proceedings, nor was any attempt made to prove it. The assumption that it was mere business reasons which caused him to neglect the execution of a distinct order always remained a possible point in his favour, although I could not understand the train of thought which must have led him to it. But I never, for my part, gave expression to this suspicion, although it was communicated to the Foreign Office and court society, by correspondence and travellers from Paris, and was carried around in these circles. It was a loss for our diplomatic service that Arnim's uncommon qualifications for it were not coupled with an equal measure of trustworthiness and credibility.

The impression made on diplomatic circles is shown, among other proofs, by the following letter written by the Secretary of State, von Bülow, on October 23, 1874:

'The "Kreuzzeitung" to-day contains a dishonest communication, evidently composed by Count Arnim himself to the tune, What harm have I done? Nothing, except saving entirely personal documents from the indiscretion of ambassadors and government clerks; I should have given them up long ago if the Foreign Office had not been so rude and inconsiderate. It is difficult, during the course of the inquiry, to answer such lies and distortions. Meantime, the "Weser Zeitung" yesterday contained a very useful notice of the contents of several of the missing documents. Yesterday, Field-Marshal von Manteuffel called on me, chiefly with the view of inquiring about the Arnim affair. He expressed in very suitable language his conviction that it would have been impossible to act differently, and his pity for the Chancellor and the Diplomatic Service, who were obliged to carry on business with such experiences. However, he had known Arnim from a child, and had suffered sufficiently under or side by side with him at Nancy, not to be surprised by the catastrophe. Arnim, he said, was a man who, on every occasion, only

asked : What personal advantage or disadvantage do I
derive from it ? Word for word, the same was the testimony of Lord Odo Russell, as the result of his Roman
experience, and of Nothomb with his memories of
Brussels. What struck me most was the Field-Marshal's
repeated assertion that Arnim had begun to conspire
against your serene Highness in the summer of 1872, had
tried to sound him (Manteuffel) in this connexion in the
summer of 1873, and, by his attitude towards Thiers, had
been really responsible for his fall and all its disastrous
political consequences. On this last matter he spoke
with considerable knowledge of the subject and persons,
not without a hint of the influence which Arnim had at
that time been able to acquire in the very highest quarters,
by incitements against the Republic and in favour of the
Legitimist succession. On the day of Thiers' fall, he had
dined with several prominent Orleanists. The bulletins
from Versailles reached him during dinner and were
greeted with joy—it was a support for the party, without
which it might not have had the moral courage for the
coup d'état of May 24. Similarly, Nothomb told me that
Thiers had said to him the previous winter, speaking of
Arnim : " Cet homme m'a fait beaucoup de mal, beaucoup
plus même que ne sait ni pense Monsieur de Bismarck." '

In the libel action against the editor of the 'Reichsglocke,' January 1877, the Attorney-General said :

'I regard as morally responsible for this criminal line
of action all the collaborators of the paper, as well as
those who support the paper in word and deed, but in
particular Herr von Loë, and next to him Count Harry
Arnim. It is impossible to doubt that all the articles
" Arnim contra Bismarck," which have, for the last
year, been devoted to attacking and depreciating the

person of Prince Bismarck, were written in the interest
of Count Arnim.'

It is my conviction that after 1866 the Roman Curia,
as well as most politicians, regarded a war between
France and Germany as probable, and thought it equally
probable that Prussia would be the loser. Assuming the
war, the reigning Pope must have considered that the
victory of France over evangelical Prussia would enable
him to push to its furthest consequences the attack which
he had made with his Council and his infallibility on
the non-Catholic world and nervous Catholics. Considering the relations then prevailing between imperial
France, and in particular the Empress Eugénie and the
Pope, it would not be too bold an assumption that France,
if its armies should reach Berlin victoriously, would not
leave the interest of the Catholic Church in Prussia
unconsidered at the conclusion of peace; similarly, the
Emperor of Russia was in the habit of using treaties of
peace for the protection of his co-religionists in the East.
Perhaps the *gesta Dei per Francos* would have been
enriched by some fresh advances of the Papal power; and
the decision of the denominational contests, which, in the
opinion of Catholic writers (Donoso Cortes de Valdegamas),
must eventually be fought out ' on the sands of the March
of Brandenburg,' would be promoted in various directions
by a preponderating position of France in Germany.
The Empress Eugénie's partiality for the warlike tendency in French politics can hardly have been unconnected with her devotion to the Catholic Church and
the Pope. If French policy and Louis Napoleon's

personal relation to the Italian movement rendered it impossible for the Emperor and Empress to satisfy the Pope in Italy, the Empress would, in case of victory, have been able to show her devotion to the Pope in Germany, and on this domain would have provided a *fiche de consolation*, even if an inadequate one, for the injuries which the Papal See had sustained in Italy with and by means of Napoleon's concurrence.

After the peace of Frankfort, if a Catholic party, no matter whether Royalist or Republican, had remained at the helm in France, it would scarcely have been possible to postpone the renewal of war for so long a time. In that case there would have been a fear that the two neighbouring powers against whom we had made war, Austria and France, would approach one another on the ground of their common Catholicism, and make a joint attack on us, and the circumstance that both in Germany and in Italy there was no lack of elements with whom denominational sympathies were stronger than national, would serve to strengthen and encourage such a Catholic alliance. It was impossible to predict whether, in face of it, we should find allies ; at any rate, it would have been in the power of Russia by joining the Austro-French alliance, to develop it into a preponderating coalition, as in the Seven Years' war, or, at any rate, to keep us in a state of dependence, under the diplomatic pressure of this possibility.

The re-establishment of a Catholic monarchy in France would have greatly increased the temptation to seek revenge with the help of Austria. On this account I considered it contrary to the interests of Germany and of peace, for us to promote the restoration of the monarchy in France, and therefore I opposed the persons who repre-

sented this idea. This opposition became personal, and
was directed against the French ambassador, Gontaut-
Biron, and our own ambassador in Paris, Count Harry
Arnim. The former was acting in accordance with the
party to which he naturally belonged, the Legitimist
Catholic ; but the latter was speculating on the Emperor's
sympathies with a view to discrediting my policy and
becoming my successor. Gontaut, an amiable diplomat
of good family, found a point of contact with the Empress
Augusta, both on account of her preference for Catholic
elements in and near the Centrum, with which the government was in conflict ; and also in his quality as Frenchman, which, recalling the Empress's youthful memories
of the German court in pre-railway days, was almost as
good a recommendation as that of being an Englishman.[1] Her Majesty had French-speaking servants ; her
French reader Gérard * had entrance to the imperial
family and correspondence. Everything foreign, except
what was Russian, had the same attraction for the
Empress as it has for so many natives of little German
towns. At the time of the old-fashioned slow means of
communication, a foreigner at the German courts, especially
an Englishman or a Frenchman, was almost always an
interesting visitor. No careful inquiries were made about
his position at home ; to make him presentable at court
it was sufficient that he should come from ' a long way
off,' in fact, not be a fellow-countryman.

[1] See vol. i., p. 131.

* This man, probably recommended by Gontaut to her Majesty, carried
on an animated correspondence with Gambetta, which, after the death of
the latter, fell into the hands of Madame Adam, and served as the main
material for the work, *La Société de Berlin*. On his return to Paris,
Gérard was for a time director of the official press, then Secretary of
Legation at Madrid, Chargé d'Affaires in Rome, and in 1890 Envoy to
Montenegro.

The interest shown at that time in exclusively evangelical circles in the unusual apparition of a Catholic, and
at Court, of a dignitary of the Catholic Church, sprang
from a similar source. In the days of Frederick William III
it was an interesting break in the general uniformity
when any one was a Catholic. A Catholic fellow-pupil
was regarded without any denominational ill-will, but
with a sort of amazement, as an exotic apparition; not
without some satisfaction at his showing no traces of
St. Bartholomew, the stake, and the Thirty Years' war.
In the household of Professor von Savigny, whose wife
was a Catholic, the children, when they reached the age
of fourteen, were allowed to choose their religion.
They all chose their father's evangelical creed, with the
exception of one, who was my own age, and afterwards
became envoy at the Federal Diet and one of the founders
of the Centrum. At the time when we were both
either in the first class at school or at the University, he
spoke without any trace of polemics about the motives of
his choice, referring to the impressive dignity of the
Catholic services, but also adducing as a reason that on the
whole it was much more distinguished to be a Catholic,
' after all, every silly boy is a Protestant.'

Conditions and feelings have changed during the last
half-century, and political and economical developments
have brought every variety of nationality, both in and out
of Europe, into closer contact one with another. At the
present day it would be impossible in any Berlin circles
to arouse any excitement or make the least impression by
the fact of being a Catholic. The Empress Augusta alone
never got rid of the impressions of her young days. In
her eyes a Catholic ecclesiastic was more distinguished
than an evangelical of equal rank and equal standing.

The task of winning over a Frenchman or an Englishman was more attractive to her than if he were one of her own countrymen; and she cared more for the applause of Catholics than of her own co-religionists. Gontaut-Biron, who came of a good family, had no difficulty in creating for himself a position in Court circles, whose connexions reached, by more than one road, even to the person of the Emperor.

The choice of a French secret agent as the Empress's reader was a proceeding so extraordinary as to be only explicable by the confidence which Gontaut's dexterity and the co-operation of part of his Catholic environment inspired in her Majesty. It was, of course, an enormous advantage for French policy and the position of the French ambassador at Berlin to have such a man as Gérard in the imper'al household. He was a very smart fellow, but incapable of overcoming his vanity in externals. He delighted in figuring as a specimen of the latest Parisian fashions, exaggerated in a manner which attracted attention at Berlin, a blunder which, however, did him no harm at the palace. The interest in exotic, and especially Parisian, types was stronger than the feeling for simple taste.

Gontaut's activity in the service of France was not confined to the domain of Berlin. In 1875 he went to St. Petersburg to concoct, together with Prince Gortchakoff, the theatrical *coup* which was to make the world believe, on the occasion of the Emperor Alexander's impending visit to Berlin, that he alone had saved defenceless France from a German attack by seizing our arm with his *Quos ego*, and that this was his object in accompanying the Emperor to Berlin.

I do not know with whom this idea originated. If it was Gontaut's, he must have found Gortchakoff very congenial soil, owing to his vanity and jealousy of me, and the resistance which I had been obliged to offer to his claims of precedency. I was obliged to say to him in a confidential conversation, 'You do not treat us like a friendly power, but "comme un domestique, qui ne monte pas assez vite quand on a sonné."' Gortchakoff made the most of the circumstance that his authority was superior to that of the ambassador, Count Redern, and the *chargés d'affaires* who succeeded him, and preferred to transact negotiations by communicating with our representative at St. Petersburg, thus avoiding the necessity of instructing the Russian ambassador at Berlin with a view to discussion with me. Probably it was a mere slander when some Russians asserted that the motive for this proceeding was that a lump sum was allowed for telegrams in the Budget of the Foreign Minister, and Gortchakoff therefore preferred to make his communications at German rather than Russian expense, by means of our *chargé d'affaires*. Doubtless he was very avaricious, still, I fancy that the motive was political. Gortchakoff was a clever and brilliant speaker, and liked to appear as such, especially before the foreign diplomatists who were accredited at St. Petersburg. He spoke French and German with equal fluency, and as envoy, and afterwards as his colleague, I used often to enjoy listening for hours to his didactic discourses. He preferred as auditors foreign diplomats, especially young *intelligent chargés d'affaires*, in whose case the oratorical impression was strengthened by the distinguished position of the Foreign Minister, to whom they were accredited. By this road Gortchakoff's opinions reached me in a form which suggested *Roma locuta est*. I complained direct to him in my private correspondence about this method of carrying on business

and about the tone of his communications, and requested
him no longer to consider me his diplomatic pupil, as I
had gladly been at St. Petersburg, but rather to reckon
with the fact that I was his colleague, and responsible for
the policy of my Emperor and of a great country.

In 1875, when the post of ambassador was vacant and
a secretary of legation was acting as Chargé d'Affaires, Herr
von Radowitz, at that time ambassador at Athens, was sent
to St. Petersburg, *en mission extraordinaire*, in order that
the conduct of business might outwardly also be placed
on a footing of equality. This gave him an opportunity, by
a determination to emancipate himself from Gortchakoff's
preponderating influence, of earning his dislike in such a
high degree that the ill-will of the Russian cabinet, in spite
of his Russian marriage, is probably not extinct to this
day. The part of peacemaker, well suited to satisfy
Gortchakoff's vanity by the impression made in Paris,
which he valued more than anything else, had been prepared in advance by Gontaut in Berlin. We may
assume that his conversations with Count Moltke and
Radowitz, which were afterwards adduced as proofs of
our warlike intentions, were cleverly led up to by him in
order to represent to Europe an image of France threatened by us and protected by Russia. Gortchakoff arrived
at Berlin on May 10, 1875, and dated from this place a
telegraphic circular, destined for publication, beginning
with the words, '*Maintenant*,' i.e. under Russian pressure, '*la paix est assurée*,' as though this had not been
the case before. One of the non-German sovereigns who
received this communication afterwards showed me the
wording.

I reproached Prince Gortchakoff sharply. It was
not, I said, a friendly part suddenly and unexpectedly to

jump on the back of a trustful and unsuspecting friend, and get up a circus performance at his cost; proceedings of this kind between us, who were the directing ministers, could only injure the two monarchies and states. If he was anxious to be applauded in Paris, he need not on that account injure our relations with Russia; I was quite ready to assist him and have five-franc pieces struck at Berlin, with the inscription *Gortchakoff protège la France;* * we might also set up a theatre in the German Embassy, where he could appear before a French audience with the same inscription, in the character of a guardian angel, dressed in white with wings, to the accompaniment of Bengal fire!

My cutting invectives made him sing rather small, but he combated the facts which I considered established, without showing his usual security and fluency; thus causing me to conclude that he was doubtful whether his imperial master would approve his proceedings. This was further confirmed on my complaining to the Emperor Alexander, with the same openness, of Gortchakoff's dishonest proceedings. The Emperor admitted all the facts and confined himself to saying, laughingly, smoking the while, that I must not take this *vanité sénile* too seriously. The disapproval thus expressed never found sufficient authentic expression to rid the world of the myth of our intending to attack France in 1875.

So far was I from entertaining any such idea at the time, or afterwards, that I would rather have resigned than lent a hand in picking a quarrel, which could have had no other motive than preventing France from recovering her breath and her strength. A war of this kind could not, in my opinion, have led to permanently tenable conditions.

* [An allusion to the inscription on the rim of five-franc pieces.]

in Europe, but might have brought about an agreement between Russia, Austria, and England, based upon mistrust of us, and leading eventually to active proceedings against the new and still unconsolidated empire; and we should thus have been entering upon the path which led the Second French Empire to destruction by a continuous policy of war and prestige. Europe would have seen in our proceedings a misuse of our newly acquired power; and the hand of every one, including the centrifugal forces within the empire, would have been permanently raised against Germany, or at any rate been ready to draw the sword. It was just the peaceful character of German policy after the astonishing proofs of the nation's military strength, which induced foreign Powers and internal opponents, even sooner than we had expected, at least to tolerate the new development of German power, and to regard either with a benevolent eye or else in the character of a guarantee of peace the development and strengthening of the empire.

It seemed strange from our point of view that the Emperor of Russia, in spite of the contemptuous manner in which he had expressed himself about his chief minister, still left the whole machinery of the Foreign Office in his hands, and thus permitted the influence on the missions which he actually exercised. Although the Emperor distinctly recognised the by-paths which his minister had been led by personal reasons to adopt, he did not submit the drafts drawn up by Gortchakoff for his autograph letters to the Emperor William to the careful examination necessary to prevent the impression that the Emperor's friendly disposition had given way on main points to Gortchakoff's exacting and threatening attitude. The Emperor Alexander wrote a tiny hand, elegant and clear, and did not dislike the labour of writing; but although the letters from Sovereign to Sovereign, which as a rule were very long and detailed, were entirely in the Emperor's handwriting, I still felt justified in concluding from their style and contents that they were usually based on a draft drawn up by Gortchakoff; as in fact my master's autograph answers were similarly drafted by me. By this means, the autograph correspondence in which the two monarchs treated the most serious political questions with decisive authority, though lacking the constitutional guarantee of a ministerial counter-signature, still had the corrective of ministerial co-operation, always supposing that the imperial correspondent kept closely to his draft. Of course its author never received any security on that point, as the fair copy either never passed through his hands at all, or reached him sealed up.

The wide ramifications of the Gontaut-Gortchakoff intrigue are evident from the following letter, which I addressed to the Emperor from Varzin, August 13, 1875 : [1]

'I received with respectful gratitude your Majesty's gracious letter from Gastein of the 8th inst., and was especially rejoiced to find that your Majesty was the better for the waters, in spite of the bad weather in the Alps. I have the honour of returning herewith Queen Victoria's letter; it would have been very interesting if her Majesty had expressed herself in further detail as to the origin of the war rumours at that time. The sources must, however, have seemed to her very sure, else her Majesty would not have referred to them afresh, and the English government would not have been induced by them to take such important steps, so unfriendly towards us. I do not know whether your Majesty would consider it

[1] *Bismarck-Jahrbuch*, iv. 35 &c.

feasible to take Queen Victoria at her word, when she
assures your Majesty that she would find it " easy to
prove that her fears were not exaggerated." Otherwise
it would certainly be of importance to discover from what
quarter such " serious errors " could have been conveyed to
Windsor. The hint about persons who must be regarded
as "representatives" of your Majesty's government is
apparently aimed at Count Münster. It is quite possible
that both he and Count Moltke may have spoken
theoretically of the utility of a timely attack on France,
although I am not aware of it, and he never received any
such instructions. It may indeed be said that it is not
conducive to peace for France to feel secure that she will
not be attacked under any circumstances, whatever she may
do. At this day, as in 1867 in the Luxemburg question, I
should never advise your Majesty to begin a war at once, on
the score of a likelihood that our enemy would afterwards
begin it better prepared. For this we can never sufficiently predict the ways of divine Providence. But, on
the other hand, it is not advantageous to give our enemy
the assurance that we shall in any case await his attack.
Therefore I should not be inclined to blame Münster if he
had let fall an occasional remark to that effect ; and this
would by no means give the English government the
right to base official action upon the unofficial speeches
of an ambassador, and *sans nous dire gare* call upon
the other Powers to bring pressure to bear on us. A step
so serious and so unfriendly leads us to suppose that
Queen Victoria must have had some other reasons for
believing in our warlike intentions, besides occasional
remarks of Count Münster's, in which I do not even
believe. Lord [Odo] Russell assured me that he always
reported his firm belief in our peaceful intentions. On

the other hand, all the Ultramontanes and their friends have attacked us both secretly and openly in the press, accusing us of wanting to begin war very shortly, and the French ambassador, who lives in these circles, has passed on their lies to Paris as certain information. But even that would not be really sufficient to give Queen Victoria that assured confidence in the untruths to which your Majesty yourself gave a denial, which she again expresses in her letter of June 20. I am too little acquainted with the Queen's character to have any opinion as to the possibility of her using the expression " it would be easy to prove " in order to cover an act of precipitation which has already been committed, instead of openly acknowledging it.

'I trust your Majesty will pardon me if my professional interest has led me to deal in detail, after three months' silence, with a point already settled.'

In the summer of 1877, Count Frederick Eulenburg declared that his health was bankrupt; and in fact his activity was greatly diminished, not by over-work so much as by unsparing indulgence from his youth in every kind of pleasure. He had plenty of ability and courage, but not always sufficient inclination for persevering labour. His nervous system was impaired and fluctuated at last between lachrymose depression and artificial excitement. Besides this, in the middle of the 'seventies he had, as I conjecture, been attacked by a certain desire for popularity which had been foreign to him as long as he had had sufficient health to enjoy himself. This attack was not without a touch of jealousy of me, even though we were old friends.

He tried to satisfy it by taking up the question of administrative reform. It must be successful, if it was to bring him honour. In order to secure its success he made unpractical concessions in the parliamentary deliberations on the subject and bureaucratised the post of district president, which is the essential support of our rural affairs, and along with it the new Local Administration. The district presidency had formerly been a Prussian peculiarity, the last offshoot of the administrative hierarchy, which brought it into immediate connexion with the people.* But in social position the district president stood above other officials of the same rank. In former days a man did not become district president as a stepping-stone to a career, but rather with the intention of spending his life as president of that particular district. His authority increased with the years of his tenure; he had no ideas to represent but those of his district and no wishes to strive for but those of its inhabitants. It is obvious how useful must be the effect of such an institution, both upward and downward, and what small resources of men and money were sufficient for performing the district business. Since that time the district president has become a mere government official, his position a stepping-stone to further promotion in the government service, facilitating his election to parliament; and in this latter capacity, if he is an energetic person, he will consider his relations as an official with his superiors more important than those with the inhabitants of his district. At the same time, the newly created official presidents are not instruments of self-government on the analogy of the municipal authorities, but rather an inferior class of the bureaucracy, doing the work of clerks. This helps to

* [See vol. i. chap. 1.]

spread over the country districts every unpractical or use-less suggestion made by the central bureaucracy, insufficiently occupied as it is and unfamiliar with the realities of life; thus the unfortunate local self-administrators are forced to prepare reports and lists in order to satisfy the curiosity of officials who have more time than business on their hands. It is impossible for agriculturists or manufacturers to comply with such demands in an office beside their own work. As a natural result their place tends to be more and more filled by paid clerks, whose expenses must be defrayed by the inhabitants and who are dependent on the nod of the higher bureaucracy.

I had cast my eye on Rudolf von Bennigsen as successor to Count Eulenburg, and in the course of the year 1877 I had two interviews with him, in July and December. It turned out that he was trying to extend the ground of our discussion beyond what was consistent with the opinions of his Majesty and my own views. I knew that it would in any case be a difficult task to render him personally acceptable to the King, but he regarded the matter in the light of a change of system, necessitated by the political situation and a surrender of the lead to the National Liberal party. Their desire to share in the government had already been apparent in the zeal with which the party had urged the 'Substitutes Bill,' expecting by these means to pave the way for an imperial ministry in the form of a board, where the solely responsible Imperial Chancellor should be replaced by independent offices and ministerial voting, as was the case in Prussia. Bennigsen was therefore not content to be merely Eulenburg's successor, but demanded that, at any rate, Forckenbeck and Stauffenberg should enter with him. The former he considered a most suitable man for the

Interior, who would exercise it with the same skill and energy he had shown in the administration of the city of Berlin ; he himself would choose the Ministry of Finance ; Stauffenberg must be put at the head of the Imperial Treasury, in order to work together with him.

I told him there was no place vacant except Eulenburg's ; I was prepared to recommend him to the King for this and should be glad if I could carry through the proposal. But if I were to advise his Majesty to set free two other ministerial posts *proprio motu*, in order to fill them with National Liberals, the Emperor would feel that it was not so much a question of filling a post suitably, as of a change of system ; and any such he would reject on principle. In any case, considering the views of the King and our whole political situation, Bennigsen must not count upon the possibility of taking, as it were, his party into the ministry with him, and as its leader exercising within the government an influence corresponding to its importance, thus, as it were, creating a constitutional majority ministry. In our country the King was actually and undeniably, according to the wording of our Constitution, President of the ministry, and Bennigsen, if he tried as minister to keep on the ·path designated, would soon have to choose between the King and his party. He must realise that if I succeeded in obtaining his appointment, this would give him and his party a powerful handle for strengthening and widening their influence ; he need but recall the example of Roon, who entered Auerswald's Liberal ministry as the only Conservative, and became the point of crystallisation around which it was transformed into a Conservative ministry. He must not ask the impossible of me ; I knew the King and the limits of my influence well enough ; parties were tolerably indifferent to me, in fact altogether indifferent, if I excepted the avowed and unavowed Republicans, who terminated to the Right in the Progressive party. My aim was the strengthening of our national safety; the nation would have time enough for its internal development when once its unity, and with it its outward security, was consolidated. At present the National Liberal party was the strongest element on the parliamentary domain for the attainment of this last object. The Conservative party, to which I had belonged in parliament, had attained all the geographical extension of which, in the present condition of the population, it was capable, and had not sufficient elements of growth to transform it into a national majority. Its natural occurrence and abiding-place were limited in our new provinces; in the west and south of Germany it had not the same substratum as in old Prussia; in Hanover, Bennigsen's home, in particular, the choice lay between Guelfs and National Liberals, and for the time being the latter supplied the best substratum of any in which the Empire could strike root. It was these political considerations which induced me to make overtures to them, as at the present time the strongest party, by seeking to win their leader as my colleague; whether for financial or internal business was indifferent to me. I regarded the matter from the purely political standpoint conditioned by my view that, for the present and until after the next great wars, the main issue was the firm consolidation of Germany, protected by its army against external dangers and by its Constitution against internal dynastic schisms. Whether our domestic Constitution turns out a little more Conservative or a little more Liberal is a question of expediency which can only be calmly considered when the building is weather-proof. I desired sincerely to persuade him, as I expressed it, to jump into my boat and help me steer; I was drawn up by the landing-stage and waiting for him to embark.

Bennigsen, however, insisted on his refusal to enter without Forckenbeck and Stauffenberg, and left me under the impression that my attempt had failed. This impression was quickly strengthened by the arrival of an exceptionally ungracious letter from the Emperor, informing me that Count Eulenburg had entered his room with the question : 'Has your Majesty heard yet of the new ministry ? Bennigsen.' This communication was followed by a violent outburst of imperial indignation at my arbitrary proceedings, and my venturing to suggest that he should cease to govern in 'Conservative fashion.' I was ill and tired out, and the wording of the imperial letter, together with Eulenburg's attack, took such a hold on my nerves that I once more fell seriously ill. I sent the Emperor an answer by Roon, to the effect that I could not propose to him a successor for Eulenburg without having previously gained the assurance that the person in question would accept the appointment. I had considered Bennigsen a suitable person, and sounded his views, but my overtures had not been received in the manner which I had expected, and I was therefore convinced that I could not propose him as minister. The ungracious condemnation conveyed to me in his Majesty's letter compelled me to renew the resignation which I had offered in the spring. This correspondence took place during the last days of 1877, and my fresh illness began during New Year's night.

In answer to Roon's letter, the Emperor replied to me that he had been deceived about the position of affairs, and desired me to regard his last letter as not written.

These events of themselves precluded my treating any further with Bennigsen ; but I did not think it for our political interest to acquaint the latter with the judgement expressed by the Emperor on his person and candidature. Although the matter was, in my mind, definitely terminated, I allowed it to appear outwardly *in suspenso* ; next time I was in Berlin, Bennigsen took the initiative, with a view to bringing the matter, which he regarded as still unsettled, in friendly fashion to a negative conclusion. He asked me in the parliament building whether it was true that I was trying to introduce the tobacco monopoly, and on my answering in the affirmative, he said that in that case he must decline his co-operation as minister. Even then I did not inform him that as early as the New Year the Emperor had cut off every possibility of treating with him. Perhaps he had assured himself by some other means that his scheme of modifying the principles of the government policy on the lines of National Liberal views would meet with insuperable obstacles on the part of the Emperor, especially after the speech made by Stauffenberg about the necessity of abolishing article 109 of the Prussian Constitution (Continued Levy of Customs).

If the National Liberal leaders had conducted their policy skilfully, they ought to have known long ago that the Emperor, whose signature they required and desired for their appointment, felt more sensitive on the subject of this article than on any other political question, and that the surest way of alienating him was by an attempt to deprive him of this Palladium. When I gave his Majesty the confidential report of my negotiations with Bennigsen, and mentioned his wish with regard to Stauffenberg, the Emperor, still under the impression of the latter's speech, said, pointing to his shoulder where

the regimental number is placed on a uniform : 'Number
109 Stauffenberg regiment.' If the Emperor had at that
time approved the admission of Bennigsen, which I desired
with the view of readjusting the conformity with the
majority in parliament, even though the latter had soon
recognised the impossibility of bringing the government
and the King over to his party, still I am now convinced
that the party programme, which inclined a good deal to
doctrinaire acrimony, could not long have been brought
into accord with the strong monarchical views of the
Emperor. At that time I did not feel sufficiently sure of
this not to attempt inducing his Majesty to draw somewhat nearer to the National Liberal views. The strength
of his resistance, increased, no doubt, by Eulenburg's
hostile interference, exceeded my expectations, although
I was aware that the Emperor cherished an instinctive
monarchical dislike to Bennigsen and his late proceedings
in Hanover. Although the National Liberal party in
Hanover, and the energy of their leader before and after
1866, had greatly facilitated the ' assimilation ' of Hanover,
and the Emperor was quite as little disposed as his father
in 1805 to abandon this acquisition, the princely instinct
was sufficiently strong in him to make him view with some
inward disapproval such proceedings on the part of a
Hanoverian subject against the Guelf dynasty.

Among the number of current untrue myths belongs
the statement that I desired to 'squeeze the National
Liberals to the wall.' On the contrary, this is what
these gentlemen tried to do to me. The breach with the
Conservatives, brought about by the whole slander episode
of the ' Reichsglocke ' and ' Kreuzzeitung,' and by the
resulting declaration of war, under the leadership of my discontented former friend, Kleist-Retzow, together with the

jealous ill-will of my own class, the country *Junkers*, all these losses, and the enmities at Court combined with Catholic and feminine influences there, had tended to weaken my supports outside the National Liberal party, so that I could now only rely on the Emperor's personal relations to me. The National Liberals did not use this opportunity to strengthen our mutual relations by giving me their support ; but, on the contrary, attempted to take me in tow against my will. With this object they entered into relations with several of my colleagues ; by help of the ministers Friedenthal and Botho Eulenburg, the latter of whom possessed the ear of my vice-president, Count Stolberg, official understandings were entered into, un-known to me, with the presidents of both parliaments, and these related not only to questions of session and adjourn-ment, but also to important proposals in opposition to my wishes, with which my colleagues were acquainted. The general attack on my position, the striving after a share in the government, or sole dominion in my stead, betrayed by the scheme of independent imperial ministers, and by the above-mentioned secret negotiations, was very clearly marked at the council meeting held by the Crown Prince on June 5, 1878, as representative of his wounded father. The subject of discussion was the dissolution of parliament after Nobiling's attempt at assassination. Half, or more, of my colleagues, at any rate the majority of the ministry and the council, voted adversely to me against dissolution, on the ground that the present parliament, now that Nobiling's attempt had followed on Hödel's, would be prepared to reverse its recent vote and meet the views of the government. The confidence expressed by my colleagues on this occasion evidently depended on a confidential understanding between them and influential parliamentarians, though not one of the latter made any utterance to me on the subject. It appeared that they had already come to an understanding about the division of my inheritance.

I was certain that the Crown Prince would accept my view, even if all my colleagues had been of a different opinion, and I also had the approval of the twenty or more generals and officials present, certainly of the former. If I wanted to keep my post as minister at all, a question really of official and personal expediency, which, on examining myself, I answered in the affirmative, I found myself compelled to stand on my defence, and try to bring about a change in the parliamentary situation and in the *personnel* of my colleagues. I intended to keep my post, because, if the Emperor were to recover from his severe wound, which was by no means certain in the case of so old a man after his severe loss of blood, I would not forsake him against his will. I also regarded it as my duty, if he should die, not to refuse to his successor unless he wished it those services which the confidence and experience I had acquired enabled me to render him. It was not I who sought a quarrel with the National Liberals, but they who plotted with my colleagues in an attempt to squeeze me against the wall. The tasteless and vulgar phrase ' to squeeze them to the wall until they squeal ' never found a place in my thoughts, and still less on my lips. It was one of the lying inventions with which people try to injure their political opponents. Besides, this phrase was not even the original product of the persons who spread it abroad, but only a clumsy plagiarism. In his memoirs,[1] Count Beust relates the following :

' The Slavs in Austria have quoted against me the expression which, I may state, was never used by me,

[1] *Aus drei Viertel-Jahrhunderten*, part i. p. 5.

" that they must be squeezed against the wall." The origin of this phrase was the following : The former minister, afterwards Stadtholder of Galicia, Count Goluchowski, used to converse with me in the French language. It was chiefly thanks to his efforts that after I became president of the ministry in 1867, the Galician parliament voted unconditionally in favour of the imperial council. At that time I had said to Count Goluchowski : " Si cela se fait, les Slaves sont mis au pied du mur," a very different expression from the other.'

Among my arguments in favour of dissolution I especially emphasized this one : that parliament could not rescind its resolution without injuring its prestige, unless it had been previously dissolved. It is of no moment whether prominent National Liberals intended at that time to become my colleagues or my successors, since the former could only have been a stepping-stone to the other alternative. But I acquired a certain conviction that the negotiations between some of my colleagues, some National Liberals and some influential persons at Court, about the division of my heritage, had reached the point of agreement, or, at any rate, were not far from it. This agreement would have necessitated a combination, like that of the Gladstone ministry, between Liberalism and Catholicism. The latter extended through the immediate environment of the Empress Augusta, including the influence of the ' Reichsglocke ' and of the Treasurer of the Household, von Schleinitz, into the very palace of the old Emperor ; and here the combined attack against me found an active ally in General von Stosch. The latter had a good position too, at the Crown Prince's court, due, partly to his own abilities, partly to the assistance of Herr von Normann and his wife, with whom he had been on intimate terms at Magdeburg, and whose migration to Berlin he had effected.

The plan of replacing me by a cabinet *à la* Gladstone was calculated with a view to Count Botho Eulenburg, who had been Minister of the Interior since March 31, 1878, and was assured by his connexions of the traditional Court influence of his own family and that of Dönhoff. He is clever, distinguished, of a nobler nature than Harry von Arnim, more polished than Robert Goltz; but in his case also it was my experience to find that gifted colleagues and eventual successors, whom I was anxious to train up, did not retain a permanent feeling of good-will towards me. My relations to him were impaired, in the first place, by an outbreak of touchiness which, though outwardly covered by all the courtesy of good-breeding, was acute enough to disturb the easy and confidential course of business relations. Geheimrath Tiedemann, at that time my assistant in confidential business, brought about a most unexpected epistolary explosion, by the form in which he delivered a message to the Count during my absence from Berlin. As my commission to Tiedemann is a matter which still possesses an actual and lively interest, I will subjoin the correspondence.

Kissingen : August 15, 1878.

'Dear Sir,—I must request you to express to the Minister Count Eulenburg and to Geheimrath Hahn my regret that the draft of the Socialist Law was officially published in the "Provincial Correspondence" before it was laid before the Federal Council. This publication is prejudicial

to any amendment on our part, and is discourteous to
Bavaria and other dissentients. From the negotiations
which I have carried on from this place with Bavaria, I
must assume that it maintains its opposition to the imperial
ministry. Wurtemberg and, as I am told, Saxony are
not opposed to the imperial ministry on the principle,
but on a special matter; they dread the calling-in of
judges. For my own part, I can but sympathise with this
ground of opposition. It is a question not of judicial but
of political functions, and the Prussian ministry, too, must
not be subordinated to a judicial board in its preliminary
decisions, for this would weaken it in its future political
proceedings against Socialism. The functions of the
imperial ministry can only, in my opinion, be exercised
either direct by the Federal Council or by delegation to
an annually appointed committee. The Federal Council
represents the governing board of the joint sovereignty of
Germany, thus corresponding to the State Council in different circumstances.

'For the present, however, I am forced to assume
that Bavaria will not agree to this expedient, which is
acceptable to Wurtemberg, Saxony, and personally to
myself. The clause in No. 3, article 23, that only
unemployed persons may be expelled, does not seem to
me sufficient for the purpose.

'Moreover, in my opinion the law requires an
addendum dealing with officials, to the effect that participation in Socialist politics will bring upon them dismissal
without a pension. The majority of the ill-paid subordinate officials in Berlin, as well as the railway guards, points-
men, and other similar classes, are Socialists; a fact of
dangerous tendency, as would be obvious in the case of
insurrections and transport of troops.

' Further, if the law is to be effective, I do not think it will be permanently feasible to allow those citizens who are legally proved to be Socialists, the enjoyment of active and passive electoral rights, and all the privileges of parliamentary members.

' Now, when once the milder form of the law has been simultaneously announced in all the papers, being doubtless officially communicated to them, there will be much less prospect of carrying these additional severities in parliament than would have been the case if no milder version had been officially communicated.

' The proposal in its present condition will do Socialism no practical harm, nor in any way suffice to render it harmless, particularly as it is quite certain that parliament will discuss away something from every proposal. I regret that my health absolutely forbids me to take part, for the present, in the deliberations of the Federal Council, I must therefore postpone my further motions in the Federal Council until the regular session of parliament in winter.

' V. BISMARCK.'

' Berlin : August 18, 1878.

' Your Serene Highness commissioned Geheimrath Tiedemann to express to me and to Geheimrath Hahn your regret that the draft of the Socialist Law was officially published in the " Provincial Correspondence " before being submitted to the Federal Council. Hahn is in no way responsible, since he did not act without my consent. This I only gave after the printed papers of the Federal Council, which contained the draft, had been given out on the previous evening, without any special directions as to confidential treatment, and I had been informed by the President of the Imperial

Chancery that, under these circumstances, the publication of the draft in the papers might be certainly expected onthe following day, i.e. the very day on which the "Provincial Correspondence" appeared—an assumption which was afterwards proved to be correct. The sitting of the Federal Council took place at two o'clock in the afternoon of the 14th inst.; the "Provincial Correspondence" was published on the afternoon of the same day. The communication in. it of the contents of the draft Bill, therefore, did not take place previously to laying the draft before the Federal Council.

'Whether it would even so have been better to omit that communication in the "Provincial Correspondence" is a matter I do not propose to discuss further. It will always be of the greatest value to me to hear your Serene Highness's enlightened judgement, even if it should happen to differ from my own. Still, I cannot pass over in silence the circumstance that your Serene Highness should have expressed your disapproval to me by means of one of your subordinates, and the contempt of my position which this implies is the more distinctly marked, that in doing so you place me in the same category as one of my own subordinates. The insulting character of this proceeding is so obvious that the assumption of its being done on purpose, with all the considerations which would naturally spring from this, seems natural. I shall not hesitate to follow their dictates as soon as I am convinced that this assumption is correct. Assuming, in the meantime, that this is not the case, I confine myself to imploring your Serene Highness most strongly not to permit a recurrence of a similar proceeding.

'Yours, &c.,

'COUNT EULENBURG.'

'Gastein : August 20, 1878.

'I learn from your favour of the 18th that your
Excellency ascribes to me the manner, apparently in-
cautious and certainly unexpected, in which Geheimrath
Tiedemann gave expression to my confidential and informal
remark, and lays full weight upon it, without even
giving me the benefit of the incomplete way in which
business can be done during a trying course of treatment
at the baths. The contents of your letter lead me to
suppose that you were subjected to a piece of tactlessness
for which I must ask your pardon, although I did not
commit it, but at most rendered it possible. That your
Excellency should have conceived the thought of any
intentional proceeding on my part is surprising and
distressing to me, for I supposed that the friendly
character of our personal relations to one another was too
well secured to make any such misunderstanding possible.

'Yours, &c.,

'v. BISMARCK.'

The circumstances under which Count Eulenburg
gave in his resignation in February 1881 are well known ;
also that in August of the same year he was appointed
head president at Cassel. His name is connected with
the following correspondence between his Majesty and
myself. I have not been able to trace the subject of my
speech of December 17, 1881, to which he refers :

'Berlin : December 18, 1881.

'I must tell you a curious dream which I had last
night, as clear as I am describing it to you here.

'It was the first meeting of the Reichstag after the
present vacation. During the discussion Count Eulenburg

entered. The discussion ceased at once. After a long
pause the President called upon the last speaker to continue. Silence ! The President dissolves the sitting.
The result is tumult and confusion. No member is to
receive a decoration during the session of the Reichstag ;
the Monarch must not be named in the session. Next day
another sitting. Eulenburg appears and is greeted with
such hisses and noise—I wake up in the middle, in a state
of nervous agitation, from which I could not recover for
a long time, and lay awake for two hours from half-past
four to half-past six.

'All this took place in my presence in the House, just
as clearly as I am writing it down here. I must hope
that the dream will not be realised, but still it is a curious
thing.

'As this dream did not begin until I had had six hours'
quiet sleep, it could scarcely be an immediate result of our
conversation.

'*Enfin*, I really had to tell you this curiosity.

'Your

'WILLIAM.'

'Berlin : December 18, 1881.

'I thank your Majesty most humbly for your gracious
autograph letter. I think after all that the dream was the
result, if not exactly of my previous discourse, still of the
general impressions of the last few days, based upon
Puttkamer's verbal reports, newspaper articles, and my
speech. The images of our waking life do not immediately
reappear on the mirror of our dreams, but only after the
mind has been quieted by sleep and rest. Your Majesty's
communication encourages me to relate a dream which I
had in the spring of 1863, in the hardest days of the

Conflict, when no human eye could see any possible issue.
I dreamed (as I related the first thing next morning to my
wife and other witnesses) that I was riding on a narrow
Alpine path, precipice on the right, rocks on the left.   The
path grew narrower, so that the horse refused to proceed;
and it was impossible to turn round or dismount, owing
to lack of space.   Then, with my whip in my left hand, I
struck the smooth rock and called on God.   The whip
grew to an endless length, the rocky wall dropped like a
curtain and opened out a broader path, with a view over
hills and forests, like a landscape in Bohemia; there were
Prussian troops with banners, and even in my dream the
thought came to me at once that I must report it to your
Majesty. . This dream was fulfilled, and I woke up rejoiced
and strengthened.   The bad dream from which your
Majesty woke in nervous agitation can only be fulfilled,
in so far that we shall still have many a stormy, noisy
meeting of parliament, such as unfortunately undermine
the prestige of parliament and hinder the progress of
business.   But your Majesty's presence is impossible, and
though I consider such occurrences as the latest sittings
of parliament regrettable as a standard of our manners
and political education, perhaps even of our political
capacity, they are not in themselves a misfortune : "l'excès
du mal en devient le remède."

'I trust your Majesty will pardon with your customary
graciousness this holiday meditation, suggested by your
Majesty's own letter, for yesterday we entered on the
vacation and peace until January 9.'

The form of Count Eulenburg's complaint about
Tiedemann, and the cabinet question which it involved, took
all the stronger hold of my nerves, that I was suffering from

the effects of a severe illness. This had been induced by the impression left by the attempt on the Emperor's life, and the labour in connexion with the presidency of the Berlin congress which I had to undertake at the same time. A sentiment of official duty helped me to fight against it, but the baths at Gastein tended rather to increase than to cure it. The treatment at this place, to which my colleague in the ministry, Bernard von Bülow, succumbed on October 20, 1879, has not a calming effect on overstrained nerves, if disturbed by work or excitement.

Immediately after my return to Berlin I had to support the introduction of the Socialist Bill in the Reichstag, and this again confirmed my experience, that the labour of oratorical delivery on the platform involves less nervous strain than the correction of a long speech, quickly spoken, the wording of which has to be defended in the leader's place. While I was occupied with a correction of this kind, a nervous crisis which had been impending for months came to a head, happily only in the more trivial form of a nettle-rash.

The task of a leading minister of a great European Power, with a parliamentary constitution, is in itself of a sufficiently wearing character to absorb a man's whole energy. This is even more the case when the minister, as in Germany and Italy, has to help a nation over the stage of its development and, as is the case with us, to combat a strong separatist tendency in parties and individuals. When a man devotes the whole of his strength and health to the solution of these tasks, he is more sensitive to any increased difficulties which are not actually necessary. Even at the beginning of the 'seventies I thought that my health was giving way, and therefore made over the Presidency of the Cabinet to Count Roon, the only one of my colleagues who

was on personal terms of intimacy with me. But at that
time there were no material difficulties to discourage me.
These were caused by the hostile intrigue of those circles
on whose support I thought I could specially reckon, and
they were characterised in the days of the 'Reichsglocke'
by the direct relations which the elements represented by
this paper had with the Court, the Conservatives, and with
many of my official colleagues. The Monarch, who was
as a rule so gracious to me, had given me no adequate
support against the court and domestic influence of the
'Reichsglocke' ring; and this circumstance specially
discouraged me, and completed the tale of those considerations which induced me to hand in my resignation on
March 20, 1877. The attack of shingles from which I
was suffering in 1878, when Count Shuvaloff called
upon me to summon the congress, was a sign of the
unsatisfactory condition of my health at that time, and of
the exhaustion of my nerves. This was due to the lack
of sincere co-operation on the part of some of my official
colleagues, even more than to the 'Reichsglocke' and its
party at court. The way in which I was represented by
the Vice-president, Count Stolberg, owing to the influence
which the ministers Friedenthal, and later Count Botho
Eulenburg, exercised over my representative, took such
a form that I ultimately had the impression of being face
to face with a system of gradual pressure which aimed at
ousting me from the political leadership. The outward
sign of this system was at that time the lack of my signature on the official announcements of the ministry. This
was not done at my wish or with my consent; but they
profited by my indifference to externals, and I allowed
these proceedings to pass unchecked, until I was no longer
able to doubt their systematic intention.

The separate occurrences which throw light on after events do not all fall into the time of the council's session in June 1878, but they illumined, to some extent retrospectively, the situation of that time and its springs of action. Count Botho Eulenburg, then Minister of the Interior, gave an uncalled-for expression of his good-will towards the deputy Rickert in the Prussian parliament, in answer to an article of the ' Nord-Deutsche Allgemeine Zeitung,' with such intentional distinctness that it revealed to me, without any possibility of doubt, the connexion which he drew between me and the article he disapproved. Just as every flash of lightning lights up a landscape by night, so the individual moves of my opponents enabled me to overlook the whole situation, produced by outward demonstrations of personal good-will, combined with an actual system of boycotting. Supposing it had been possible to form a cabinet à la Gladstone, whose mission would be indicated by the names of Stosch, Eulenburg, Friedenthal, Camphausen, Rickert, and other dilutions of the generic concept ' Windthorst ' with Catholic Court influence, the question whether it could have maintained itself is one which the persons concerned do not seem to have considered. The main object was the negative one of getting rid of me, and in that all the holders of drafts on the future were agreed. Each of them might then hope afterwards to drive out the others, as is with us always the natural result of heterogeneous coalitions, agreed only in their dislike to the existing order of things. The whole combination was at that time unsuccessful, because they failed to win over either the King or the Crown Prince. As to the relations of this latter to me, my place-hunting opponents were always misinformed at that time, and afterwards in 1888. To the end of his life he maintained the same confidence in me as his father and his wife's desire to undermine it never amounted to the same pugnacious determination as in the case of the Empress Augusta, who had a freer choice of methods.

Besides the harassing struggles of a personal character, material difficulties and exhausting labour were necessitated by the breach with the Free Trade policy, which is characterised by my letter to Freiherr von Thüngen on a Protective Tariff,[1] and afterwards by the secession and the transition of the secessionists to the Centrum. My health broke down in such a manner as to paralyse my work, until Dr. Schweninger recognised the true nature of my illness, introduced the right treatment, and procured me a feeling of relative health to which I had been a stranger for many years.

Herr von Gruner, who during the new era had been Under-Secretary in the Ministry of Foreign Affairs, was pensioned off soon after I took over the ministry, and replaced by Herr von Thile. Ever since my appointment as Federal Ambassador he had been among the number of my enemies, since he regarded this post as an inheritance from his father, Justus Gruner. He remained hostile to me, and was politically incapable. In November 1863 he addressed to his Majesty a letter about the Budget dispute, in the same sense in which Lieutenant-Colonel von Vincke at Olbendorf (cf. vol. i. p. 330) and Roggenbach had thought good to take the same step. These gentlemen, in laying their proposals before the King, started from the assumption that if he were to follow their

---

[1] April 16, 1879 : *Politische Reden*, viii. 54, 55.

advice, and give way to the House of Deputies, a new minister, or at any rate a new President of the Ministry and Minister of Foreign Affairs, would be appointed—a result for which influences were at work even outside the domain of public life, assisted by the Treasurer of the Household and other persons closely connected with the Court. Afterwards Herr von Gruner still continued to associate with the circles which in 1876 had protected and nourished the ' Reichsglocke.'

After the condemnation of the editor of this journal, in January 1877, and when I had renewed in March the resignation which his Majesty had declined to accept, I learned by official means, while taking the baths at Kissingen, that Herr von Gruner had been appointed to the Household ministry, and without the counter-signature of any responsible minister had been nominated as actual privy councillor; also that Herr von Schleinitz had requested the manager of the ' Imperial and State Gazette ' to publish this appointment in the official paper.

On this subject I wrote, on June 8, to the head of the Chancery, Geheimrath Tiedemann, requesting him to communicate my views to the ministry :

' In my opinion the official part of the " Imperial and State Gazette " is destined for those communications which deal with imperial and Prussian state affairs, and for which the imperial Chancellor, or the Prussian ministry, as the case may be, is responsible. If Gruner's promotion is inserted in the official part without further explanation, it is impossible to avoid the presumption, even by a previous mention of his appointment to the household treasury, that the ministry makes itself responsible for Gruner's nomination as an acting privy councillor. Public opinion and the Prussian parliament would scarcely

assume that the ministry could have desired to confer this
distinction on its notorious opponent ; they would probably
guess the truth that the ministry is not held in sufficient respect at Court, and does not enjoy sufficient
influence with his Majesty to prevent this nomination ;
nor would there be the least doubt in their minds that this
appointment, published in the " State Gazette," had been
countersigned *more solito* by the ministry.   The belief
that the ministry possesses the influence upon his Majesty's
decisions, which is assumed by the Constitution, would not
be promoted by the published communication of his
Majesty's ungracious marginal comment, and the ensuing
answer of the ministry.   People might be tempted to
compare the contents and their effect with the proceedings
in France, which have brought about the latest change of
ministry there.

' I am not without some anxiety if we ought not to
regard the proceedings in the Gruner case as only a probe
used by Herr von Schleinitz and his advisers (not by his
Majesty the Emperor) for sounding us, in order to see
how much we will stand, and how highly we rate our
ministerial authority.   In my opinion, to yield to these
unjustifiable ways of influencing his Majesty's decisions is
not the best method of putting an end to them.   On the
contrary, they will only increase, and the conflict, which is
now a merely formal one, would soon be repeated on a
more unfavourable domain, confused with great party issues.

' In my present position I might refrain from any
official utterance ; but I have a feeling that my return to
business, which is a very important matter for me personally, may be prejudiced by these means, quite apart from
any considerations of health.   As I hope that my health
will improve, and as in this case I should wish to keep

open the possibility of returning to business, if this is in accordance with his Majesty's wishes, I feel a personal interest in adequately guarding the prestige of the ministerial position in such a way that I may be able conscientiously to maintain my resumption of it.

'In my opinion the proper and logical solution of the first decision would have been the refusal of the request made by the Minister of the Household to insert the nomination in the official part of the " State Gazette." This official insertion cannot be protected from misinterpretation by public opinion, and must always remain a partial victory of the " Reichsglocke " intrigues over the present government. Announcements concerning the royal household have properly no place in the " Imperial and State Gazette." Even if the latter is also to be a " Royal Household Gazette," the orders of the Household Minister have, in my opinion, no right to a place in the *official* portion, since he has no responsibility for the contents of the official journal. These announcements must, in some form or other, bear the *placet* of a responsible minister, which the Household Minister must seek to obtain before they are printed off. This *placet* was not sought in the present case; the Household Minister assumed a right of disposal over the " State Gazette," and on this account alone his request ought properly to have been refused on the ground of its informality. If a command to insert any matter relating to the royal household is given by his Majesty the King himself, there can be no hesitation about executing it in the majority of cases; but even in perfectly straightforward cases it is advisable to keep the official announcements of the royal household apart in position from those of the state. The separation might, in my view, be managed by publishing the regula-

tions referring to the royal household, not promiscuously
with those of the ministry, but in a third column, side by
side with the two great official headings of the " State
Gazette," " German Empire " and " Kingdom of Prussia."
A place between the two would show the greatest courtesy ;
if necessary, it might follow the " Kingdom of Prussia,"
and bear the designation " Royal Household," separated
from the two other headings by continuous lines, just as
" Prussia " and " Empire " are now separated. That would
settle the formal question for the future in a manner
which, it seems to me, can give no offence to either side.

'It is quite a different matter, however, when a resolution of his Majesty's is officially announced, which,
in spite of assurances to the contrary confined to official
documents, proclaims to the public what in constitutional
language is usually called a want of confidence in his
ministers on the part of the Monarch. Of course, in such
a case, there is no remedy open to the ministers but resignation. Undoubtedly the present case, in as far as it has
this character, is aimed rather at me than at my colleagues. The " Reichsglocke " and other papers which
represented the tendencies of Herren von Gruner, von
Schleinitz, Count Nesselrode, and Nathusius-Ludom, did
not libel them publicly, or at any rate not in the same
degree as myself.

'The pardon of Herr von.Nathusius, the distinction
conferred on Count Nesselrode and Herr von Gruner, at
the very time when the libels of the organ which represented those gentlemen were occupying public opinion
and the law courts, and the connexion of those gentlemen
with these papers was becoming apparent, pointed to an
act of royal favour towards persons who were only known
for their hostility to the government and their open

attacks on my honour. But as long as I was his Majesty's servant, this last ought to be under his protection. If I experience the opposite of this protection, it must be due to a personal motive, which urges me far more imperatively to leave the service than any considerations of health could ever do. These reasons for taking the resolution are only personal to myself, but, according as matters develop, will be decisive as to the possibility of my return to my post.

'I do most earnestly call upon my colleagues, in the interest of their ministerial future, to take care that the official publication of Gruner's appointment, if his Majesty is not willing to abandon it altogether, may still be made in a form which will make the absence of counter-signature evident. This could be obtained by the above-mentioned division into three parts, the Empire, Prussia, and the household, especially if the press received an explanation on the subject. But in my view it would be desirable that Gruner's appointment to the royal household should be previously published separately in the household column, and it would then announce next day that his Majesty had been graciously pleased to confer upon the person appointed to the household ministry, &c. &c., the title of an acting privy councillor, &c. &c. A slightly different form of wording from that of the usual announcements, no matter how slight, would still be an advantage.'

This letter, addressed to Geheimrath Tiedemann, and forwarded under flying-seal to the Minister von Bülow, contained an addition meant for this latter, requesting him to make confidential use of it among his colleagues.

'. . . This occurrence, to my mind, hits me more severely than my colleagues, who have not been libelled by the " Reichsglocke " party, with the exception perhaps of Camphausen, nor was he subjected to the same measure of malignity as I. He was attacked by unworthy means about actual facts connected with his office, but his personal honour was left untouched. The ministry, as a whole, is certainly in a position to feel itself aggrieved by the *mode* of Gruner's appointment, and must take notice of this treatment in order to secure its rights and dignity for the future. But the insult conveyed in the *fact* of Gruner's appointment is aimed at me alone. It is only his long-continued enmity to me personally which has succeeded in drawing attention to him, for he lacks both talent and merit. While at the Foreign Office he was a real hindrance, in consequence of his incapacity, which at critical moments bordered on idiotcy. For the last fifteen years he has done nothing but write, speak, and intrigue against me with all the bitterness of overweening self-conceit which thinks it lacks appreciation. I am momentarily disregarding the fact that it was these very " Reichsglocke " elements which increased the difficulty of performing my official duties to an extent with which I had not sufficient strength to cope. I speak now only of the blow to be aimed at me personally in the possibility of successfully recommending this man to his Majesty. In face of this, if I say in my letter to Tiedemann that this Gruner case does not supply a sufficient motive to compel my colleagues to resign, my own position in reference to it appears to me an essentially different one.

' I should be very grateful to you if you would speak confidentially in this sense to Camphausen, Friedenthal, and Falk. Wilmowski's attitude is different from what I should have expected. I had hitherto counted on him as a safe ally against the Schleinitz Camarilla ; but I do not understand his action in this case. Together with

Eulenburg and Leonhardt he will cause the ministry to lose the measure of self-esteem and consideration which it enjoys in this country, and without which in these difficult situations at Court and in the country the state business cannot be carried on. In speaking to Eulenburg you must only use those expressions which will bear repeating. What is Hofman's attitude in the matter?

' The baths seem to suit me very well, but every relapse, caused by unpleasant impressions, is very strongly marked, and makes me realise that the state of my health will scarcely be sufficient for carrying on business. I should not shrink from the simple performance of official business ; but I am no longer able to bear as I could formerly the *faux frais* of Court intrigues, perhaps because they have increased so alarmingly in extent and influence. Three months ago I kept silence about these, the real reasons of my continued intention to resign, although they were essentially the same as now. At the present time too I shall mention no other motive for resignation, out of consideration for the Emperor, than the state of my health.'

The matter was terminated by the non-publication in the ' State Gazette ' of Gruner's appointment as an acting privy councillor.

CHAPTER XXVII

THE GOVERNMENT DEPARTMENTS

MY frequent absences caused me to lose touch with my colleagues. The fact that I had raised them all, in some cases from very unimportant posts, to the rank of minister, and had not troubled them with any interference in their departments, made me over-estimate their personal regard for me. I seldom interfered with the current business of their departments, and only when I saw that an important public interest ran a risk of being sacrificed to private interests. Thus, for instance, I opposed the canalisation of the Rhine through the Rheingau, projected for the sake of the navigation, which would in the course of thirty years have transformed the river bed, between the banks and the two dikes to be constructed, into a marsh ; as also the plan of macadamising the Elector's Embankment only for the usual width of the *chaussées*, and building on it close up to the edge of the old road. In both cases I crossed the intentions of the authorities immediately concerned, and I believe that in so doing I effected a lasting benefit. Nor did I trouble my colleagues or the subordinate imperial offices with patronage. The Constitution would have allowed me to appoint all the post office, telegraph, and railway officials, and to fill all the posts in the separate imperial departments. But I do not believe that I ever asked Herr von Stephan or any one else for a post for a candidate recommended by me, not even for a postman. I had however frequently to oppose the tendency to create new far-reaching laws or organisations, the tendency to regulate from the green table, because I knew that even if they did not exaggerate this law-mongering themselves, their officials did, and that many a reporting official in the home departments, ever since taking his degree, had carried about projects concerning his own speciality, which aimed at promoting the happiness of the subjects of the Empire as soon as he could find a chief ready to agree to them.

In spite of my non-interference the majority of my official friends seemed to have felt as though relieved from pressure after my resignation. In many cases this could be explained by the resistance which I showed to the rampant tendency to unnecessary attacks on the stability of our legislation. In the domain of the schools I continually but unsuccessfully combated the theory that the Minister of Education, without any law and without being limited by the existing school property, might determine, as a matter of administration, and without any regard to its capacity to pay, the amount which each parish must contribute to the school. This absolute authority, which existed in no other branch of administration, and the application of which was in some cases carried so far that the parishes were unable to exist, was based not upon any law, but upon a rescript of the former Minister of Education, von Raumer, making the School Budget dependent on the disposition of the government department in question, and in the last resort on that of the minister. The endeavour to consolidate this ministerial absolutism by a law was an obstacle which prevented my giving my adhesion to the various proposals for school bills presented to me from time to time.

In the domain of finance, my assent to any reform in taxation was always subordinate to the desire not to use those direct taxes which are independent of the tax-payer's property as a standard for future annual additions. Although the injustice once committed by the imposition of a ground and house tax could not be removed, it is not on that account consistent with justice to repeat it by annual additions. Scholz, my last colleague in the Finance Ministry, with whom I always maintained friendly relations, shared this view, but had to contend against the parliamentary and ministerial difficulties in the way of a remedy. The combative forces among his officials were doubtless glad of the freer movement which they experienced after I had left the ministry. Demands with which I could for many years find no agreement in the Finance Ministry were self-assessment and a higher taxation of income from foreign securities than from German, a sort of protective tariff for German securities, and of interest on invested capital compared with money which had to be earned afresh every year. In the domain of agriculture, the removal of the agrarian pressure which I was supposed to exercise chiefly benefited diseased swine and the cattle plague, as well as those higher and lower officials to whose lot fell the task of combating in parliament and in the country the lying party-cry about raising the price of food. The disposition to yield in this domain and the facilities given to French communication with Alsace (revoked, after unpleasant experiences, in February 1891) are to my mind the common expression of a cowardice which is ready to sacrifice the future for a little more comfort in the present. The desire of obtaining cheap pork will be no more permanently furthered by any lax treatment of the danger of contagion than the detachment of Alsace from France will be promoted by the weak striving after applause which shows itself in the treatment of local grievances and frontier difficulties.

As regards the imperial offices, I always, during the time of Scholz as during that of Maltzahn, kept up a good feeling with the Treasury. The task assigned to this office was of no greater range than to assist the Chancellor with technical knowledge and trained powers of work, in his discussions and understandings with the Prussian Minister of Finance. In questions of finance, the Prussian Minister of Finance and the ministry of state remained the decisive authority. The characters of both men enabled one to settle differences of opinion, without ill-feeling, by fair discussion. The idea which has lately been represented in the press, and even put into practice, that there could be a financial policy of the Chancellor or even of the Imperial Treasury, which is subordinate to him, on the one side, and of the Prussian Minister of Finance on the other, independent of one another, was in my time considered unconstitutional. Differences between the departments found their solution in the common deliberations of the ministry of state to which the Chancellor as Foreign Minister belonged, and without whose implied or express assent he is not empowered to give the Prussian votes in the Federal Council, or to propose a project of law.

My relations with the Imperial Post Office were less clear to me. During the French war there were occurrences which brought me very near a breach with Herr von Stephan; but I was then already so convinced of his unusual ability, not only as regards his special department, that I successfully supported him against his

Majesty's displeasure. Herr von Stephan had addressed to his subordinates an official circular in which he instructed them to supply certain newspapers for all the military hospitals in France, and in explanation of this order referred to the wishes of her Royal Highness the Crown Princess. How far he was justified in that I do not know, but whoever knew the old master will be able to imagine his state of mind when this postal edict was brought to his knowledge through military reports. The political colour of the papers which were recommended would alone have sufficed to bring Stephan under his Majesty's displeasure, but still more irritating was the appeal to a member of the royal family, and especially to the Crown Princess. I restored the peace with his Majesty. The desire for recognition in high quarters is one of the encumbrances that weigh upon most men of unusual ability. I assumed that, as Stephan grew older and became more distinguished, the weaknesses which he brought from his early employments into his higher posts would disappear. I can only wish that he may grow old in office, and preserve his health, and I should regard his loss as one very difficult to make up for;[1] but I conjecture that he also formed one of those who thought that they experienced a feeling of relief at my departure. I have always been of opinion that the transport and correspondence traffic should contribute to the good of the state, and that the contribution should be included in the cost of postage and carriage. Stephan is more of a departmental patriot, and as such has certainly been useful, not only to his department and its officials, but also to the Empire, in a measure to which any successor would find it difficult to attain. I always treated his arbitrary dealings with the

[1] Stephan died April 8, 1897.

indulgence inspired by my respect for his eminent ability, even when they interfered with my jurisdiction as Chancellor and as the representative who had to give the Prussian votes at the council, or when he spoiled the financial results by his love of fine buildings.

CHAPTER XXVIII

THE BERLIN CONGRESS

In the autumn of 1876 I received at Varzin a ciphered
telegram from General von Werder, our military plenipotentiary at Livadia, in which, on behalf of the Emperor
Alexander, he demanded from me some expression on the
question whether, if Russia went to war with Austria, we
should remain neutral.   In replying to it I had to take into
consideration that General von Werder's cipher was not
inaccessible within the Emperor's palace ; for I had learned
that even in our embassy at St. Petersburg the secret of
the cipher could not be preserved by any ingenious
method of locking it up, but only by constantly changing
it.   I was convinced that I could telegraph nothing to
Livadia that would not come to the knowledge of the
Emperor.   That such a question should be asked in such
a way at all presupposed a dislocation of the traditional
method of doing business. If one cabinet desires to
address questions of this kind to another, the correct way
is to sound them in confidential conversation, either by
means of its own ambassador or by a personal interview
between the Sovereigns.   That there are serious objections
to sounding by means of an inquiry addressed to the
representative of the Power which is being sounded,
Russian diplomacy experienced in the transactions between the Emperor Nicholas and Sir H. Seymour. Gort-

chakoff's preference for asking questions of us by telegraph not through the Russian representative at Berlin, but through the German one at St. Petersburg, compelled me to remind our missions at St. Petersburg more often than those at any other Court, that their duty lay not in repre- senting to us the desires of the Russian cabinet, but in placing our wishes before Russia. The temptation for a diplomatist to foster his official and social position by doing favours to the government to which he is accredited is great, and is the more dangerous if the Foreign Minister can work on our agent and win him over to his wishes, before the latter knows all the circumstances that make acquiescence, or even the suggestion, inopportune for his government.

But it lay beyond all, even beyond Russian usages, for the German military plenipotentiary at the Russian Court to place before us, and that in my absence from Berlin, by order of the Russian Emperor, a political question of far- reaching importance in the categorical style of a telegram. I had, inconvenient as I found it, never been able to procure a change in the old custom whereby our military plenipotentiaries at St. Petersburg made their communi- cations not, like the others, through the Foreign Office, but direct to his Majesty in letters in their own hand—a custom which had its origin in the fact that Frederick William III gave to Lucadou, formerly commandant of Kolberg, and the first military attaché at St. Petersburg a particularly intimate position with the Emperor. In these letters the military attaché certainly wrote down everything that the Russian Emperor told him in the course of ordinary confidential conversation at Court, and not seldom that was much more than Gortchakoff told the ambassador. The 'Pruski Fligel-adjutant,' as he was called at Court, saw the Emperor almost every day, and in any case much oftener than Gortchakoff; the Emperor did not talk to him of military matters only, and the messages entrusted to him for our Sovereign were not confined to family affairs. The diplomatic negotiations between both cabinets often found their centre of gravity, as at the time of Rauch and Münster, far more in the reports of the military attachés than in those of the officially accredited envoys. But as the Emperor William never omitted to communicate to me in course of time, although often too late, his correspondence with the military attaché at St. Petersburg, and as he never came to a political decision without reference to his official advisers, the disadvantages of this direct intercourse were confined to the retardment of such information and announcements as were contained in direct reports of this kind. It lay, therefore, beyond this usage in the transaction of business that the Emperor Alexander, undoubtedly at the instigation of Prince Gortchakoff, should employ Herr von Werder as the means of placing before us that leading question. Gortchakoff was at that time anxious to prove to his Emperor that my devotion to him, and my sympathy with Russia, was insincere, or at least 'platonic,' and also to shake his confidence in me, in which he afterwards succeeded.

Before positively answering Werder's question, I made an attempt to do so by dilatory replies referring to the impossibility of expressing myself on such a question without higher authorisation, and when I was repeatedly pressed, I recommended them to put the question, in an official, though confidential, manner, by means of the Russian ambassador at Berlin, to the Foreign Office. However, repeated interpellations through

Werder's telegrams put an end to this evasive method. In the meantime I had begged his Majesty to recall Herr von Werder by telegram to the Imperial Court, as he was being misused at Livadia for diplomatic purposes without being able to defend himself, and to forbid him to undertake political commissions, as that belonged to the Russian but not to the German service. The Emperor did not accede to my wish, and as, at length, the Emperor Alexander, on the ground of our personal relations, desired from me the expression of my own opinion through the Russian ambassador at Berlin, it was no longer possible for me to evade replying to the indiscreet question. I asked the ambassador von Schweinitz, who was just at the end of his leave, to visit me at Varzin before his return to St. Petersburg, in order to receive my instructions. Schweinitz was my guest from the 11th to the 13th of October. I commissioned him to repair as soon as possible *via* St. Petersburg to the Czar's Court at Livadia. My instructions to Schweinitz were to the effect that our first care was to preserve the friendship between the great monarchies, which in a struggle with one another had more to lose as regarded their opposition to the revolution than they had to win. If, to our sorrow, this was not possible between Russia and Austria, then we could endure indeed that our friends should lose or win battles against each other, but not that one of the two should be so severely wounded and injured that its position as an independent Great Power taking its part in the councils of Europe would be endangered. The result of the unequivocally plain declaration that Gortchakoff prevailed on his Sovereign to wrest from us, in order to prove to him the Platonic character of our love, was that the Russian storm passed from Eastern Galicia to the Balkans, and

that Russia, in place of the negotiations with us which
were broken off, began similar negotiations with Austria
—first of all, so far as I remember, at Pesth—in the
sense of the settlement come to at Reichstadt, where
the Emperors Alexander and Francis Joseph had met on
July 8, 1876, and requested that they should be kept secret
from us. This treaty,[1] and not the Berlin congress, is
the foundation of the Austrian possession of Bosnia and
Herzegovina, and during her war with the Turks secured
to Russia the neutrality of Austria.

That the Russian cabinet in the settlement at
Reichstadt conceded to the Austrians the acquisition of
Bosnia as an equivalent for their neutrality makes us
assume that Herr von Oubril did not speak the truth
when he assured us that the Balkan war would be only
a question of a ' promenade militaire,' of giving occupation
to the ' trop plein ' of the army, and of Turkish horses'
tails and crosses of St. George ; in that case Bosnia
would have been too high a price to pay. Probably at
St. Petersburg they had reckoned on Bulgaria, when it was
separated from Turkey, remaining permanently in dependence on Russia. Even if the peace of San Stefano had
been carried out intact, this calculation would probably
have proved false. In order not to be held responsible for
this error by their own people, they sought with success
to lay the guilt of the unsuccessful issue of the war on
the German policy, on the ' disloyalty ' of the German
friend. It was a dishonest fiction ; we had never let
them expect anything but a benevolent neutrality, and the

[1] Concluded January 15, 1877.

honesty of our intentions is manifested by the fact that
we did not let ourselves be disturbed by the demand of
Russia that the Reichstadt arrangement should be kept
secret from us, but readily acceded to the desire communicated to me at Friedrichsruh by Count Shuvaloff to
summon a congress at Berlin. The desire of the Russian
government to arrive at peace with Turkey by means of a
congress proved that they did not feel themselves strong
enough on the military side to let the matter come to
a war with England and Austria, after they had once
let slip the opportunity of occupying Constantinople.
Prince Gortchakoff doubtless shares the responsibility
for the blunders of the Russian policy with younger and
more energetic men holding similar views, but he is not
free from it. How strong, measured by Russian traditions, his position as against the Emperor was is shown
by the fact that he took part in the Berlin congress as
representative of Russia, although he knew that this was
against the wish of his master. When, relying on his
character as chancellor and foreign minister, he took his
seat, the peculiar situation arose that the chancellor,
who was at the head of the state, and the ambassador
Shuvaloff, who was subordinate to his department,
figured side by side, but the holder of the Russian plenary
powers was not the chancellor but the ambassador.

This, which, by what I observed, was undoubtedly the
situation, though we could perhaps not find documentary
proof of it, except in the Russian archives, and perhaps
not even in them, shows that even in a government with
so absolute and despotic a ruler as Russia, the unity of
political action is not secured. It is so, perhaps, in a greater
degree in England, where the chief minister and the communications he receives are exposed to public criticism,

while in Russia only the Emperor ruling at the time is
in a position to judge, according to his knowledge of men
and to his capacity, which of the servants who make reports
to, and advise, him on current affairs is in error or lies to
him, and from which he learns the truth. By this I do
not mean to say that the current business of the Foreign
Office is more cleverly carried on in London than in St.
Petersburg, but the English government falls less often
than the Russian into the necessity of repairing by insin-
cerity the errors of its subordinates. Lord Palmerston did
indeed on April 4, 1856, say in the House of Commons,
with an irony which was probably not understood by the
mass of the members, that the selection of the papers
regarding Kars, to be laid before the House, had demanded great care and attention from persons occupying
not a subordinate, but a high position in the Foreign Office.
The Blue Book on Kars, the castrated dispatches of Sir
Alexander Burnes from Afghanistan, and the communications of ministers regarding the origin of the note which
the Vienna conference of 1854 recommended to the Sultan
for signature instead of that of Mentchikoff, are proofs
of the ease with which parliament and the press in England
can be deceived. That the archives of the Foreign Office in
London are more carefully guarded than those of other
places makes us suspect that many similar proofs might
be found in them. But on the whole it may be said that
it is easier to deceive the Czar than the parliament.

It was expected at St. Petersburg that in the diplomatic
discussion for carrying out the decisions of the Berlin
congress we should immediately in every case support
and carry through the Russian interpretation as opposed
to that of Austria and England, and especially without
any preliminary understanding between Berlin and St.

Petersburg. The demand which I at first only indicated, but afterwards unequivocally expressed, that Russia should tell us confidentially, but plainly, her wishes, so that they might be discussed, was evaded, and I had the impression that Prince Gortchakoff expected from me, as a lady from her admirer, that I should guess at and represent the Russian wishes without Russia having herself to utter them, and thereby to undertake any responsibility. Even in cases where we could assume that we were completely certain of Russian interests and intentions, and where we believed ourselves able to give a voluntary proof of our friendship towards the Russian policy without injuring our own interests, instead of the expected acknowledgement we received a grumbling disapproval, because, as it was alleged, in aim and degree, we had not met the expectations of our Russian friends. Even when that was undoubtedly the case, we had no better success. In the whole proceeding lay a calculated dishonesty, not only towards us, but towards the Emperor Alexander, to whose mind the German policy was to be made to appear dishonest and untrustworthy. 'Votre amitié est trop platonique,' said reproachfully the Empress Marie to one of our representatives. It is true that the friendship of the cabinet of one Great Power for the others always remains Platonic to a certain point; for no Great Power can place itself exclusively at the service of another. It will always have to keep in view not only existing, but future, relations to the others, and must, as far as possible, avoid lasting fundamental hostility with any of them. That is particularly important for Germany, with its central position, which is open to attack on three sides.

Errors in the policy of the cabinets of the Great Powers bring no immediate punishment, either in St. Petersburg or

Berlin, but they are never harmless.   The logic of history
is even more exact in its revisions than our chief audit
office.   In carrying out the decrees of the congress, Russia
expected and required that, in the local discussions about
them in the East, when there was any difference of
opinion between the Russian and the other interpreta-
tions, the German commissioners should, on principle,
support Russia.[1]   In many questions the objective decision
might certainly be fairly indifferent to us ; therefore it was
only incumbent on us to explain the stipulations honestly,
and not to disturb our relations with the other Great Powers
by party support of local questions that did not affect
German interests.   The passionate and bitter language of
all the Russian organs, the instigation of Russian popular
opinion against us which was authorised by the censorship
of the press, seemed to make it advisable that we should
not alienate from us the sympathies which we might still
possess among the non-Russian Powers.

    In this situation there now came a letter from the
Emperor Alexander, written in his own hand, which, in
spite of all the respect shown for his aged friend and
uncle, contained in two passages decided menaces of war
in the form which is customary by the laws of nations,
something to this effect : if the refusal to adapt the
German vote to the Russian is adhered to, peace between
us cannot last.   In two passages was a variation of this
theme in sharp and unequivocal terms.   That Prince Gortchakoff, who on September 6, 1879, made France a very
striking declaration of love in an interview with Louis
Peyramont, the correspondent of the Orleanist ' Soleil,'
had also had a share in that letter, I could see in it ; my

    [1] *Cf.* the estima'e of the situation quoted from a dispatch in the
Bismarck-Jahrbuch, i. 125 ff.

suspicion was confirmed through two later observations. In October a lady in Berlin society, whose room in the Hotel del'Europe at Baden-Baden was next Gortchakoff's, heard him say : ' I should have wished to go to war, but France has other intentions.' And on November 1 the Paris correspondent of the ' Times ' was in a position to inform his paper that before his arrival at Alexandrovo, the Czar had written to the Emperor William complaining of the attitude of Germany, and using the phrase : ' Your Majesty's chancellor has forgotten the promises of 1870.' *

In face of the attitude of the Russian press, the increasing excitement of the great mass of the people, and the aggregation of troops all along the Russian frontier, it would have been levity to doubt the serious nature of the situation and of the Emperor's threats to the friend whom he had formerly so much honoured. The Emperor William, in going by the advice of Field-Marshal von Manteuffel to Alexandrovo on September 3, 1879, in order to give a verbal and propitiatory answer to the written threats of his nephew, acted contrary to my feeling and my judgement as to what was necessary.

Considerations analogous to those which dissuaded any attempt at solving the complicated difficulties of 1863 by means of a Russian alliance were in the second

* The correspondent, Herr Oppert from Blowitz in Bohemia, doubtless undertook the more willingly to spread this news, which must have come to him from Gortchakoff, because he bore me a grudge ever since the congress. At the desire of Beaconsfield, who wished to keep him in good humour, I procured for him the third class of the Crown Order. Angry at what, according to Prussian ideas, is considered an unusually high distinction, he refused it, and demanded the second class.

half of the 'seventies opposed in the same way to any
stronger accentuation of the Russian alliance without
Austria. I do not know how far Count Peter Shuvaloff,
before the beginning of the last Balkan war, and during
the congress, was expressly commissioned to discuss the
question of a Russo-German alliance. He was not
accredited to Berlin but to London; his personal relations
with me, however, enabled him on his occasional visits to
Berlin on his journeys to and from England, as well as
during the congress, to discuss with me without restraint
all eventualities.

In the beginning of February 1877, I received a long
letter from him from London; my answer and his reply
here follow.

'Berlin : February 15, 1877.

' Dear Count,*—I thank you for the kind words you
have been good enough to write me, and I am much obliged
to Count Münster for having on this occasion so well interpreted the sentiments which since our first acquaintance
have formed between us a bond that will survive the
political relations that now draw us together. Among
the regrets which official life will leave me, that which
will arise from the remembrance of my relations with you
will be the most poignant.

' Whatever the political future of our two countries may
be, the part I have played in the past allows me the satisfaction of knowing that, respecting the necessity of their
alliance, I have always been in agreement with the statesman most worthy of esteem among your compatriots. As
long as I am in office, I shall be faithful to the traditions
by which I have been guided for five-and-twenty years,

---

*·[In the German original this and the following letter are in French.]

and of which the principles coincide with the ideas expressed in your letter in regard to the reciprocal services which Russia and Germany can render to one another, and have rendered for more than a century, without harming the particular interests of either. It was that conviction which guided me in 1848, in 1854, in 1863, as in the present instance, and for which I succeeded in gaining the suffrages of the great majority of my countrymen. It is a work that will perhaps be easier to destroy than it was to create, especially if it happens that my successors do not use the same patience as I have done in cultivating traditions the experience of which they will lack, as well as sometimes the self-abnegation necessary for subordinating appearances to realities, personal susceptibilities to great monarchical interests. An old stager of my stamp does not let himself be easily put out by false alarms, and in the interests of my Sovereign and of my country, I can forget the mortifications that, during the past two years, have not been spared me from your direction. I pay no heed to the " flirtations " in which my old friend and protector at St. Petersburg and my young friend at Paris [1] are indulging ; but it will perhaps be easier to lead astray the judgement of the chancellors who will come after me, by giving them a glimpse, as has been done for the last three years, of the facility with which, on your part, a coalition could be built up on the basis of revenge. The calmness with which I regard this eventuality I shall not be able to bequeath to my successors. With the menaces of semi-official journals, with Parisian blandishments in feuilletons, and in letters to political ladies, it will not be very difficult one of these days to derange the compass of a German minister dismayed by the idea

[1] Orloff.

of isolation. To avoid this he will commit himself to maladroit pledges which it will be difficult to discharge. In any case it will not be my affair; as soon as I have satisfied, well or ill, the requirements of the Diet, which opens on the 22nd, and which should only last a few weeks, I shall go to the baths, and shall return no more to office. I have the faculty's certificate that I am " *untauglich,*" the official phrase for permission to retire, which in this case only expresses the sad truth. I have no more interest in it.

' Before that period I must reply to the latest enigma of your policy ; I am not clever at divination ; I need to be enlightened on a deep-seated thought which, as it seems, I have not rightly understood in the past. Without instructions or advice, I cannot find the narrow line between the reproach of encouraging Turkey by speaking of peace, and the suspicion of treacherously urging war. I have just passed under the fire of those incompatible accusations, and I have no desire to expose myself to them afresh without a pilot, and even without a lighthouse, which will indicate the port at which you desire us to disembark.

'BISMARCK.'

From Count Shuvaloff to Bismarck

'London : February 25, 1877.

' My dear Prince,—I was very deeply touched by your kind letter, but I feel genuine remorse when I think of the trouble you have taken in writing it, and of the time, so precious when it is yours, which it cost you.

' The letter will form one of the pleasantest souvenirs of my political career, and I shall bequeath it to my son.

' Having been for a year far away from Berlin and St. Petersburg, doubt had taken possession of me.

' I thought that what had existed—perhaps existed no longer. You have given me proof of the contrary. As a good Russian I rejoice with all my heart.

' If, my dear Prince, I had not again found in you the man who never changes, either in policy or in goodwill towards his friends, I should this time have sold my Russian stock, as you wanted to do three years ago, because you had too high an opinion of me.

' I have copied some passages in your letter and sent them to my Emperor. I know it will give him pleasure to read them. On every occasion on which he has come into *direct* contact with you, the result has been beneficial and useful ; and to read what you write to one whom you honour with the title of friend is for the Emperor exactly as if he was in direct communication with you.

' It is needless to add that I have left out everything that concerns Gortchakoff because I regarded your allusions to him as a proof of your confidence in my discretion.

' Ill-informed as I am (and for good reasons) of what they want at St. Petersburg, postponement and disarmament appear to me probable.

' It is said that peace is to be concluded with Servia and Montenegro. The Grand Vizier has sent letters to Decazes and Derby informing them that the Sultan promises to carry out of his own accord all the reforms demanded by the conference. Europe is going to ask us to grant Turkey time. Would it be a favourable moment for us to declare war, and alienate still further from us the feelings of Europe ?

' As private business imperiously summons me to

Russia, I intend to ask for a short leave of absence as soon as we arrive at a decision one way or another. I hope, my dear Prince, that when I pass through Berlin you will permit me to see you—I am immensely anxious to do so.

'Pardon the length of this letter for the reason that you have not to reply to it.

'Accept, once again, my dear Prince, my cordial thanks for your "kindness" [in English], and for your letter, to which I make only one objection : it is the way in which I am sorry to see you speak of your health. God will keep it from failing, I am sure, as He preserves all that is useful to millions of men, and for the maintenance of vast and great interests.

'Rest assured, my dear Prince, that you will always find in me more than an admirer—the number of them is large enough without me—but a man who is with all his heart sincerely and devotedly attached to you.

'SCHUVALOFF.'

Even before the congress Count Shuvaloff touched on the question of a Russo-German offensive and defensive alliance, and put it to me directly. I discussed openly with him the difficulties and prospects that the question of the alliance offered us, and especially the choice between Austria and Russia if the triple alliance of the Eastern Powers were not maintained. Among other things he said, during the discussion : 'Coalitions are your nightmare,' to which I replied : 'Necessarily.' He pointed out that a firm and steadfast alliance with Russia would be the safest means against this, because, by the exclusion of the latter Power from the circle of our coalition-adversaries, no combination which would endanger our existence would be possible.

I admitted as much, but expressed a fear that if the German policy confined its possibilities to the Russian alliance, and in accordance with the wishes of Russia, refused all other states, Germany would with regard to Russia be in an unequal position, because the geographical situation and the autocratic constitution of Russia made it easier for her to give up the alliance than it would be for us, and because the maintenance of the old traditions of the Russo-Prussian alliance after all rests on a single pair of eyes—that is it depends on the moods of the reigning Emperor of Russia. Our relations to Russia rested essentially on the personal relations of the two sovereigns to one another, and upon the proper fostering of this by the tact of the Courts and diplomatists and the sentiments of the representatives on either side. We had had an example that even with somewhat helpless Prussian ambassadors at St. Petersburg, the intimacy of our mutual relations had been maintained by the tact of military attachés like the Generals von Rauch and Count Münster, notwithstanding much justifiable sensitiveness on either side. We had also learned that hasty, irritable, quick-tempered representatives of Russia like Budberg and Oubril by their attitude at Berlin, and by their official reports when they were personally out of humour, engendered impressions which might react dangerously on the whole mutual relations of two peoples numbering a hundred and fifty millions.

I remember that Prince Gortchakoff, when I was envoy at St. Petersburg, and enjoyed his unbounded confidence, used, if he had to keep me waiting, to give me unopened dispatches from Berlin to read before he had looked through them himself. I was at times astonished to learn from them with what malevolence my former friend

Budberg subordinated the task of maintaining the existing relations to his personal sensitiveness over some
occurrence in society, or merely to the desire of introducing
a witty sarcasm on the affairs of the Berlin Court or
ministry. His dispatches were naturally laid before the
Emperor, and this was done without comment or explanation. The imperial marginal notes, which Gortchakoff,
in the course of further business correspondence, at times
permitted me to glance at, gave me undoubted proof how
susceptible the Emperor Alexander, well disposed towards
us though he might be, was to the ill-natured dispatches
of Budberg and Oubril, and inferred from them not false
statements on the part of his representatives, but a pre-
valent lack of intelligent and friendly policy at Berlin.
When Prince Gortchakoff gave me things of this kind to
read with their seals unbroken, in order to coquet with his
confidence, he used to say : 'Vous oublierez ce que vous
ne deviez pas lire,' which I, after I had looked through
the dispatches in the next room, naturally agreed to do,
and as long as I was at St. Petersburg, kept my promise ;
for it was not my business to render the relations of the
two Courts worse by complaints of the Russian representative at Berlin, and I feared that my information
would be clumsily turned to account in fostering intrigues
and quarrels at Court.

It is especially to be wished that we should be represented at every friendly Court by diplomatists who, without
encroaching on the general policy of their own country,
should as far as possible foster the relations of both interested states, suppress as far as possible ill-humour and
gossip, bridle their desire to be witty, and rather bring
forward the practical side of the matter. I have often not
shown dispatches from our representatives at German

Courts in the highest quarters, because they had a tendency to be piquant, or to relate and give importance to annoying expressions or occurrences, rather than to foster and improve the relations between the two courts, so long as the latter, as in Germany is always the case, was the task of our policy. When I was in St. Petersburg and Paris I always considered myself justified in suppressing things which would merely have caused useless ill-feeling at home, or were only adapted for satirical representations; and when I was minister I did not lay dispatches of this kind before those who filled the highest place in the state. In the position of an ambassador at the Court of a Great Power there is no obligation to report mechanically all the foolish talk and spiteful things that arise at the ambassador's place of residence. Not only an ambassador, but also every German diplomatist at a German Court ought to avoid writing dispatches like those which Budberg and Oubril sent home from Berlin, and Balabin from Vienna, under the calculation that they would be read with interest and complacent gaiety as witty effusions; but as long as the relations between the Courts are friendly, he ought to refrain from stirring up irritation and from gossip. A man who looks only at the formal part of the course of business will certainly consider it the most correct thing that the ambassador shall report all that he hears without reserve and leave it to the minister to decide what is to be passed over and what is to be emphasised. Whether such a method is practically useful depends on the personality of the minister. As I considered that I had quite as much insight as Herr von Schleinitz, and as I took a deeper and more conscientious interest in the fate of our country than he did, I considered myself entitled,

nay, bound not to bring to his knowledge many things
that in his hands might have served the cause of provocations and intrigues at Court in the sense of a policy
which was not that of the King.

I return from this digression to the conversations
which I had with Count Peter Shuvaloff at the time of
the Balkan war. I told him that if we sacrificed our
relations with all the other Powers to the firmness of our
alliance with Russia, we should find ourselves, with our
exposed geographical situation, in a dangerous dependence
on Russia in the event of an acute manifestation of French
or Austrian desire of revenge. The friendliness of Russia
with Powers which could not exist without her goodwill
had its bounds, especially in a policy like that of Prince
Gortchakoff—a policy that occasionally reminded me of
Asiatic conceptions. He had often simply beaten down
every political objection with the argument : ' L'Empereur
est fort irrité,' to which I used ironically to reply : ' Eh,
le mien donc ! ' On that Shuvaloff remarked : ' Gortchakoff est un animal,' which, in the slang of St. Petersburg, is not so rude in meaning as in sound,' il n'a aucune
influence.' He owed it in the main only to the Emperor's
respect for his age, and his esteem for his past services,
that he still formally conducted affairs. About what
could Russia and Prussia seriously fall into dispute ?
There was absolutely no question between them of
sufficient importance for such an issue. I admitted the
latter, but reminded him of Olmütz and the Seven Years'
war, and how a quarrel might arise out of an unimportant
cause, even from questions of form. Even without
Gortchakoff it would be difficult for many Russians to
consider and treat a friend as having equal rights ; I was
not personally sensitive on points of form, but modern

Russia had for the future not merely Gortchakoff's methods of procedure but also his pretensions.

I declined at that time also the 'option' between Austria and Russia, and recommended the alliance of the three Emperors, or at least the preservation of peace between them.

CHAPTER XXIX

THE TRIPLE ALLIANCE

THE triple alliance which I originally sought to conclude after the peace of Frankfort, and about which I had already sounded Vienna and St. Petersburg, from Meaux, in September 1870, was an alliance of the three Emperors with the further idea of bringing into it monarchical Italy. It was designed for the struggle which, as I feared, was before us; between the two European tendencies which Napoleon called Republican and Cossack, and which I, according to our present ideas, should designate on the one side as the system of order on a monarchical basis, and on the other as the social republic to the level of which the anti-monarchical development is wont to sink, either slowly or by leaps and bounds, until the conditions thus created become intolerable, and the disappointed populace are ready for a violent return to monarchical institutions in a Cæsarean form. I consider that the task of escaping from this *circulus vitiosus*, or, if possible, of sparing the present generation and their children an entrance into it, ought to be more closely incumbent on the strong existing monarchies, those monarchies which still have a vigorous life, than any rivalry over the fragments of nations which people the Balkan peninsula. If the monarchical governments have no understanding of the necessity for holding together in the interests of political and social order, but make themselves subservient to the chauvinistic impulses of their subjects, I fear that the international revolutionary and social struggles which will have to be fought out will be all the more dangerous, and take such a form that the victory on the part of monarchical order will be more difficult. Since 1871 I have sought for the most certain assurance against those struggles in the alliance of the three Emperors, and also in the effort to impart to the monarchical principle in Italy a firm support in that alliance. I was not without hope of a lasting success when the meeting of the three Emperors took place at Berlin in September 1872, and this was followed by the visits of my Emperor to St. Petersburg in May, of the King of Italy to Berlin in September, and of the German Emperor to Vienna in the October of the next year. The first clouding over of that hope was caused in 1875 by the provocations of Prince Gortchakoff,[1] who spread the lie that we intended to fall upon France before she had recovered from her wounds.

At the time of the Luxemburg question (1867) I was on principle an adversary of preventive wars, that is of offensive wars to be waged because we thought that later on we should have to wage them against an enemy who would be better prepared. According to the views of our military men it was probable that in 1875 we should have conquered France; but it was not so probable that the other Powers would have remained neutral. Even during the last months of the negotiations at Versailles the danger of European intervention had been daily a cause of anxiety

---

[1] Cf. Chap. xxvi. *supra*, p. 186.

to me, and the apparent hatefulness of an attack undertaken merely in order not to give France time to recover
her breath would have offered a welcome pretext first for
English phrases about humanity, but afterwards also to
Russia for making a transition from the policy of the
personal friendship of the two Emperors, to that of the
cool consideration of Russian interests which had held the
balance at the delimitation of French territory in 1814
and 1815. That for the Russian policy there is a limit
beyond which the importance of France in Europe must
not be decreased is explicable. That limit was reached,
as I believe, at the peace of Frankfort—a fact which in
1870 and 1871 was not so completely realised at St.
Petersburg as five years later. I hardly think that during
our war the Russian cabinet clearly foresaw that, when it
was over, Russia would have as neighbour so strong and
consolidated a Germany. In 1875 I had the impression
that some doubt prevailed on the Neva as to whether it
had been prudent to let things go so far without interfer-
ing in their development. The sincere esteem and friendship of Alexander II for his uncle concealed the uneasiness
already felt in official circles. If we had wished to renew
the war at that time, so as not to give invalided France
time to recover, after some unsuccessful conferences for
preventing the war, our military operations in France
would undoubtedly have come into the situation which I
had feared at Versailles during the dragging on of the
siege. The termination of the war would not have been
brought about by a peace concluded *tête-à-tête*, but, as in
1814, in a congress to which the defeated France would
have been admitted, and perhaps, considering the enmity
to which we were exposed, just as in those days, at the
dictation of a new Talleyrand.

Even at Versailles I had feared that the participation of France in the London conference upon the clauses of the treaty of Paris dealing with the Black Sea might be used in order, with the assurance that Talleyrand had shown at Vienna, to graft the Franco-German question on to the programme for discussion. For that reason, notwithstanding recommendations from many quarters, I prevented, by influences at home and abroad, the participation of Favre in the conference. Whether France in 1875 would have been so weak in her defence against our attack, as our military men assumed, seems questionable when one remembers that in the Franco-Anglo-Austrian agreement of January 3, 1815, France, although defeated, partly occupied by foreign troops, and exhausted by twenty years of fighting, was still prepared to lead at once into the field, for the coalition against Russia and Prussia, 150,000 men, and shortly after 300,000 men. The 300,000 trained soldiers who had been our prisoners were back in France, and we should not, as in January 1815, have had the Russian power behind us in benevolent neutrality, but very likely in hostility. From the Gortchakoff circular telegram of May 1875 to all Russian embassies, it is clear that Russian diplomacy was already urged to activity against our alleged inclination to disturb the peace.

On this episode followed the Russian chancellor's uneasy efforts to disturb our, and especially my, friendly personal relations to the Emperor Alexander; among other ways, he extorted from me, as is related in Chapter xxviii, through General von Werder, a refusal to promise neutrality in the event of an Austro-Russian war. That the Russian cabinet should have then immediately and secretly turned to Austria again shows a phase of the

Gortchakoff policy which was not favourable to my effort towards a monarchical conservative triple alliance.

Count Shuvaloff was perfectly right when he said that the idea of coalitions gave me nightmares. We had waged victorious wars against two of the European Great Powers; everything depended on inducing at least one of the two mighty foes whom we had beaten in the field to renounce the anticipated design of uniting with the other in a war of revenge. To all who knew history and the character of the Gallic race, it was obvious that that Power could not be France, and if a secret treaty of Reichstadt was possible without our consent, without our knowledge, so also was a renewal of the old coalition—Kaunitz's handiwork—of France, Austria, and Russia, whenever the elements which it represented, and which beneath the surface were still present in Austria, should gain the ascendency there. They might find points of connexion which might serve to infuse new life into the ancient rivalry, the ancient struggle for the hegemony of Germany, making it once more a factor in Austrian policy, whether by an alliance with France, which in the time of Count Beust and the Salzburg meeting with Louis Napoleon, August 1867, was in the air, or by a closer accord with Russia, the existence of which was attested by the secret convention of Reichstadt. The question of what support Germany had in such a case to expect from England I will not answer without more in the way of historical retrospect of the Seven Years' war and the congress of Vienna. I merely take note of the probability that, but for the victories of Frederick the Great, the cause of the King of Prussia would have been abandoned by England even earlier than it actually was.

This situation demanded an effort to limit the range of the possible anti-German coalition by means of treaty arrangements placing our relations with at least one of the Great Powers upon a firm footing. The choice could only lie between Austria and Russia, for the English constitution does not admit of alliances of assured permanence, and a union with Italy alone did not promise an adequate counterpoise to a coalition of the other three Great Powers, even supposing her future attitude and formation to be considered independently not only of French but also of Austrian influence. The area available for the formation of the coalition would therefore be narrowed till only the alternative remained which I have indicated.

In point of material force I held a union with Russia to have the advantage. I had also been used to regard it as safer, because I placed more reliance on traditional dynastic friendship, on community of conservative monarchical instincts, on the absence of indigenous political divisions, than on the fits and starts of public opinion among the Hungarian, Slav, and Catholic population of the monarchy of the Habsburgs. Complete reliance could be placed upon the durability of neither union, whether one estimated the strength of the dynastic bond with Russia, or of the German sympathies of the Hungarian populace. If the balance of opinion in Hungary were always determined by sober political calculation, this brave and independent people, isolated in the broad ocean of Slav populations, and comparatively insignificant in numbers, would remain constant to the conviction that its position can only be secured by the support of the German element in Austria and Germany. But the Kossuth episode, and the suppression in Hungary itself of the German elements that remained loyal to the Empire, with other symptoms showed that among Hungarian hussars and lawyers self-confidence is apt in critical moments to get the better of political calculation and self-control. Even in quiet times many a Magyar will get the gypsies to play to him the song, ' Der Deutsche ist ein Hundsfott ' (' The German is a blackguard').

In the forecast of the future relations of Austria and Germany an essential element was the imperfect appreciation of political possibilities displayed by the German element in Austria, which has caused it to lose touch with the dynasty and forfeit the guidance which it had inherited from its historical development. Misgivings as to the future of an Austro-German confederation were also suggested by the religious question, by the remembered influence of the father confessors of the imperial family, by the anticipated possibility of renewed relations with France, on the basis of a *rapprochement* by that country to the Catholic Church, whenever such a change should have taken place in the character and principles of French statesmanship. How remote or how near such a change may be in France is quite beyond the scope of calculation.

Last of all came the Austrian policy in regard to Poland. We cannot demand of Austria that she should forgo the weapon which she possesses as against Russia in her fostering care of the Polish spirit in Galicia. The policy which in 1846 resulted in a price being set by Austrian officials on the heads of insurgent Polish patriots was possible because, by a conformable attitude in Polish and Eastern affairs, Austria paid (as by a contribution to a common insurance fund) for the advantages which she derived from the holy alliance, the league of the three Eastern Powers. So long as the triple alliance of the Eastern Powers held good, Austria could place her relations with the Ruthenes in the foreground of her policy ; as soon as it was dissolved, it was more advisable to have the Polish nobility at her disposal in case of a war with Russia. Galicia is altogether more loosely connected with the Austrian monarchy than Poland and West Prussia with the Prussian monarchy. The Austrian trans-Carpathian eastern province lies open without natural boundary on that side, and Austria would be by no means weakened by its abandonment provided she could find compensation in the basin of the Danube for its five or six million Poles and Ruthenes. Plans of the sort, but taking the shape of the transference of Roumanian and Southern-Slav populations to Austria in exchange for Galicia, and the resuscitation of Poland under the sway of an archduke, were considered officially and unofficially during the Crimean war and in 1863. The Old-Prussian provinces are, however, separated from Posen and West Prussia by no natural boundary, and their abandonment by Prussia would be impossible. Hence among the preconditions of an offensive alliance between Germany and Austria the settlement of the future of Poland presents a problem of unusual difficulty.

While occupied with the consideration of these questions I was compelled by the threatening letter of Czar Alexander (1879) to take decisive measures for the defence and preservation of our independence of Russia.

An alliance with Russia was popular with nearly all parties, with the Conservatives from an historical tradition, the entire consonance of which, with the point of view of a modern Conservative group, is perhaps doubtful. The fact, however, is that the majority of Prussian Conservatives regard alliance with Austria as congruous with their tendencies, and did so none the less when there existed a sort of temporary rivalry in Liberalism between the two governments. The Conservative halo of the Austrian name outweighed with most of the members of this group the advances, partly out of date, partly recent, made in the region of Liberalism, and the occasional leaning to *rapprochements* with the Western Powers, and especially with France. The considerations of expediency which commended to Catholics an alliance with the preponderant Catholic Great Power came nearer home. In a league, having the form and force of a treaty, between the new German Empire and Austria the National-Liberal party discerned a way of approximating to the quadrature of the political circle of 1848, by evading the difficulties which stood in the way of the complete unification, not only of Austria and Prussia-Germany, but also of the several constituents of the Austro-Hungarian Empire. Thus, outside of the social democratic party, whose approval was not to be had for any policy whatever which the government might adopt, there was in parliamentary quarters no opposition to the alliance with Austria, and much partiality for it.

Moreover, the traditions of international law from the time of the Holy Roman Empire, German by nation, and of the German confederation tended to the theory that between Germany as a whole and the Habsburg monarchy there existed a legal tie binding these central

European territories together for purposes of mutual support. Practical effect had indeed rarely been given to this *consortium* in former ages; but it was possible to vindicate in Europe, and especially in Russia, the position that a permanent confederation of Austria and the modern German Empire was, from the point of view of international law, no new thing. These questions, whether the alliance would be popular in Germany, how far it could be justified by international law, were to me matters of subordinate importance, merely subsidiary to its eventual completion. In the foreground stood the question whether the execution of the design should be begun at once or deferred for a time, and with what degree of decision it would be advisable to combat the opposition which might be anticipated on the part of Emperor William—an opposition sure to be determined rather by his idiosyncrasy than by policy. So cogent seemed to me the considerations which in the political situation pointed us to an alliance with Austria that I would have striven to conclude one even in the face of a hostile public opinion.

When Emperor William went to Alexandrovo (Sept. 3), I had already made arrangements at Gastein for a meeting with Count Andrassy, which took place on August 27–28. When I had explained the situation to him he drew therefrom the following conclusion: To a Russo-French alliance the natural counterpoise is an Austro-German alliance. I answered that he had formulated the question to discuss which I had suggested our meeting, and we came readily to a preliminary understanding for a

merely defensive alliance against a Russian attack on one
of the two sides; but my proposition to extend the alliance
to other than Russian attacks found no favour with the
Count. When, not without difficulty, I had obtained his
Majesty's authorisation to commence official negotiations,
I travelled home for that purpose by Vienna.

Before my departure from Gastein I addressed
(Sept. 10) the following letter to the King of Bavaria :

'Gastein : September 10, 1879.

'Your Majesty was so gracious on a former occasion
as to express your most exalted satisfaction with the
efforts which I directed to the object of securing for the
German Empire peace and friendship with both her great
neighbours, Austria and Russia alike. In the course of the
last three years this problem has increased in difficulty, as
Russian policy has come to be entirely dominated by the
partly warlike revolutionary tendencies of Panslavism. Already in the year 1876 we received from Livadia repeated
demands for an answer in such form as might be binding
upon us to the question whether the German Empire
would remain neutral in a war between Russia and
Austria. It was not possible to avoid giving this answer,
and the Russian warcloud drew for a time Balkanward.
The great results which, even after the congress, Russian
policy reaped from this war have not subdued the restlessness of Russian policy in the degree which would be
desirable in the interests of peace-loving Europe. Russian
policy has remained unquiet, unpacific; Panslavistic
Chauvinism has gained increasing influence over the mind
of Czar Alexander, and the serious (as, alas, it seems) disgrace of Count Shuvaloff has accompanied the Czar's
censure of the Count's work, the Berlin congress. The

leading minister, in so far as such a minister there is at present in Russia, is the War Minister, Milutin. At his demand the peace, in which Russia is threatened by no one, has yet been followed by the mighty preparations which, notwithstanding the financial sacrifice involved in the war, have raised the peace footing of the Russian army by 56,000 men, and the footing of the army of the West, which is kept ready for active service, by about 400,000 men. These preparations can only be intended as a menace to Austria or Germany, and the military establishments in the kingdom of Poland correspond to such a design. The War Minister has also, in presence of the technical commissions,* unreservedly declared that Russia must prepare for a war " with Europe."

' If it is indubitable that Czar Alexander, without desiring the war with Turkey, nevertheless waged it under stress of Panslavist influence, and if, meanwhile, the same party has gained in influence in consequence of the greater and more dangerous impression which the agitation at the back of it now makes on the mind of the Czar, we may readily apprehend that it may also succeed in obtaining Czar Alexander's sanction for further warlike enterprises on the western frontier. The European difficulties, which Russia might encounter by the way, have few or no terrors for a minister like Milutin or Makoff, if it is true, as the Conservatives in Russia fear, that the party of movement, while seeking to involve Russia in grievous wars, is less concerned to secure Russia's victory over the foreigner than to bring about an internal revolution.

' In these circumstances I cannot resist the conviction

---

* Appointed to carry out certain decisions of the Berlin treaty of July 13, 1878.

that in the future, perhaps in the near future, peace is threatened by Russia, and perhaps only by Russia. The attempts which, according to our intelligence, have been made of late to ascertain whether Russia, on the commencement of hostilities, would find support in France and Italy have certainly yielded only a negative result. The impotence of Italy has been revealed, and France has declared that at present she has no desire for war, and does not feel strong enough for an offensive war against Germany without other ally than Russia.

'In this situation of affairs Russia has in the course of the last few weeks presented to us demands which amount to nothing less than that we should make a definite choice between herself and Austria, at the same time instructing the German members of the Eastern committees to vote with Russia in doubtful questions; while, in our opinion, the true construction of the decisions of the congress is that taken by the majority formed by Austria, England, and France, with which Germany has accordingly voted, so that Russia, partly with, partly without Italy, forms by herself the minority. Though these questions, e.g. the position of the bridge at Silistria, the concession to Turkey by the congress of the military road in Bulgaria, the administration of the postal and telegraphic system, and the frontier dispute (which concerns only a few villages), are in themselves very unimportant in comparison with the freedom of great empires, yet the Russian demand that we should vote upon them no longer with Austria, but with Russia, was accompanied not once, but several times, by unambiguous threats of the consequences prejudicial to the international relations of both countries which our refusal would eventually entail. This surprising circumstance, coinciding as it did with the withdrawal of Count Andrassy,* was calculated to awaken a misgiving that between Russia and Austria a secret understanding had been established to the prejudice of Germany. This misgiving, however, is unfounded. Austria regards the restless Russian policy with as much disquietude as we, and seems to be inclined for an understanding with us for common defence against a possible Russian attack on either of the two Powers.

' If the German Empire were to come to such an understanding with Austria, an understanding which should have in view the cultivation of peace with Russia as sedulously as before, but should also provide for joint defence in the event of an attack by her upon either of the allied powers, I should see in it an essential security for the peace of Europe. Thus mutually assured, both empires might continue their efforts for the further consolidation of the Three Emperors' Alliance. The German Empire in alliance with Austria would not lack the support of England, and the peace of Europe, the common interest of both empires, would be guaranteed by 2,000,000 fighting men. In this alliance, purely defensive as it would be, there would be nothing to excite jealousy in any quarter: for in the German Confederation the same mutual guarantee subsisted with the sanction of international law for fifty years after 1815. If no such understanding is come to, Austria will not be to blame if, under the influence of Russian threats, and uncertain of the attitude of Germany, she finally seeks an *entente cordiale* with either France or

---

* On August 14 the Emperor Francis Joseph had sanctioned in principle the discharge requested by Count Andrassy, but had deferred letting him go definitively until his successor should be appointed. The Count agreed to retain his position a little longer in order to complete the alliance with Germany. On October 8 his resignation and the appointment of his successor Haymerle were published.

Russia. In the latter case, Germany, by reason of her relation to France, would be in danger of entire isolation on the Continent. Supposing, however, that Austria were to effect an *entente cordiale* with France and England, as in 1854, Germany, unless prepared for isolation, would be forced to unite with Russia alone, and, as I fear, to follow in the mistaken and perilous course of Russian domestic and foreign policy.

'If Russia compel us to choose between her and Austria, I believe that the disposition which Austria would display towards us would be conservative and peaceable, while that of Russia would be uncertain.

'I venture to entertain the hope that your Majesty, consistently with what I know of your most exalted political views, shares the sentiments which I have expressed, and would hail their corroboration with satisfaction.

'The difficulties of the problem which I propose to myself are great in themselves, and will be yet more materially increased by the necessity to which I am reduced of treating so large and many-sided a subject in writing, and that too at this place where I have nothing to rely on but my own energy, which previous excessive strain has rendered quite inadequate for the purpose. Considerations of health have already compelled me to protract my sojourn here. I hope, however, to be able to start on my journey homeward by Vienna after the 20th instant. If in the interim we do not succeed in coming to an understanding, at least on the question of principle, I fear that the present favourable opportunity will be missed, and the retirement of Andrassy forbids us to calculate on its return at any future time. In deeming it my duty respectfully to submit to your Majesty my view of the political

situation of the German Empire, I pray your Majesty
graciously to bear in mind that Count Andrassy and I
are bound by mutual promises to keep secret the
plan of which the foregoing is an exposition, and that
hitherto only their Majesties, the two Emperors, are
acquainted with the design of their principal ministers to
bring about a coalition of their two most exalted Majesties.'

For completeness sake I subjoin the answer of the
King, and my reply thereto.

' My dear Prince von Bismarck,—With sincere regret I
learned from your letter of the 10th instant that the strain
and excitement of attending to business prevented you
from deriving full benefit from the baths of Kissingen and
Gastein.   I have followed with the greatest interest your
detailed exposition of the present state of politics, for which
I tender you my most hearty thanks.   Were the German
Empire to become involved in war with Russia, a change
so deeply to be regretted in the mutual relations of the
two empires would cause me the most poignant grief, and
I still entertain the hope that success may attend an effort
to prevent such a turn of affairs by influence brought to
bear in the cause of peace on the mind of his Majesty the
Czar of Russia.   Under all circumstances, however, your
exertions to bring about a close union between the German
Empire and Austria-Hungary have, I may assure you, my
full approval, and I most earnestly desire that they may
be crowned with success.   I trust that you may return
home with health restored, and I heartily add and reiterate
my assurance of the especial esteem in which you are, and
ever will continue to be, held by Your sincere friend,

' LEWIS.

' Berg : Sept. 16, 1879.'

'Gastein : Sept. 19, 1879.

'With respectful gratitude I acknowledge the receipt of your Majesty's gracious letter of the 16th instant, from which I am delighted to find that your Majesty is in accord with me in my endeavours to bring about an alliance for mutual defence with Austria-Hungary. In regard to the relations with Russia I remark, with the utmost submission, that the danger of hostile complications, which not only from a political, but also from a personal, point of view I should most deeply deplore, does not in my respectful judgement confront us immediately, but would only become imminent in the event of France being ready to make common cause with Russia. So far this is not the case, and it is the intention of his Majesty the Emperor that our policy should leave no stone unturned in order now, as heretofore, to promote and assure peaceable relations between the Empire and Russia by such influences as may best operate upon the mind of his Majesty Czar Alexander. The negotiations for a closer alliance with Austria are only directed to assure peace, provide for common defence, and promote neighbourly intercourse.

'I think of leaving Gastein to-morrow, and hope to enter Vienna on Sunday. With humblest thanks for your Majesty's gracious expression of concern for my health, I remain, with profound respect,

'Your Majesty's most obedient servant,

'von Bismarck.'

During the long journey from Gastein by Salzburg and Linz my sense of being in true German territory and among a German population was deepened by the reception

which I met with from the public at the stations. At
Linz the crowd was so great, its frame of mind so animated,
that, from fear of giving occasion to misapprehensions in
Viennese circles, I drew the blinds of my carriage-windows.
made no response to any of the greetings of welcome, and
allowed the train to leave the station without even showing
myself. In Vienna I found the people in the streets in a
similar frame ; the greetings of the closely-packed throng
were so continuous that, as I was in civilian dress, I was
reduced to the awkward necessity of driving to the hotel
with a head as good as bare the whole way. Moreover,
during the days which I spent at the hotel I could not
show myself at the window without eliciting friendly
demonstrations from watchers or passers by it. These
manifestations were multiplied after the Emperor Francis
Joseph had paid me the honour of a visit. All these
phenomena were the unequivocal expression of the desire
of the population of the capital, and of the German provinces which I had traversed, to witness the formation of
a close friendship with the new German Empire, as pledge
of the future of both powers. I could not doubt that
community of blood would meet with similar sympathies
in the German Empire, in the South yet more than in the
North, among Conservatives yet more than among the opposition, in the Catholic West more than in the Evangelical
East. The nominally religious struggles of the Thirty
Years' war, the purely political struggles of the Seven
Years' war, and the strife of rival diplomacies that went
on between the death of Frederick the Great and 1866,
had not stifled the sense of this community of blood,
notwithstanding the otherwise strong disposition of the
German to fight his fellow-countryman, when occasion
serves, with more zeal than the foreigner. It is possible

that the wedge of Slav (Czech) population by which the true German stock of the Austrian Fatherland is separated from the people of the north-west provinces has mitigated the results which are commonly produced by neighbourly shoulder-rubbing with Germans of similar stock, but owing allegiance to different dynasties, and intensified in the German-Austrian those German sympathies which have only been over-laid, not extinguished, by the débris deposited by the struggles of the past.

I met with a very gracious reception from the Emperor Francis Joseph, who evinced willingness to conclude with us. In order to make sure of the assent of my most gracious master I had daily spent at the writing-table part of the time which ought to have been devoted to the 'course,' explaining the necessity under which we stood of limiting the number of possible coalitions against us, and that an alliance with Austria was the expedient most conducive to that end. I had, of course, little hope that the dead letters of my argumentation would alter the view of his Majesty, which rested rather on mental idiosyncrasy than political calculation. To conclude a treaty, which though merely defensive in form yet contemplated the possibility of war, and thus evinced suspicion of a friend and nephew, from whom he had only just parted at Alexandrovo amid mutual tears and heartfelt pledges of the continuance of the cordial relations of the past, ran too directly counter to the chivalrous feelings with which the Emperor regarded a friend and equal. I had no doubt whatever that the sentiments of Czar Alexander were equally frank and honourable, but I knew that he brought to political affairs neither the native acumen nor the close study which would have afforded him permanent protection against the insidious influences by which he was surrounded, nor yet the scrupulous trustworthiness in personal relations which characterised my lord. Czar Nicholas, for good or for evil, had displayed a frankness of which his more yielding successor had not inherited his full share ; nor was the son superior to feminine influences in the same high degree as his father. Now the sole security for the permanence of Russian friendship is the personality of the ruling Czar, and whenever that security falls below the standard set by Alexander I, who in 1813 evinced a loyalty to the Prussian dynasty not always to be expected on the same throne, the Russian alliance cannot be counted upon to afford in the hour of need a resource adequate to every occasion.

Even in the last century it was perilous to reckon on the constraining force of the text of a treaty of alliance when the conditions under which it had been written were changed ; to-day it is hardly possible for the government of a great Power to place its resources unreservedly at the disposal of a friendly state when the sentiment of the people disapproves it. No longer, therefore, does the text of a treaty afford the same securities as in the days of the 'cabinet wars,' which were waged with armies of from 30,000 to 60,000 men ; a family war, such as Frederick William II waged on behalf of his brother-in-law in Holland, could hardly to-day be put upon the European stage, nor could the conditions preliminary to such a war as Nicholas waged on Hungary be readily again found. Nevertheless the plain and searching words of a treaty are not without influence on diplomacy when it is concerned with precipitating or averting a war ; nor are even treacherous and violent governments usually inclined to an open breach of faith, so long as the *force majeure* of imperative interests does not intervene.

All the well-pondered arguments which I reduced
to writing at Gastein, and thence transmitted to the King
at Baden, as also those which I afterwards sent him from
Vienna, and finally from Berlin, were entirely without
effect. In order to secure the Emperor's approval for the
projet de traité, which I had concerted with Andrassy,
and which had been sanctioned by the Emperor Francis
Joseph under the impression that the Emperor William
would also concur, I was compelled to bring the cabinet
into play, a method of procedure extremely against my
grain. I succeeded, however, in gaining the approval of
my colleagues. As I was myself so worn out by the
exertions of the last few weeks, which, as I said before,
had broken in upon the time required for the treatment at
Gastein, as to be unfit to travel to Baden-Baden, Count
Stolberg went thither in my stead. He brought the
negotiations, notwithstanding the stout opposition of his
Majesty, to a successful issue. The Emperor was not
convinced by the arguments of policy, but gave the
promise to ratify the treaty only because he was averse
to ministerial changes.

The Crown Prince was from the outset a strong advocate of the Austrian alliance, but had no influence on his
father.

The Emperor's chivalrous temper demanded that the
Czar of Russia should be confidentially informed that in
the event of his attacking either of the two neighbour-
powers he would find himself opposed by both, in order
that Czar Alexander might not make the mistake of
supposing that he could attack Austria alone. I deemed
this solicitude groundless inasmuch as the cabinet of St.
Petersburg must by our answer to the questions sent us
from Livadia have already learned that we were not going

to let Austria fall, and so our treaty with Austria had not created a new situation, but only legalised that which existed.

A renewal of Kaunitz's coalition might be confronted without despair by a United Germany which conducted her campaigns with skill; nevertheless it would be a very serious combination, the formation of which it must be the aim of our foreign policy, if possible, to prevent. If the united Austro-German power had by the closeness of its cohesion and the unity of its counsels as assured a position as either the Russian or the French power regarded *per se*, I should not consider a simultaneous attack by our two great neighbour-empires, even though Italy were not the third in the alliance, as a matter of life and death. But if in Austria anti-German proclivities, whether national or religious, were to gain strength; if Russian tentatives and overtures in the sphere of eastern policy, such as were made in the days of Catherine and Joseph II, were to be thrown into the scale, if Italian ambitions were to threaten Austria's possession on the Adriatic sea, and require the exertion of her strength to the same degree as in Radetzky's time—then the struggle, the possibility of which I anticipate, would be unequal. And if we suppose the French monarchy restored, and France and Austria in league with the Roman Curia and our enemies for the purpose of making a clean sweep of the results of 1866, no words are needed to show how greatly aggravated would then be the peril of Germany. This idea, pessimistic, but by no means chimerical, nor without justification in the past, induced me to raise the

question whether it might not be advisable to establish
between the German Empire and Austria-Hungary an
organic connexion which should not be published like
ordinary treaties, but should be incorporated in the
legislation of both Empires, and require for its dissolution
a new legislative Act on the part of one of them.

Such a guarantee has a tranquillising effect on the mind;
but whether it would stand the actual strain of events may
reasonably be doubted, when it is remembered that the constitution of the Holy Roman Empire, which in theory had
much more effective sanctions, yet failed to assure the cohesion of the German nation, and that we should never be
able to embody our relation with Austria in any more
binding treaty-form than the earlier confederation treaties,
which in theory excluded the possibility of the battle of
Königgrätz.   All contracts between great states cease
to be unconditionally binding as soon as they are tested
by 'the struggle for existence.'   No great nation will
ever be induced to sacrifice its existence on the altar of
fidelity to contract when it is compelled to choose between
the two.   The maxim ' ultra posse nemo obligatur ' holds
good in spite of all treaty formulas whatsoever, nor can any
treaty guarantee the degree of zeal and the amount of force
that will be devoted to the discharge of obligations when the
private interest of those who lie under them no longer
reinforces the text and its earliest interpretation.   If, then,
changes were to occur in the political situation of Europe
of such a kind as to make an anti-German policy appear
salus publica for Austria-Hungary, public faith could no
more be expected to induce her to make an act of self-
sacrifice than we saw gratitude do during the Crimean
war, though the obligation was perhaps stronger than any
can be established by the wax and parchment of a treaty.

An alliance under legislative sanction would have realised the constitutional project which hovered before the minds of the most moderate members of the assembly of the Paulskirche, both those who stood for the narrower Imperial-German and those who represented the wider Austro-German confederation ; but the very reduction of such a scheme to contractual form would militate against the durability of its mutual obligations. The example of Austria between 1850 and 1866 was a warning to me that the political changes which such arrangements essay to control outrun the credits which independent states can assure to one another in the course of their political transactions. I think, therefore, that to ensure the durability of a written treaty it is indispensable that the variable element of political interest, and the perils involved therein, should not be left out of account. The German alliance is the best calculated to secure for Austria a peaceful and conservative policy.

The dangers to which our union with Austria are exposed by tentatives towards a Russo-Austrian understanding, such as was made in the days of Joseph II and Catherine, or by the secret convention of Reichstadt, may, so far as possible, be minimised by keeping the strictest possible faith with Austria, and at the same time taking care that the road from Berlin to St. Petersburg is not closed. Our principal concern is to keep the peace between our two imperial neighbours. We shall be able to assure the future of the fourth great dynasty in Italy in proportion as we succeed in maintaining the unity of the three empire states, and in either bridling the ambition of our two neighbours on the east or satisfying it by an *entente cordiale* with both. Both are for us indispensable elements in the European political equilibrium ;

the lack of either would be our peril—but the maintenance
of monarchical government in Vienna and St. Petersburg,
and in Rome as dependent upon Vienna and St. Petersburg,
is for us in Germany a problem which coincides with the
maintenance of our own state régime.

The treaty which we concluded with Austria for
common defence against a Russian attack is *publici
juris*. An analogous treaty between the two powers for
defence against France has not been published. The
German-Austrian alliance does not afford the same protection against a French war, by which Germany is
primarily threatened, as against a Russian war, which is
to be apprehended rather by Austria than by Germany.
Germany and Russia have no divergencies of interest
pregnant with such disputes as lead to unavoidable ruptures.
On the other hand, coincident aims in regard to Poland,
and in a secondary degree the ancient solidarity which
unites their dynasties in opposition to subversive efforts,
afford both cabinets the bases for a common policy.
They have been impaired by the false bias given now for
ten years past to public opinion by the Russian press.
This has assiduously planted and fostered in the mind
of the reading part of the population an antipathy to
everything German, with which the dynasty will have
to reckon, even though the Czar may wish to cultivate
German friendship. Scarcely, however, could anti-German
rancour acquire in Russia a keener edge than it has among
the Czechs in Bohemia and Moravia, the Slovenes of the
countries comprised within the earlier German confederation, and the Poles in Galicia. In short, if in deciding be-

tween the Russian and the Austrian alliance I gave the preference to the latter, it was not that I was in any degree blind to the perplexities which made choice difficult. I regarded it as no less enjoined upon us to cultivate neighbourly relations with Russia after, than before, our defensive alliance with Austria; for perfect security against the disruption of the chosen combination is not to be had by Germany, while it is possible for her to hold in check the anti-German fits and starts of Austro-Hungarian feeling so long as German policy maintains the bridge which leads to St. Petersburg, and allows no chasm to intervene between us and Russia which cannot be spanned. Given no such irremediable breach Vienna will be able to bridle the forces hostile or alien to the German alliance. Suppose, however, that the breach with Russia is an accomplished fact, an irremediable estrangement. Austria would then certainly begin to enlarge her claims on the services of her German confederate, first by insisting on an extension of the *casus fœderis,* which so far, according to the published text, provides only for the measures necessary to repel a Russian attack upon Austria; then by requiring the substitution for this *casus fœderis* of some provision safeguarding the interests of Austria in the Balkan and the East, an idea to which our press has already succeeded in giving practical shape. The wants, the plans of the inhabitants of the basin of the Danube naturally reach far beyond the present limits of the Austro-Hungarian monarchy, and the German imperial constitution points out the way by which Austria may advance to a reconciliation of her political and material interests, so far as they lie between the eastern frontier of the Roumanian population and the Gulf of Cattaro. It is, however, no part

of the policy of the German Empire to lend her subjects,
to expend her blood and treasure, for the purpose of
realising the designs of a neighbour Power. In the interest
of the European political equilibrium the maintenance of
the Austro-Hungarian monarchy as a strong independent
Great Power is for Germany an object for which she
might in case of need stake her own peace with a good
conscience. But Vienna should abstain from going outside this security, and deducing from the alliance claims
which it was not concluded to support.

Peace between Germany and Russia may be imperilled
by the systematic fomentation of ill-feeling, or by the
ambition of Russian or German military men like
Skobeleff, who desire war before they grow too old to dis-
tinguish themselves, but is hardly to be imperilled in
any other way. The Russian press must needs be characterised by stupidity and disingenuousness in an unusual
degree for it to believe and affirm that German policy
was determined by aggressive tendencies in concluding
the Austrian, and thereafter the Italian, defensive
alliance. The disingenuousness was less of Russian
than of Polish-French, the stupidity less of Polish-
French than of Russian origin. In the field of Russian
credulity and ignorance Polish-French finesse won a
victory over that want of finesse in which, according
to circumstances, consists now the strength, now the
weakness of German policy. In most cases an open and
honourable policy succeeds better than the subtlety of
earlier ages, but it postulates, if it is to succeed, a degree of
personal confidence which can more readily be lost than
gained. The future of Austria, regarded in herself, cannot
be reckoned upon with that certainty which is demanded
when the conclusion of durable and, so to speak, organic

treaties is contemplated. The factors which must be taken into account in this shaping are as manifold as is the mixture of her populations, and to their corrosive and occasionally disruptive force must be added the incalculable influence that the religious element may from time to time, as the power of Rome waxes or wanes, exert upon the directing personalities. Not only Panslavism and the Bulgarian or Bosnian, but also the Servian, the Roumanian, the Polish, the Czechish questions, nay even to-day the Italian question in the district of Trent, in Trieste, and on the Dalmatian coast, may serve as points of crystallisation not merely for Austrian, but for European crises, by which German interests will be directly affected only in so far as the German Empire enters into a relation of close solidarity with Austria. In Bohemia the antagonism between Germans and Czechs has in some places penetrated so deeply into the army that the officers of the two nationalities in certain regiments hold aloof from one another even to the degree that they will not meet at mess. There is more immediate danger for Germany of becoming involved in grievous and dangerous struggles on her western frontier, by reason of the aggressive, plundering instincts of the French people, which have been greatly developed by her monarchs since the time of Emperor Charles V, in their lust of power at home as well as abroad.

Austria's help is more readily to be had by us in a struggle with Russia than in a struggle with France, seeing that the jealousies which sprang from their courtship of Italy no longer exist for these two Powers in their old form. Should France once more become monarchical and Catholic she need not abandon the hope of recovering such relations with Austria as she held during the Seven Years' war, and at the congress of Vienna before the return

of Napoleon from Elba, such as were threatened during
the agitation of the Polish question in 1863, and bade fair to
be actually established during the Crimean war, and in the
time of Count Beust, 1866-70, at Salzburg and Vienna.

In the event of the possible restoration of monarchy in
France the mutual attraction of the two great Catholic
Powers, no longer counteracted by the Italian rivalry,
would induce enterprising politicians to try the experi-
ment of reviving the old alliance.

In taking account of Austria it is even to-day an error
to exclude the possibility of a hostile policy such as was
pursued by Thugut, Schwarzenberg, Buol, Bach, and
Beust. May not the policy which made ingratitude a
duty, the policy on which Schwarzenberg plumed himself
in regard to Russia, be again pursued towards another
Power? The policy which from 1792 to 1795, while we
stood in the field by Austria's side, led us into difficulties,
and left us in the lurch in order thereby to retain the
power of settling the Polish question to our disadvantage ;
which in fact was pushed so far as all but to involve us
in a war with Russia, while we as nominal allies were fighting for the German Empire against France ; which at the
congress of Vienna all but resulted in a war between
Russia and Prussia. Spasmodic symptoms of a tendency
towards a similar policy will for the present be sup-
pressed by the personal honour and loyalty of the Emperor
Francis Joseph, who is neither so young nor so inex-
perienced as when he allowed Count Buol's personal
antipathy to Czar Nicholas to dictate a policy hostile to
Russia, a few years after Vilagos ; but he affords only a
personal guarantee, which disappears so soon as another
succeeds to his place, and the elements which from time
to time have served to support a policy of rivalry with

Germany may acquire fresh influences. The love of the Poles of Galicia, of the Ultramontane clergy, for the German Empire is of a fitful and opportunist nature; nor have we any better guarantee that a perception of the value of German support will permanently outweigh the contempt with which the Magyar of full blood regards the Suabian.

In Hungary, in Poland, French sympathies are still lively, and the restoration of monarchy upon a Catholic basis in France might cause the renewal of those relations with the clergy of the united Habsburg monarchy which in 1863 and between 1866 and 1870 found expression in common diplomatic action, and more or less mature schemes of union by treaty. The security which, in regard to these contingencies, is to be found in the person of the present Emperor of Austria and King of Hungary is, as has been said, manifest enough, but a far-sighted policy must take account of all eventualities which lie within the region of possibility. The possibility of a rivalry between Vienna and Berlin for the friendship of Russia may return upon us just as in the days of Olmütz, or when, under the auspices (propitious for us) of Count Andrassy, it once more attested its existence by the convention of Reichstadt.

In face of this eventuality it makes in our favour that Austria and Russia have opposing interests in the Balkan, while none such in strength enough to occasion an open breach and actual struggle exist between Russia and Prussia with Germany. This advantage, however, may be taken from us—thanks to the peculiar character of the Russian constitution—by personal misunderstanding and maladroit policy, no less easily to-day than when Czarina Elizabeth was induced by the bitter *bons mots* of Frederick the Great to accede to the Franco-Austrian alliance. Mischief-making intrigues, such as then served to irritate Russia, scandalous fabrications, indiscreet utterances or acts, will not be wanting even to-day at either Court; but it is possible for us to maintain our independence and dignity in face of Russia without wounding Russian sensitiveness or damaging Russia's interests. The wanton stirring up of bad and bitter feeling reacts to-day with no less effect on the course of history than in the times of Czarina Elizabeth of Russia and Queen Anne of England. But this reaction exerts to-day a much more powerful influence upon the present and future weal of the nations than a hundred years ago. An anti-Prussian coalition like that of the Seven Years' war between Russia, Austria and France, in union perhaps with other discontented dynasties, would to-day expose our existence to just as grave a peril, and if victorious would be far more disastrous. It is irrational, it is criminal by fomenting personal misunderstandings to cut off the way of access to an *entente cordiale* with Russia.

We must and can honourably maintain the alliance with the Austro-Hungarian monarchy; it corresponds to our interests, to the historical traditions of Germany, to the public opinion of our people. The influences and forces under and amid which the future policy of Vienna must be shaped are, however, more complex than with us, by reason of the manifold diversity of the nationalities the divergence of their aspirations and activities, the influence of the clergy, and the temptations to which the Danubian countries are exposed in the Balkan and Black Sea latitudes.

We cannot abandon Austria, but neither can we lose sight of the possibility that the policy of Vienna may willy-nilly abandon us. The possibilities which in such a case remain open to us must be clearly realised and steadily borne in mind by German statesmen before the critical moment arrives, nor must their action be determined by prejudice or misunderstanding, but by an entirely dispassionate weighing of the national interests.

It has always been my endeavour to promote not merely the security of the country against Russian attacks, but also in Russia itself a peaceful tone, and a belief in the unaggressive character of our policy. Nor (thanks to the personal confidence which Czar Alexander III reposed in me) did I ever fail so long as I remained in office to turn the edge of the mistrust which again and again was aroused in his mind by misrepresentations on the part both of his own subjects and of foreigners, and occasionally by subterranean influences of a military kind from this side of the frontier.

At my first interview with him after his accession (in the Dantzig roads), and at all subsequent meetings, he was prevented neither by falsehoods disseminated in regard to the congress of Berlin, nor by the knowledge which he possessed of the Austrian treaty, from displaying towards me a good-will which at Skiernevice and at Berlin received authentic expression—a good-will which rested on personal trust in me. Even the affair of the forged letters placed in his hands at Copenhagen—an intrigue which by its shameless audacity was capable of producing the worst impression—was rendered innocuous by my mere disavowal. No less success had I at the meeting in October 1889 in

dissipating the doubts which he had brought with him
from Copenhagen, including the last, which concerned my
own continuance in office. He was far better instructed
than I when he put the question, whether I was quite
sure of retaining my place under the new Emperor. I
answered, as I then thought, that I was convinced that I
possessed the confidence of Emperor William II, and did
not believe that I should ever be dismissed against my
will, because his Majesty, by reason of my prolonged experience in office, and the confidence which I had won for
myself, not only in Germany, but in foreign Courts, had
in my person a servant whom it was very difficult to
replace. My assurance elicited from his Majesty an expression of great satisfaction, though he hardly seemed
to share it unreservedly.

International policy is a fluid element which under
certain conditions will solidify, but on a change of
atmosphere reverts to its original diffuse condition. The
clause *rebus sic stantibus* is tacitly understood in all
treaties that involve performance. The Triple Alliance
is a strategic position, which in the face of the perils
that were imminent at the time when it was concluded
was politic, and, under the prevailing conditions, feasible.
It has been from time to time prolonged, and may be
yet further prolonged, but eternal duration is assured to
no treaty between Great Powers; and it would be unwise
to regard it as affording a permanently stable guarantee
against all the possible contingencies which in the future
may modify the political, material, and moral conditions
under which it was brought into being. It has the significance of a strategic position adopted after strict scrutiny
of the political situation of Europe at the time when it

was concluded, but it no more constitutes a foundation capable of offering perennial resistance to time and change than did many another alliance (triple or quadruple) of recent centuries, and in particular the Holy Alliance and the German Confederation.　It does not dispense us from the attitude of *toujours en vedette*.

CHAPTER XXX

THE FUTURE POLICY OF RUSSIA

THE danger of foreign wars, the danger that the next war on our west frontier might bring the red flag into the struggle, just as a hundred years ago it brought the tricolor, was present at the time of Schnäbele and Boulanger, and is still present. The probability of a war on two sides has been to some extent diminished by the death of Katkoff and Skobeleff; a French attack upon us would not necessarily bring Russia into the field against us with the same certainty as a Russian attack would bring France; but the inclination of Russia to sit still depends not only on moods and feelings, but still more on technical questions of armament by land and sea. As soon as Russia is in her own opinion 'through' with the construction of rifles, the choice of powder, and the strength of the Black Sea fleet, then the tone in which at present the variations of Russian policy are maintained will perhaps make room for a freer one.

It is not probable that Russia when she has completed her armaments will, calculating on French assistance, use them in order at once to attack us. A German war offers to Russia just as few immediate advantages as a Russian war offers to Germany, at most in regard to the war contribution. The Russians, if victorious, would be in a more favourable position than the Germans, but even so they would scarcely recover their expenses. The thought

of acquiring East Prussia which appeared during the
Seven Years' war will scarcely find adherents now. If
the German element in the population of the Baltic
provinces is already more than they can do with, we
cannot suppose that Russian policy would be directed
towards strengthening this minority, which is considered
dangerous, by so vigorous an addition as East Prussia.
Just as little can a Russian statesman desire an increase of
the Polish subjects of the Czar by Posen and West Prussia.
If we consider Germany and Russia as isolated, it is difficult on either side to discover a compelling or even a justifiable ground of war. The mere satisfaction of pugnacity,
or the desire to avoid the dangers of an unoccupied army,
might perhaps make them enter on a war in the Balkans;
a German-Russian war is, however, too serious for either
side to use it simply as a means for occupying their army
and their officers.

I also do not believe that Russia, when she is ready,
would at once attack Austria, and I am still of the
opinion that the massing of troops in the west of Russia
is not calculated for any directly aggressive tendency
against Germany, but merely for defence, in case Russia's
advance against Turkey should decide the Western Powers
to attempt to check it. When Russia considers herself
sufficiently armed—and for this an adequate strength of
the fleet in the Black Sea is requisite—then, I think, the
St. Petersburg cabinet will act as it did in 1833 at the
treaty of Hunkiar-Iskelessi; they will offer the Sultan to
guarantee to him his position in Constantinople and in
the provinces which remain to him, on condition that he
will give to Russia the key to the Russian house—that is
to the Black Sea—in the form of a Russian control of the
Bosphorus. It is not only possible, but, if the affair is

cleverly managed, it is probable that the Porte would agree to a Russian protectorate in this form. In former years the Sultan could believe that the jealousy of the European Powers would give him guarantees against Russia. For England and Austria the maintenance of Turkey was a traditional policy; but Gladstone's public utterances have deprived the Sultan of this support not only in London but also in Vienna, for one cannot suppose that the cabinet of Vienna would at Reichstadt have dropped the traditions of the Metternich period (Ypsilanti, hostility to the liberation of Greece), had it been sure of English support. The check of gratitude to the Emperor Nicholas had already been broken by Buol during the Crimean war, and at the congress of Paris the attitude of Austria had turned back to the old Metternich direction; this was all the more evident, since it was not softened by the financial relations of that statesman to the Russian Emperor, but rather had been intensified by the injury done to Count Buol's vanity. The Austria of 1856 would, but for the dissolving effects of the blundering English policy, not have cut itself adrift from England, or from the Porte, even for the sake of Bosnia. As things are at the present day, it is not probable that the Sultan expects from England, or Austria, as much assistance and protection as Russia could promise without surrendering her own interests, and in virtue of her proximity successfully afford.

If Russia, as soon as she is sufficiently ready, if necessary, to fall upon and overrun the Sultan and the Bosphorus by land and sea, makes a personal and confidential proposal to the Sultan to guarantee him his position in the Seraglio and all his provinces, not only against foreign countries but also against his own subjects, in return for permission to erect sufficient fortifications and maintain a sufficient number of troops at the northern entrance to the Bosphorus—this would be an offer which he would be much tempted to accept. Let us assume the case, however, that the Sultan of his own impulse or under foreign pressure rejects the advances of Russia, then the new Black Sea fleet might be destined, even before trying conclusions, to secure that position on the Bosphorus which Russia believes she requires, in order to come into possession of the key to her own house.

Whatever may be the future course of this phase of the Russian policy the existence of which I have assumed, anyhow it will produce a state of things in which Russia, as in July 1853, takes some security and waits to see whether and by whom it will be taken away again. The first step of Russian diplomacy after these long-prepared operations would probably be to find out by cautious sounding in Berlin, whether Austria or England, if they opposed by war the Russian advance, could reckon upon the support of Germany. In my opinion this question would have to be met by an unconditional negative. I believe that it would be advantageous for Germany if the Russians in one way or another, physically or diplomatically, were to establish themselves at Constantinople and had to defend that position. We should then cease to be in the condition of being hounded on by England and occasionally also by Austria, and exploited by them to check Russian lust after the Bosphorus, and we should be able to wait and see if Austria were attacked and thereby our *casus belli* arose.

It would be better for the Austrian policy also to withdraw itself from the influence of Hungarian Chauvinism, until Russia had taken up a position on the Bosphorus, and had thereby considerably intensified its friction with the Mediterranean states—that is with England, and even with Italy and France—and so had increased the necessity of coming to an understanding with Austria à l'amiable. Were I an Austrian minister I would not prevent the Russians going to Constantinople, but I would not begin an understanding with them until they had made the move forward. Under any circumstances, the share which Austria has in the inheritance of Turkey will be arranged in understanding with Russia, and the Austrian portion will be all the greater the better they know at Vienna how to wait, and to encourage Russian policy to take up a more advanced position. As regards England, the position of modern Russia might perhaps be considered as improved if it ruled Constantinople ; but as regards Austria and Germany, Russia would be less dangerous as long as it remained in Constantinople. It would no longer be possible for Prussia to blunder as it did in 1855, and to play ourselves out and hazard our stake for Austria, England, and France, in order to earn a humiliating admission to the congress and a *mention honorable* as a European Power.

If the inquiry whether Russia, if it be attacked on its advance towards the Bosphorus by other Powers, can reckon on our neutrality so long as Austria is not endangered, is answered at Berlin in the negative, or indeed with threats, then Russia will first of all enter on the road she took in 1876 at Reichstadt, and again attempt to win Austrian fellowship. The field in which Russia can make offers is a very wide one ; there is not only the East at the expense of the Porte, but Germany at our expense. How far we can rely on our alliance with Austria-Hungary against temptations of this kind will depend not only on the letter of agreement, but also to some extent on the character of the personalities and the political and confessional currents, which at the time are influential in Austria. If Russian policy succeeds in winning Austria, then the coalition of the Seven Years' war against us is complete, for France will always be to be had against us, her interests on the Rhine being more important than those in the East and on the Bosphorus.

Anyhow, in the future not only military equipment but also a correct political eye will be required to guide the German ship of state through the currents of coalitions to which we are exposed in consequence of our geographical position and our previous history. We shall not avoid the dangers which lie in the bosom of the future by amiability and commercial *pourboires* to friendly Powers. We should only increase the greed of our former friends and teach them to reckon on our anxieties and necessities. What I fear is, that by following the road in which we have started our future will be sacrificed to small and temporary feelings of the present. Former rulers looked more to the capacity than the obedience of their advisers; if obedience alone is the criterion, then demands will be made on the general ability of the monarch, which even Frederick the Great himself would not satisfy, although in his time politics, both in war and peace, were less difficult than they are to-day.

Our reputation and our security will develop all the more permanently, the more, in all conflicts which do not immediately touch us, we hold ourselves in reserve and do not show ourselves sensitive to every attempt to stir up and utilise our *vanity*. Attempts of this kind were made during the Crimean war by the English press and the English Court, and the men who tried to push them-

selves forward at our own Court by depending on England ;
we were then so successfully threatened with the loss
of the title of a Great Power, that Herr von Manteuffel
at Paris exposed us to great humiliations in order that we
might be admitted to take part in signing a treaty, which
it would have been useful to us not to be bound by. Now
also Germany would be guilty of a great folly if in
Eastern struggles which did not affect her interests she
were to take a side sooner than the other Powers who
were more directly concerned. Even during the Crimean
war there were moments in which Prussia, weaker though
she then was, by resolutely arming to support Austrian
demands, and even going beyond them, could command
peace and further an understanding with Austria on
German questions ; and just in the same way in future
Eastern negotiations Germany, by holding back, will be
able to turn to its advantage the fact that it is the Power
which has least interest in Oriental questions, and will
gain the more the longer it holds up its stake, even if the
advantage were to consist in nothing more than a longer
enjoyment of peace. Austria, England, Italy will always
have to take up a position with regard to a Russian move
forward upon Constantinople sooner than the French, for
the Oriental interests of France are less imperative, and
must be considered more in connection with the question
of the German frontier. In Russo-Oriental crises France
would not be able to entangle herself either in a new
policy for gaining power in the West, or in threats
against England based upon friendship with Russia, unless
she had previously come to an understanding or a breach
with Germany.

If Germany has the advantage that her policy is free
from direct interests in the East, on the other side is the

disadvantage of the central and exposed position of the German Empire, with its extended frontier which has to be defended on every side, and the ease with which anti-German coalitions are made. At the same time Germany is perhaps the single Great Power in Europe which is not tempted by any objects which can only be attained by a successful war. It is our interest to maintain peace, while without exception our continental neighbours have wishes, either secret or officially avowed, which cannot be fulfilled except by war. We must direct our policy in accordance with these facts—that is, we must do our best to prevent war or limit it. We must reserve our hand, and not allow ourselves before the proper time to be pushed out of a waiting into an active attitude by any impatience, by the desire to oblige others at the expense of the country, by vanity or other provocation of this kind ; otherwise *plectuntur Achivi*.

Our non-interference cannot reasonably be directed to sparing our forces so as, after the others have weakened themselves, to fall upon any of our neighbours or a possible opponent. On the contrary, we ought to do all we can to weaken the bad feeling which has been called out through our growth to the position of a real Great Power, by honourable and peaceful use of our influence, and so convince the world that a German hegemony in Europe is more useful and less partisan and also less harmful for the freedom of others than that of France, Russia, or England. That respect for the rights of other states in which France especially has always been so wanting at the time of her supremacy, and which in England lasts only so long as English interests are not touched, is made easy for the German Empire and its policy, on one side owing to the practicality of the German character, on the other by the fact (which has nothing to do with our deserts) that we do not require an increase of our immediate territory, and also that we could not attain it without strengthening the centrifugal elements in our own territory. It has always been my ideal aim, after we had established our unity within the possible limits, to win the confidence not only of the smaller European states, but also of the Great Powers, and to convince them that German policy will be just and peaceful, now that it has repaired the *injuria temporum*, the disintegration of the nation. In order to produce this confidence it is above everything necessary that we should be honourable, open, and easily reconciled in case of friction or *untoward events*. I have followed this recipe not without some personal reluctance in cases like that of Schnäbele (April 1887), Boulanger, Kauffmann (September 1887) ; as towards Spain in the question of the Caroline Islands, towards the United States in that of Samoa, and I imagine that in the future also opportunities will not be wanting of showing that we are appeased and peaceful. During the time that I was in office I advised three wars, the Danish, the Bohemian, and the French ; but every time I first made myself clear whether the war, if it were successful, would bring a prize of victory worth the sacrifices which every war requires, and which now are so much greater than in the last century. Had I had to say to myself that after one of these wars we should find some difficulty in discovering conditions of peace which were desirable, I should scarcely have convinced myself of the necessity for these sacrifices as long as we were not actually attacked. I have never looked at international quarrels which can only be settled by a national war, from the point of view of the Göttingen student code or the honour which

governs a private duel, but I have always considered
simply their reaction on the claim of the German people,
in equality with the other great states and Powers of
Europe, to lead an autonomous political life, so far as is
possible on the basis of our peculiar national capacity.

The traditional Russian policy, which was based partly
on community of faith and partly on blood relationship—
the thought of freeing from the Turkish yoke and thereby
binding to Russia the Roumanians, the Bulgarians, the
Greeks, occasionally also the Roman Catholic Servians
who under various names are to be found on either side
of the Austro-Hungarian frontier—has not stood the test.
It is not impossible that in the far future all these races
will be forcibly incorporated in the Russian system; but
the Greek race has been the first to show that liberation
alone does not change them into adherents of the Russian
power. After Tchesme (1770) the Greeks were regarded
as the support of Russia, and as late as the Russo-Turkish
war of 1806 to 1812 the aims of the Imperial Russian
policy seemed to be unchanged. It is immaterial whether
the undertakings of the Hetæria at the time of Ypsilanti's
rebellion (and this, which had been made popular also in
the West, was the outcome of the Hellenising Eastern
policy of which the Fanariots were the intermediaries)
had the united support of the different currents of Russian
life which crossed one another from Araktcheyeff down
to the Decembrists; anyhow the Greeks, the firstborn of
the Russian policy of liberation, were a disappointment to
Russia, if not a decisive one. The policy of the liberation
of Greece has, from the time of Navarino, ceased, even in
the eyes of the Russians, to be a Russian speciality. It
was a long time before the Russian cabinet drew the conclusion from this critical event. The *rudis indigestaque*

moles of Russia is too heavy to be easily moved by every observation of political instinct. They went on liberating, and the experience they had had with the Greeks repeated itself with the Roumanians, Servians, and Bulgarians. All these races have gladly accepted Russian help for liberation from the Turks ; but since they have been free they have shown no tendency to accept the Czar as successor of the Sultan. I do not know whether in St. Petersburg they share the conviction that even 'the only friend' of the Czar, the Prince of Montenegro, will continue to hoist the Russian flag only so long as he expects equivalents in gold and power, though this, considering his distant and isolated situation, would to some extent be excusable ; but it cannot be unknown in St. Petersburg that the Vladika was ready and perhaps is still ready to some forward as constable for the Grand Turk at the head of the Balkan peoples, if this idea were to find at the Porte an acceptance and support sufficiently favourable to make it profitable for Montenegro.

If at St. Petersburg they wish to draw conclusions from their previous mistakes, and profit by their experience, the natural thing would be for them to limit themselves to the less fantastical progress which can be attained by the weight of regiments and cannons. Experience has not pronounced its *placet* on the historical and poetical side which was in the mind of the Empress Catherine when she gave her second grandson the name of Constantine. Liberated nations are not grateful but exacting ; and it seems to me that the advance of Russian policy in dealing with Eastern questions in the present realistic time would be rather technical than enthusiastic. Their first practical requirement for developing their power in the East is to make the Black Sea safe. If they succeed in attaining a firm control over the Bosphorus by laying down torpedoes and placing guns in position, then the south coasts of Russia will be even better protected than the Baltic; and in the Crimean war the superior English and French fleets could do little to the latter.

This is the form which the calculation of the St. Petersburg cabinet may take if its first object is to close the Black Sea and to win over the Sultan for this purpose by love, by money, or by violence. If the Porte rejects the friendly approach of Russia and draws the sword against the threatened violence, then Russia will probably be attacked from another side, and in my opinion the massing of troops on the western frontier is calculated to meet this event. If they succeed in closing the Bosphorus by goodwill, then perhaps the Powers who find themselves injured by this will sit still for a time, since each one would wait for the initiative of the other and the decision of France. Our interests are more easily reconciled with the gravitation of the Russian power to the south than those of other Powers; one can even say that they are advanced by it. We can await longer than the others the unravelling of the new knot which has been tied by Russia.

CHAPTER XXXI

THE Council of State which was introduced by the law of March 20, 1817, was intended to advise the absolute King. In his place has now been put the King who by the constitution is advised by his ministers, and thereby the ministry of state has been absorbed into that governing factor which has to be assisted by the previous discussion in the council—a factor which in former days was represented by the King alone. The discussions in the council are nowadays for the information not only of the King, but also of the responsible ministers. When it was brought into activity again in 1852, the object was to prepare not only the decisions of the King, but the votes of the ministers.

The preparation of drafts of law by the ministry of state is incomplete. A reporting secretary is in a position to determine the fate of a bill right down to the time of its promulgation, for, supposing the subject is difficult and the number of paragraphs large, he can divert all attempts to influence the contents, which are made either in the ministry of state or in the different stages of parliamentary discussion, to the outward form of the draft. Even within the ministry the departmental ministers do not always really comprehend the matter which the secretaries lay before them in the form of a draft bill

accompanied by motives and explanations. Much less
do the other ministers spend time and trouble in making
themselves acquainted with the contents and importance
of a new law in every detail, unless it will affect their
own department. If this is the case, then the feeling of
independence and the particularism which animates each
one of the eight federated ministerial provinces, and every
secretary in his own sphere, are set in motion. The departmental minister, however, will not be in a condition to
judge the effect of an intended law on practical life, if he
himself be a one-sided product of the bureaucracy; much
less will his colleagues. Not five per cent. of those whom
I have had the opportunity of observing are conscious
of being not merely departmental ministers, but also
ministers of state who share in the common responsibility for their joint policy. The others confine themselves to attempting to administer their own departments
free from blame, to getting the necessary supplies from
the Minister of Finance, and having them passed by the
Diet, and to defending themselves successfully against
parliamentary attacks on their department by their eloquence and, if necessary, by throwing over their subordinates. The receipts which come to them in the form
of the royal signature and parliamentary grants are sufficient to prevent the question whether the law is in itself
desirable from coming before the bureaucratic ministerial
conscience. The interference of a colleague whose
department is not directly concerned arouses the sensitiveness of the departmental minister, and, as a rule, this
is spared in return for the similar consideration which
each one expects for his own proposals. I can remember
that the discussions of the old Council of State before
1848, some prominent members of which I knew, were

carried on with more pointed exertion of the individual judgment and stronger stirrings of the conscience than the ministerial consultations which I have been in a position to observe for more than forty years.

It is also, I consider, misleading to assume that the draft of a bill which leaves the ministry badly drawn is sufficiently discussed in the Diet. It can and, let us hope, will as a rule be rejected. If, however, the question with which it has to do is pressing, then there is a danger that ministerial nonsense goes smoothly through the parliamentary stages, especially if the author of the scheme succeeds in winning for his product some influential or eloquent friend. Considering the great number of members who have been at the universities, and who hold judicial or administrative posts, there must, one would suppose, be some who give themselves the trouble to read a draft bill of more than a hundred paragraphs, or who might even be able to read it with understanding ; but few have the love of work and the feeling of duty, and these are divided among groups and parties which are in constant conflict with one another, and whose tendencies make it difficult for them to come to a judgment on the matter itself. Most members read without criticising, and ask the party leaders, who work and speak for their own ends, when they are to attend the sitting and how they are to vote. This all is to be explained by human nature, and nobody is to be blamed that he cannot change his skin ; only we must not deceive ourselves, and it is a serious error to suppose that our laws nowadays have that investigation and preparatory work which they require, or even that which they enjoyed before 1848.

The Reichstag has set up a monument of this superficiality in the constitution of the North German confederation, which has been transferred to the constitution of the German Empire. Article 68 of the draft constitution, which was imitated from a resolution of the Frankfort Diet, enumerated five forms of crime which, if they were committed against the confederation, were to be punished in the same way as though they had been committed against a single federal state. The fifth number was introduced with the word ' lastly.' Twesten, whose thoroughness was well known, proposed as an amendment to strike out the three first numbers ; he had, however, obviously not read to the end the article which he proposed to amend, and left the word ' lastly ' in it. His proposal was accepted, and retained in all stages of the discussion, and the article (now No. 74) has the remarkable reading :

' Every undertaking against the existence, the integrity, the safety, or the constitution of the German empire, lastly insults against the Federal Council, the Reichstag,' &c.

Before 1848 people took trouble to find out what was right and reasonable ; now they are satisfied with a majority and the signature of the King. I can only regret that in preparing laws the co-operation of wider circles of the kind which was given in the Council of State and in the Board for Economics has not been made sufficiently powerful against ministerial or monarchical impatience. When I found leisure to occupy myself with these problems, I occasionally expressed to my colleagues the wish that they should begin their legislative activity by publishing the draft of laws, exposing them to the criticism of publicists, listening to the greatest possible number of circles who understood the matter and were interested in the question—that is the Council of State, the Economic Board, and, under circumstances, the provincial Diets—before they brought them up for discussion in the ministry. I attribute the repression of the Council of State and similar consultative bodies chiefly to the jealousy with which these unprofessional advisers in public affairs are regarded by the professional secretaries and the parliaments, at the same time also to the discomfort with which ministerial omnipotence within its own department looks on the interference of others.

The first meetings of the Council of State which I attended after 1884, under the presidency of the Crown Prince Frederick William, made a businesslike and favourable impression not only on me, but, as I believe, on all others who took part in them. The Prince listened to the speeches without showing any desire to influence the speakers. It was noticeable that the speeches of two former officers of the guards, von Zedlitz-Trützschler, afterwards chief President in Posen and Minister of Religion and Education, and von Minnigerode, made such an impression that the Crown Prince afterwards appointed both of them to draw up reports, and in this acted in accordance with the opinion of the meeting, although without doubt the speeches which showed more theoretic knowledge of the subject were made by the specialist professors who were present. The influence which in this way men who had formerly been officers in the guard exercised in projects of law confirmed me in my conviction that the mere testing of drafts in the ministry is not the right way of avoiding the danger that unpractical, harmful, and dangerous proposals, drawn up in very incorrect language, should make their way from the compositions of the dilettante legislative activity of a single reporting secretary unchecked, or at any rate without any sufficient correction, through all the stages of the ministry of state, the parliaments, and the cabinet, into the collections of laws, and then, until some remedy is found, form a portion of the burden which creeps among us and drags on like a disease.

CHAPTER XXXII

THE EMPEROR WILLIAM I

ABOUT the middle of the 'seventies the Emperor's intellect began to work less easily, he had difficulty in comprehending what others said and in developing his own statements; at times he lost the thread in listening and speaking. Curiously enough a change for the better began after Nobiling's attempt on his life. Moments like those I have described did not occur; the Emperor was freer, had more life, and was also more easily moved. When I expressed my delight at the good state of his health he was moved to the jest, 'Nobiling knew better than the doctors what I wanted—a good letting of blood.' The last illness was short; it began on March 4, 1888. On the 8th at midday I had my last interview with the Emperor, at which he was still conscious, and I obtained from him the authorisation to publish the order, which had been drawn up as long ago as November 17, 1887, in which Prince William was commissioned to act as the Emperor's representative in cases where his Majesty should believe that he required one. The Emperor said he expected me to remain in my position and stand at the side of his successors; at first there seemed to be in his mind chiefly the anxiety that I should not be able to get on with the Emperor Frederick. I expressed myself so as to calm his apprehensions, so far as it seemed fitting to speak to a dying man of that which his successors and

I would do after his death. Then, thinking of his son's illness, he required from me the promise that I would allow his grandson to have the benefit of my experience and remain at his side, if, as seemed probable, he should soon come to the government. I gave expression to my readiness to serve his successor with the same zeal as himself. His only answer was a slightly more noticeable pressure of my hand; then his mind began to wander, and the occupation with his grandson came so much into the front, that he thought the Prince, who in September 1886 had paid a visit to the Czar at Brest Litewsk, was sitting in my place at his bedside, and suddenly addressing me with 'Du,' he said, 'Thou must always keep touch with the Russian Emperor; there no conflict is necessary.' After a long interval of silence the hallucination had disappeared; he dismissed me with the words, 'I still see you.' He saw me once more when I came in the afternoon, and again at four o'clock in the night on the 9th, but he can scarcely have recognised me among the many who were present; there had been a return of full clearness and consciousness late in the evening of the 8th, and he was able to speak with those who were standing round his deathbed in the narrow bedroom in clear and connected words. It was the last flicker of that strong and brave spirit. At half-past eight he drew his last breath.

Under Frederick William III only the Crown Prince had been consciously educated as successor to the throne; the education of the second son had been on the other hand exclusively military. It was natural that throughout his whole life military influences should have

in themselves a stronger influence on him than civil,
and I myself thought that my influence on him was to
some extent strengthened by the impression of the military uniform which I used to wear in order to avoid the
necessity of changing my clothes many times a day.
Among the people who, so long as he was only Prince
William, could have influence on his development, officers
without political duties took the first place, after General
von Gerlach, who had been his aide-de-camp for many
years, had temporarily dropped out of political life. He
was the ablest among the aides-de-camp whom the Prince
had had ; he was not a theoretical fanatic in politics and
religion like his brother the President, but still he was
enough of a doctrinaire not to find so much response in
the practical understanding of the Prince as he did with
the brilliant intellect of the King, Frederick William.
' Pietism ' was a word and an idea which were easily connected with the name of Gerlach, on account of the *rôle*
which the general's two brothers, the President and the
clergyman, who was author of an extensive work on the
Bible, played in the political world.

A conversation connected with the name of Gerlach,
which I had in 1853 with the Prince at Ostend, where
I had been brought into closer connexion with him, has
remained in my memory, for I was much struck by the
Prince's want of acquaintance with our public institutions
and the political situation.

One day he spoke with a certain animosity about
General von Gerlach, who as it seemed, in consequence
of a want of agreement, had in bad humour resigned his
post as adjutant.   The Prince spoke of him as a ' Pietist.'

I.—What does your Royal Highness mean by a
pietist ?

He.—A man who plays the hypocrite in religion in order to advance in his career.

I.—There is nothing of that in Gerlach: what could he become? In the language of the present day the word pietist has quite another meaning, viz. a man who believes in the Christian religion according to the orthodox creed and makes no secret of his belief; and there are many of them who have nothing to do with political life and do not think of making a career.

He.—What do you mean by orthodox?

I.—For example, one who seriously believes that Jesus is the Son of God and died for us as a sacrifice for the pardon of our sins. At the moment I cannot give a more accurate definition, but that is the essential part in the difference of belief.

He (growing very red).—Who is there, then, so forsaken by God that he does not believe that?

I.—If what you have just said were publicly known, your Royal Highness would yourself be counted among the pietists.

In the further course of the conversation we touched on the question of the 'regulation for districts and villages' which at that time was in suspense. On this the Prince spoke as follows:

He was, he said, no enemy to the nobility, but he could not allow that the peasant should be ill-treated by the nobleman.

I answered:

'How can the nobleman set to work? If I wanted to ill-treat my Schönhausen peasants, I should be without any means of doing so, and the attempt would end with my ill-treatment either by the peasants or by the law.'

He rejoined: 'That may be the case with you in Schönhausen; but it is an exception, and I cannot allow that the poor in the country should be cruelly used.'

I asked for permission to lay before him a short explanation of the origin of our rural conditions and the relation between landlord and peasant. He accepted the offer with pleasure, and afterwards in Norderney I devoted my spare hours to explaining to the heir to the throne, who was already fifty-six years old, the legal position of manors and peasants in 1853, quoting the passages from the laws. I sent him the work not without some fear that the Prince would answer curtly and ironically that I had told him nothing which he had not already known for thirty years. On the contrary, however, he thanked me warmly for the interesting collection of facts which were new to him.

From the moment when the regency began, Prince William felt so keenly the want of a proper business education that he shunned no labour by day or night in order to make good the deficiency. When he was 'transacting public affairs,' then he really worked, seriously and conscientiously. He read *all* papers which were sent in to him, not merely those which attracted him, and studied the treaties and laws so that he might form an independent judgement. He knew no pleasure which would have taken away time from affairs of state. He never read novels or other books which did not concern his duties as ruler. He did not smoke or play cards. When there was a shooting party at Wusterhausen and after dinner they went into the room where Frederick

William I used to collect the *tabakscollegium* in order that the others might be able to smoke in his presence, he had a long Dutch clay pipe handed to him, took a few puffs at it, and then put it down with a wry face. Once when he was in Frankfort, while he was still Prince of Prussia, he came into a room where hazard was being played, and said to me, ' I will just try my luck once, but I have no money with me ; give me some.' As I also did not carry money about with me, Count Theodor Stolberg came to our help. The Prince staked a thaler several times, lost each time, and left the room. His only recreation was, after a hard day's work, to sit in his box at the theatre ; but even there I, as minister, was allowed to seek him out for pressing business, and make reports to him in the small room behind the box and receive his signature. A good night's rest was so necessary to him that he would complain of a bad night if he was disturbed twice, and of sleeplessness if he were disturbed three times, and yet I never saw the slightest touch of annoyance when in difficult circumstances I had to wake him up at two or three o'clock to ask for a hasty decision.

Besides the diligence to which he was impelled by his strong sense of duty, he was helped in fulfilling his duties as ruler by an unwonted measure of clear and healthy human understanding, *common sense*, which was neither dependent on nor limited by acquired knowledge. He was hindered in understanding affairs by the tenacity with which he clung to princely, military, and local traditions ; it was always difficult for him to give them up, or to turn into new paths when the course of circumstances made it necessary, and it easily appeared to him in the light of something unpermissible or undignified. He clung firmly

to impressions and convictions just as he did to the
persons by whom he was surrounded and the things he
used ; the remembrance of what his father had done in
similar cases, or would have done, always had much
influence on him; especially during the French war he
always had before his eyes the remembrance of the parallel
course of the wars of liberation.

King William once during the Schleswig-Holstein
episode asked me reproachfully : 'Are you then not also
a German?' because I opposed his intention, which was
predisposed by domestic influences, to create at Kiel a
new grand duchy which would vote against Prussia ; and
yet when he followed his own natural feelings without
being weakened by political thoughts, he was one of the
most resolute particularists among the German princes,
following the line of a patriotic and conservative Prussian
officer of his father's time.   In riper years the influence
of his wife brought him into opposition to the traditional
principle; the incapacity of his ministers of the new era
and the precipitate blunders of the Liberals in parliament
during the Conflict once more made his pulse beat like a
Prussian prince and officer, the more so that he never
considered whether the road on which he was entering
was dangerous.   If he was convinced that duty and
honour, or one of the two, required him to enter on a
path, he went his way without caring for the dangers to
which he might be exposed, in politics as much as on the
field of battle.   He was not to be intimidated ; the Queen
was : the necessity of living in domestic peace being with
her a force, the result of which one could never foresee ;
but parliamentary rudeness or threats had no effect but
to strengthen his resolution not to give in.   The ministers
of the new era and their parliamentary supporters and

followers had never taken this quality into account. Count Schwerin went so far in his want of comprehension of this fearless officer on the throne, that he thought he could intimidate him by an overbearing manner and want of courtesy. This was the turning point of the influence of the ministers of the new era, the old Liberals and the Bethmann-Hollweg party, and from this time the current turned in the opposite direction; the lead fell into Roon's hands; and the Minister-President, Prince Hohenzollern, with his adjutant Auerswald, desired my entrance into the ministry. The Queen and Schleinitz prevented this for a time when I was in Berlin in the spring of 1860, but the scenes which had passed between the ruler and his ministers had made a rent in their mutual relations which was never healed.

During the reign of Frederick William IV the Princess Augusta generally was in opposition to the policy of the government; she regarded the new era of the regency as *her* ministry, at least until the retirement of Herr von Schleinitz. Before and after that it was a necessity for her to be in opposition to the attitude of the government, whatever it might be, both to that of her brother-in-law and afterwards of her husband. Her influence changed, and in such a way that to the very last years of her life it always fell into the scale against the ministers. If the policy of the government was Conservative, then Liberal persons and Liberal tendencies were marked out for distinction and advance in her domestic circle; when the government of the Emperor in its task of strengthening the new Empire entered the path of

Liberalism, then her favour inclined to the side of the
Conservative elements, and especially to the Catholics;
as under a Protestant dynasty these were often and, to a
certain point, regularly in opposition, the support of the
Catholics was of much interest to the Empress.

During the periods when our foreign policy could go
hand in hand with Austria, her mood towards Austria
was distant and unfriendly; when our policy made opposition to Austria necessary, then the Queen became
the representative of Austrian interests, and this was the
case right into the beginning of the war of 1866. Even
after fighting had begun on the Bohemian frontier, the
organ of Herr von Schleinitz, under the patronage of her
Majesty, kept up relations and negotiations of a very
dubious nature. After I became Minister of Foreign
Affairs, and Herr von Schleinitz Minister of the Royal
House, he held the position of a kind of opposition
minister to the Queen, who could provide her Majesty
with material for criticism and for influencing the King.
He used for this purpose the connexions which, when he
was my predecessor, he had made by private correspondence, and concentrated in his hands a system of regular
diplomatic reports. I received the proof of this by accident; some of these reports came into my hands by a
mistake of the courier or of the post; they were so drawn
up that one could see they were not isolated, and they so
closely resembled official reports that I noticed nothing
till I was startled by some references in the text; then
I looked for the envelope in the wastepaper basket and
found on it the address of Herr von Schleinitz. To the
officials with whom he maintained connexions of this
kind belonged, among others, a consul about whom Roon
wrote to me on January 25, 1864, that he was in the pay

THE 'REICHSGLOCKE'   309

of Drouyn de Lhuys, and, under the name of Siegfeld, wrote articles for the 'Mémorial Diplomatique,' which among other things supported the occupation of the Rhine by Napoleon and compared it to our occupation of Schleswig. At the time of the 'Reichsglocke' and the venomous attacks of the Conservative party and the 'Kreuzzeitung' against me, I was able to find out that the distribution of the 'Reichsglocke' and similar libellous publications was managed in the office of the ministry of the royal family. The person employed was one of the higher subordinate officials of the name of Bernhard, who cut Frau von Schleinitz's pens and kept her writing table in order. By his means thirteen copies of the 'Reichsglocke' had gone to the very highest personages only, of which two went to the imperial palace and others to nearly related Courts.

One morning, when I had to visit the Emperor, who had been made ill through annoyance, in order to lodge what, under the circumstances, was a complaint of pressing importance about a demonstration of the Court in favour of the Centrum, I found him in bed, and with him was the Empress in a costume from which one would conclude that she had come down after I had been announced. On my request to be allowed to speak alone with the Emperor she went away, but only as far as a chair which was just outside the door, which she had not quite shut; and she took care to let me know by her movements that she heard everything. I did not allow myself to be prevented by this attempt at intimidation (and it was not the first) from completing my report. On the evening of the same day I was at a party in the palace. Her Majesty addressed me in a manner which made me suppose that the Emperor had supported my remonstrance to her. The conversation took the turn that I begged the Empress to spare the health of her husband, which already was unsatisfactory, and not expose him to conflicting political influences. This suggestion, which, according to all Court traditions, was quite unexpected, had a remarkable effect. During the last ten years of her life I never saw the Empress Augusta so beautiful as she was at this moment; her figure drew itself up, her eyes brightened with a fire which I have never seen there before or since. She broke off the conversation, left me standing alone, and, as I was told by one of the courtiers who was a friend of mine, said, 'Our most gracious Chancellor is very ungracious to-day.'

The experience of many years had enabled me by degrees to judge with some certainty whether the Emperor opposed suggestions, which seemed to me logically necessary, from his own conviction or in the interest of his domestic peace. In the first case I could as a rule reckon on coming to an understanding if I awaited the time when the clear understanding of my master had assimilated the matter; or he would appeal to the council of ministers. In such cases the discussion between me and his Majesty always remained practical and confined to the subject at issue. It was different when the cause of the royal opposition to ministerial opinions lay in the previous discussion of the question which her Majesty had aroused at breakfast, and carried on till he had positively expressed his agreement with her. When the King at such moments, influenced by letters and newspaper articles which had been written for the purpose, had been brought to hasty expressions opposed to the ministerial policy, then her Majesty was accustomed to confirm the success she had obtained by giving utterance to doubts whether the Emperor would be in a condition to uphold the purpose or opinion he had expressed 'against Bismarck.' When his Majesty opposed me not from his own conviction, but as a result of repeated feminine pressure, I could see what had happened, for his arguments were not to the point and illogical. When he could not find any more arguments against what I said, then he would end the discussion with the expression: 'Ei der Tausend, da muss ich doch sehr bitten' ('Oh, come, I say! *please*'). Then I knew that I had met not the Emperor, but his wife.

All the opponents belonging to the most different regions, whom during my political struggles I had been compelled to make in the interest of the public service, found in their common hatred of me a bond of union which sometimes was stronger than their mutual antipathies. They made a truce in their feuds in order for the time to serve the stronger hostility to me. The Empress Augusta formed the point about which their agreement crystallised; her temperament when it was a matter of getting her way did not always observe the limits required by regard for the age and health of her husband.

During the siege of Paris, as frequently before and afterwards, the Emperor had often to suffer in the struggle between his understanding and his feeling of duty as a King on one side, and the requirements of domestic peace and female assent to his policy on the other. His chivalrous feeling towards his wife, his mystical feeling towards the crowned Queen, his sensitiveness to interruptions in his domestic life and his daily habits, put obstacles in my way, which were at times more difficult to overcome than those caused by foreign Powers or hostile parties; in consequence of the hearty attachment which I had for the person of the Emperor, this considerably increased the exhausting effect of the struggles which I had to go through when in my reports to the Emperor my duty compelled me to defend my convictions.

The Emperor felt this, and in the last years of his life he made no secret to me of his domestic relations, and used to discuss with me what ways and forms we should choose so as to spare his household peace without injury to interests of state; when in a confidential mood, with a mixture of annoyance, respect, and goodwill, he used to speak of her as *Feuerkopf*, and accompanied this expression with a motion of his hands as though he would say, ' I cannot alter it.' I found this designation extraordinarily happy; the Queen was a spirited woman as long as physical dangers did not threaten; she was upheld by a high feeling of duty, but her royal feelings made her indisposed to recognise other authorities than her own.

The great influence which, after his accession to the government, the will and convictions of the Prince of Prussia, afterwards Emperor, exercised outside the military and in the political sphere was simply the result of the powerful and distinguished nature which was inborn in this prince, and quite independent of the education he had received. The expression ' königlich vornehm ' (royal distinction) is characteristic of his appearance. With monarchs vanity can be a spur to action and to labour for the happiness of their subjects. Frederick the Great was not free from it; his impulse to his first actions sprang from the desire for historical fame. I will not discuss the question whether this motive degenerated towards the end of his reign, as was said, or whether he secretly gave ear to the wish that posterity should notice the difference between his government and that of his successors. He dated one of his political effusions from the day before a battle and communicated it in a letter with the words 'Pas trop mal à la veille d'une bataille.'

The Emperor William 1 was completely free from vanity of this kind; on the other hand he had in a high degree a peculiar fear of the legitimate criticism of his contemporaries and of posterity. In this he was completely the Prussian officer, who, as soon as he is protected by a higher command, goes without wavering to most certain death, but through fear of the blame of his superior officer or public criticism falls into such doubt and uncertainty as to choose the wrong path. No one would have dared to flatter him openly to his face. In his feeling of royal dignity he would have thought, 'if any one had the right of praising me to my face, he would also have the right of blaming me to my face.' He would not admit either.

Monarch and parliament had learnt to know and respect one another by long internal struggles; the King's noble dignity and quiet confidence had at last won the respect even of his opponents, and the King himself was enabled justly to judge the two sides of the situation owing to his own high feeling of personal honour. He was governed by the feeling of justice, not only towards his friends and servants, but also in the struggle against his opponents. He was a gentleman expressed in terms of a king, a nobleman in the primary sense of the word, who never felt himself dispensed from the principle *Noblesse oblige* by any temptations of the power which belonged to him ; his attitude both in home and foreign policy was always subordinated to the principles of a cavalier of the old school and to the normal feeling of a Prussian officer. He held fast to honour and loyalty not only towards princes but also towards his servants, even down to his valet. If in momentary excitement he trespassed on his fine feeling for royal dignity and duty, he soon recovered and remained at the same time ' every inch a king,' and moreover a just and kindly king, and an honour-loving officer whom the thought of his Prussian *porte-épée* kept in the right way.[1]

The Emperor could lose his temper, but did not let himself be infected by the ill-temper of any one with whom he was conversing; he would break off the discussion in a friendly and dignified manner. Outbreaks like that at Versailles, when he refused the title of Emperor, were very rare. If he got angry with any one to whom he was well disposed, as Count Roon and myself, then he was either excited by the subject itself, or he had beforehand been bound by unofficial promises which could not be defended. Count Roon listened to explosions of this kind as a soldier at the front listens to the rebuke of a superior officer, which he believes to be undeserved, but his nerves suffered from it and they affected his physical health. I did not experience outbreaks of anger on the part of the Emperor so often as Roon, and they never had a contagious but rather a cooling effect on me. I had thought it out for myself in this way: any irregularities in a ruler who showed me confidence and goodwill to such a degree as did William I should be for me of the nature of *vis major* which it was not for me to resist; I must look on it as the weather or the sea, or any natural event to which I must accommodate myself. This im-

[1] Cf. vol. i. p. 312.

pression rested on my personal love for the Emperor William I, not on my general conception of the relation of a king by the grace of God to his servants. Towards him I was not personally sensitive; he could treat me with much injustice without creating feelings of indignation in me. The feeling that I had been insulted was one which I had towards him as little as I should have had in my father's house. This did not prevent me from being led into a passive opposition to him by the nervous excitement which was engendered by uninterrupted struggles, when I found him without understanding for political matters and interests or prejudiced against them by her Majesty or by the religious or masonic Court intrigues. Now, in thinking over this quietly, I disapprove of this feeling and regret it, as in remembering points of disagreement one has similar feelings after the death of one's father.

His natural uprightness, the genuine kindliness of his disposition, and the amiability which with him came from the heart, enabled him to perform with ease and success one of the duties which at times causes much trouble to the intellectual activity of constitutional rulers and ministers. The annually recurring utterances of those monarchs who are regarded as the patterns of constitutionalism contain a rich storehouse of expressions useful for public utterances; but, notwithstanding all their linguistic skill, both Leopold of Belgium and Louis Philippe pretty well exhausted constitutional phraseology, and a German monarch will scarcely be in a position to enlarge the circle of available expressions in writing and

print. I found no work more disagreeable and difficult than the provision of the necessary supply of phrases
for speeches from the throne and similar utterances.
When the Emperor William himself drew up proclama-
tions or when he wrote letters with his own hand, then,
even if the language was incorrect, they still had something winning and often inspiring. They moved one in
an agreeable way by the warmth of his feeling and the
security which shone from them that he not only required
loyalty but gave it. ' Il était de relation sûre ; ' he was one
of those figures, princely alike in soul and body, whose
qualities belong more to the heart than the understanding,
and explain the life-and-death devotion of their servants
and adherents which appears now and again in the German character. The extent of monarchical devotion is
not identical as regards every prince ; it makes a difference
whether the limit is drawn by political understanding or
by feeling. A certain measure of devotion is determined
by the laws, a still greater by political conviction; anything beyond that requires a personal feeling of reciprocity, and this it is which brings it about that loyal
masters have loyal servants whose devotion extends
beyond what is required by public considerations. It is a
peculiarity of royalist feeling that any one who is moved
by it does not cease to feel himself the servant of the
monarch, even when he is conscious that he influences
the decisions of the King. One day (in 1865) the King
spoke to his wife with admiration of my skill in guessing
his intentions, and, as he added after a pause, of directing them. In acknowledging this he did not lose the
feeling that he was the master and I the servant—a
useful but a respectful and devoted servant. This did not
leave him even when, after an excited discussion about my

resignation in 1877, he broke out into the words : 'Am I
to make a fool of myself (*blamiren*) in my old age? It is
disloyal of you to desert me.' Even with feelings like
this he stood so high in his own royal estimation and in
his sense of justice, that he was never accessible to any
feeling of Saul-like jealousy of me. He had the true
kingly feeling ; not only was the possession of a powerful
and respected servant not disagreeable to him, but the
thought was an elevating one to him. He was too distinguished to feel like a nobleman who cannot endure to
have a rich and independent peasant in the village. This
royal and noble character was displayed for the public and
history in a proper light by the cheerful way in which,
when I celebrated in 1885 the fiftieth anniversary of my
entrance into the public service,* he did not order and
arrange the celebrations, but allowed them and shared in
them. It was not commanded by him, but he permitted it
and cheerfully assisted. Never for a moment did the
thought of jealousy towards his servant and subject come
into his mind, and never for a moment did the royal
consciousness that he was master leave him, just as with
me all the homage that was paid me, exaggerated though
it were, never affected my feeling that I was the servant
of my master and was it gladly.

Our relations and my attachment to him were in
principle based on the fact that I was by conviction a
royalist ; but the special form which it took is only
possible by the exercise of a certain reciprocity of good-
will between master and servant, just as our feudal law
assumed 'loyalty' on both sides. Relations like those in
which I stood to the Emperor William are not exclusively

---

* By the wish of the Emperor it was joined with the celebration of my
seventieth birthday.

of a political or feudal nature ; they are personal and they must be won by the master as well as the servant if they are to be effective ; they are easily transferred to one generation rather personally than logically, but to give them a permanent character and require them as a matter of principle answers more to the feelings and character of the Romance than of the German races! We cannot transfer the Portuguese *porteur du coton* into German ideas.

Certain characteristics of the Emperor will be more clearly seen in the following letters than in any description :

'Berlin: Jan. 13, 1870.

' Unfortunately I have always forgotten to give you the medal of victory, which really ought to have been in *your* hands *first*, and so I send it to you now as a seal of your historical achievements.

'Yours,

'WILLIAM.'

On the same day I wrote to the Emperor :

' I present to your Majesty my humble duty, and offer my heartfelt thanks for your gracious presentation of the medal, and for the honourable place which your Majesty has been pleased to assign to me on this historical monument. The remembrance which this engraved document will maintain for posterity wins for me and mine a special importance by the gracious lines with which your Majesty has accompanied the presentation. If my self-esteem finds a great satisfaction that it is given to me to see my name go down to posterity under the wings of the royal eagle which points her way to Germany, my heart derives still more satisfaction from the feeling that under God's visible blessing I serve an hereditary master, to whom I am attached with full personal love, and the possession of whose approbation is for me the most desirable reward in this life.'

'Berlin : March 21, 1871.

'With to-day's opening of the first German Reichstag, after the restoration of a German Empire, begins its first public activity.   Prussia's history and fate have for long pointed to an event like that which has now been completed by her summons to the head of the newly-founded Empire.   Prussia owes this not so much to the extent of her territory and her power, although both have been increased together, as to her intellectual development and the organisation of her army.   In the course of the last six years the fortunes of my country have with unexpectedly rapid succession developed themselves to the culmination at which it now stands.   To this period belongs an activity for which I summoned you to me ten years ago. All the world can see how you have justified the confidence from which I then summoned you.   To your counsel, to your wisdom, to your untiring activity, Prussia and Germany owe the historical event which to-day takes place in my residency.

'Although the reward for these deeds lies within yourself, I am still forced and bound to express to you in public and enduring form the thanks of my Fatherland and myself.   I therefore raise you into the Prussian Order of Princes, and decree that the rank shall always be hereditary in the eldest male member of your family.

'May you see in this distinction the never failing gratitude of your Emperor and King

'WILLIAM.'

'Berlin: March 2, 1872.

'We celebrate to-day the first anniversary of the conclusion of that glorious peace which, won by courage and sacrifices of every kind, by your wisdom and energy, led to unthought-of results. Again to-day I repeat to you with grateful emotion the recognition and thanks to which I have already given public expression in iron and the noble metals. One metal still remains—bronze. I to-day place at your disposition a token of this metal, and one in the form which a year ago you brought to silence; I have arranged that some of the captured cannon, which you yourself shall choose, should be handed over to you, and you shall erect them on your own estates as a lasting memorial of the great services you rendered to me and the Fatherland.

'Your truly devoted and grateful

'WILLIAM.'

'Coblenz: July 26, 1872.

'On the 28th of this month you will celebrate a happy family festival, which the Almighty in His grace grants to you. Therefore I can and must not remain behind in my sympathy at this festival, and I ask that you and the Princess your wife will accept my sincere and warmest congratulations at this festival. That among all the many gifts of fortune which Providence has chosen for you, for both of you domestic happiness stands above all— this it is for which your prayers and thanksgivings rise to heaven. Our and my thanksgiving go further, for they include our gratitude that at the decisive hour God set you at my side, and thereby opened to my government a course which went far beyond my thoughts and under- standing. But for this also you will send your feelings of gratitude above, that God in His mercy granted you to achieve such great things. Through all your labours you ever found recreation and joy in your home, and that it is which preserves you for your difficult calling. I never cease to urge you that you will maintain and strengthen yourself for this, and I am glad to hear from your letter to Count Lehndorff and from himself that you will now think more of yourself than of the papers.

'As a reminiscence of your silver wedding a vase will be handed over to you, representing a grateful Prussia, which, fragile though the material may be, still in every fragment shall express what Prussia owes to you for raising her to the height at which she stands.

'Your truly devoted, grateful King,

'WILLIAM.'

'Coblenz: November 6, 1878.

'It has been granted to you within a quarter of a year, by your insight, wisdom, and courage, partly to restore, partly to maintain, peace in Europe, and in Germany by legal means to oppose an enemy who threatened destruction to all public institutions. These two historical events are understood by all who are well disposed, and their acknowledgement has been imparted to you; I myself have been able to give proof of my acknowledgement of that which I have first named, the congress of Berlin, and it is now again my duty publicly to express to you my acknowledgement for the decisive manner in which you have defended the basis of law. The law * which I have in my mind, and which owes its origin to an event painful to my heart and feeling, will insure that the

---

* The law of October 21, 1878, against social democracy and its efforts, perilous to the community.

German states, and therefore also Prussia, will continue to be based on law and justice.

' I have chosen as signs of my acknowledgement of your great deserts for my Prussia, the emblems of her power—crown, sceptre, and sword—and had them added to the Grand Cross of the Red Eagle which you always wear ; and I now send you the decoration.

' The sword speaks for the courage and insight with which you know how to protect my sceptre and my crown.

' May Providence grant you the power for long years to devote your patriotism to my government and the weal of the Fatherland.

'Your truly devoted, grateful

' WILLIAM.'

'Berlin : April 1, 1879.

' Unfortunately I cannot personally and verbally bring you my good wishes for to-day, for although I am to drive out to-day for the first time, I may not yet go upstairs.

' Above all, I wish for you good health, for from that all activity depends, and this you are developing now more than for a long time, a proof that activity also keeps one in health. May it so continue for the good of the Fatherland, large and small alike.

' I use the day to appoint your son-in-law, Count Rantzau, a councillor of legation, for I believe I shall in this do you a pleasure.

' I shall also send you a copy of my great ancestor, the Great Elector, as he stands on the Long Bridge, as a memorial of the present day, which will I hope often recur for you and us.

'Your grateful

' WILLIAM.'

At Christmas 1883 the Emperor presented to me a copy of the Niederwald monument, on which was fastened a small leaf with the following words :

'Christmas 1883.

' The corner-stone of your policy, a celebration which was chiefly for you and which you were unfortunately * unable to attend.'

'Berlin : April 1, 1885.

' My dear Prince,—If a warm desire has appeared in the German country and people to assure you, at the celebration of your seventieth birthday, that the remembrance of all which you have done for the greatness of the Fatherland lives in so many grateful hearts, I feel deeply the necessity of expressing to you to-day how much pleasure it gives me that this wave of gratitude and respect runs through the nation. I rejoice at it, for it is an acknowledgement which you have truly deserved in the highest degree ; and it warms my heart that these feelings find such widespread utterance, for it is an adornment to the nation in the present, and it strengthens our hope for the future, if it recognises what is true and great, and honours and celebrates men of great deserts. To take part in a celebration of this kind is a special pleasure for me and my house, and we wish to express to you by the accompanying picture (the proclamation of the Emperor at Versailles) with what feelings of grateful remembrance we do this. It recalls to us one of the greatest moments in the history of the House of Hohenzollern, of which we can never think without at the same time remembering your services. You, my dear Prince, know how I shall always have the fullest confidence, the most genuine and the warmest gratitude towards you.

* Owing to ill-health.

y 2

'I therefore in this say nothing which I have not often enough already told you, and I think that this picture will place before the eyes of your distant descendants that your King and Emperor and his house will know what we owed to you. With these feelings and thoughts I end these lines, as lasting beyond the grave,

'Your grateful, truly devoted Emperor and King,

'WILLIAM.'

'Berlin : September 23, 1887.

'To-day, my dear Prince, you celebrate the day on which, twenty-five years ago, I summoned you to my ministry, and after a short time appointed you President of it. The services which up to that time you had rendered to the Fatherland in the most varied and important commissions justified me in giving you this highest post. The history of the last quarter of the century proves that I did not err in my choice.

'A shining picture of true love to the Fatherland, of unwearied activity, often to the neglect of your own health, with unwearied zeal you kept clearly in your eye the often overwhelming difficulties in war and peace, and guided them to good ends which with honour and glory led Prussia to a position in history of which we had never dreamt. Such achievements may well cause us to celebrate the twenty-fifth anniversary of September 23 with thanks to God that He has put you at my side in order to carry out His work on earth.

'And these thanks I once more lay to your heart, as I have so often before been able to express and assure you of them.

'With thankful heart I wish you happiness on the

celebration of such a day, and from my heart I wish that your powers may long remain unimpaired to the blessing of throne and Fatherland.

'Your ever grateful King and friend,

'WILLIAM.'

'P.S. As a remembrance of the twenty-five years which have passed I send you the view of the building in which we had to discuss and carry out such decisive resolutions, which I hope will always be for the honour and good of Prussia, and now I hope also of Germany.'

I received the last letter of the Emperor on December 23, 1887. Compared with the previous ones it shows, both in the structure of the sentences and in the hand-writing, that during the last three months both writing and expressing himself in writing had become much more troublesome to the Emperor; but these difficulties did not interfere with the clearness of the thoughts, the fatherly regard for the feelings of his invalid son, or the anxiety which as ruler he felt for the proper education of his grandson. It would be wrong in reproducing this letter to attempt to improve anything in it.

'Berlin: December 23, 1887.

'Enclosed I send you the appointment of your son to be an actual Privy Councillor with the title of Excellency, that you may give it to your son—a pleasure of which I did not wish to deprive you. The pleasure will, I think, be threefold—for you, for your son, and for me.

'I take the opportunity of explaining to you my previous silence as to your proposal to introduce my grandson Prince William more into state affairs in the melancholy state of health of the Crown Prince my son. In principle I am quite agreed that this should be done,

but it is very difficult to carry it out. You will know that
the decision (natural enough in itself) which at your
advice I adopted, that my grandson W., if I were prevented, should sign the current orders of the civil and
military cabinet under the words " by order," that this
decision has much irritated the Crown Prince, as though
in Berlin they were already thinking of a substitute for
him. When he has considered it more quietly my son
will probably have calmed himself. This consideration
would be more difficult if he were to hear that his son is
allowed still greater insight into affairs of state, and that
even a " civil aide-de-camp " is given him—as I in my time
called the secretary who had to make reports to me.
At that time, however, the position of affairs was quite
different, for no reason could induce my royal father to
appoint an understudy to the then Crown Prince, although it had long been possible to foresee my succession
to the crown, and my introduction was omitted till
my forty-fourth year, when my brother at once appointed me a member of the ministry with the
addition of the title Prince of Prussia. With this
position the appointment of an experienced man of
business was necessary to prepare me for every meeting
of the ministry. At the same time I daily received the
political dispatches after they had gone through four,
five, six hands, to judge by the seals ! Merely for conversation, as you propose, to assign a statesman to my
grandson is not, as in my case, justified by the preparation for a definite object, and would decidedly irritate my
son again and still more, which we must certainly avoid. I
therefore propose that the previous method of learning the
business and management of, and the way-about of public
affairs be maintained, i.e. be assigned to single ministries

and perhaps be extended to two, as during this winter, when my grandson should be allowed as a volunteer to visit the Foreign Office as well as the Ministry of Finance, and then at the new year this might cease to be left to his own free will, and perhaps also the Ministry of the Interior, and at the same time my grandson might be allowed in cases to make himself acquainted with the Foreign Office. This continuation of the present procedure can irritate my son less, although you will remember that he was sharply opposed to this procedure also. I beg, therefore, for your opinion in this matter. Wishing you all a pleasant festival,

' Your grateful

' WILLIAM.

' Will you be so good as to sign the accompanying patent before delivering it?   W.'[1]

I very rarely received letters from the Empress Augusta; her last letter, during the composition of which she doubtless thought of the struggles which I had to wage with her as much as I did in reading it, runs as follows:

(Dictated.)

' Baden-Baden : December 24, 1888.

' Dear Prince,—If I write these lines to you it is simply in order to fulfil a duty of gratitude at the turning-point of a grave year of my life. You have stood loyally by our departed Emperor and fulfilled my request to care for his grandson. In hours of bitterness you have shown sympathy to me, therefore I feel myself called upon, before I complete this year, to thank you once again and

---

[1] A larger number of letters of the Emperor William I to Bismarck are published in the *Bismarck-Jahrbuch*, i. 140–141 ; iv. 3–12 ; v. 254-5 ; vi. 203.

at the same time to reckon on the continuance of your
help in the midst of the painful events of a stirring time.
I am about to celebrate the end of the year quietly in the
circle of my family, and send a friendly greeting to you
and your wife.

'AUGUSTA.'

The signature is in her own hand, but very different
from the firm strokes with which the Empress was wont
to write in former times.

CHAPTER XXXIII

THE EMPEROR FREDERICK III

IT was a widespread error that the change of government from the Emperor William I to the Emperor Frederick must be associated with a change of ministry and that a tame successor would be appointed. In the summer of 1848 I had for the first time an opportunity of becoming acquainted with the young Prince, who was then seventeen years of age, and received from him proofs of personal confidence; this may from time to time have wavered up till 1886, but was clearly and decidedly shown at the settlement of the Dantzig episode at Gastein in 1863.[1] During the war of 1866, especially in the struggle with the King and the higher military authorities regarding the wisdom of the conclusion of peace at Nikolsburg, I enjoyed a confidence from the Crown Prince which was quite independent of political principles and differences of opinion. Attempts to shake this confidence were made from many sides, not excluding the Extreme Right; many excuses were made and many pretexts invented, but they had no permanent success. At any time after 1866 a personal conversation between the Prince and myself was all that was necessary to make them unavailing.

When the state of William I's health in 1885 gave occasion to serious anxiety, the Crown Prince summoned me to Potsdam and asked whether, in case of a

[1] Cf. vol. i. p. 351.

change on the throne, I would remain in office; I declared that I was ready to do so under two conditions: no parliamentary government and no foreign influence in politics. The Crown Prince with a corresponding gesture answered, ' Not a thought of that.'

I could not assume that his wife had the same kindly feeling for me; her natural innate sympathy for her home had, from the beginning, shown itself in the attempt to turn the weight of Prusso-German influence in the groupings of European power into the scale of her native land; and she never ceased to regard England as her country. In the differences of interests between the two Asiatic Powers, England and Russia, she wished to see the German power applied in the interests of England if it came to a breach. This difference of opinion, which rested on the difference of nationality, caused many a discussion between her Royal Highness and me on the Eastern question, including the Battenberg question. Her influence on her husband was at all times great, and it increased with years to culminate at the time when he was Emperor. She also, however, shared with him the conviction that in the interests of the dynasty it was necessary that I should be maintained in office at the change of reign.

It is not my intention, and it would in fact be an impossible task, expressly to contradict every legend and malicious invention. As, however, the story that in 1887, after his return from Ems, the Crown Prince signed a document in which, in the event of his surviving his father, he renounced his succession to the throne in favour of Prince William, has found its way into an English work on the Emperor William II, I will state that there is not a shadow of truth in the story. It is also a fable that, as in 1887 was maintained in many circles and believed in others, an heir to the throne who suffers from an incurable physical complaint is by the family laws of the Hohenzollern excluded from the succession. The family laws contain no provision on the matter, any more than does the text of the Prussian constitution. On the other hand there was one point in which a question of a public nature compelled me to interfere in the treatment of the sufferer, which otherwise belonged to medical science. The doctors who were treating him were at the end of May 1887 determined to make the Crown Prince unconscious and to carry out the removal of the larynx without having informed him of their intention. I raised objections, required that they should not proceed without the consent of the Prince, and, as they were dealing with the successor to the throne, that the approval of the head of the family should also be required. The Emperor, after being informed by me, forbade them to carry out the operation without the consent of his son. Of the few discussions which during his short government I had with the Emperor Frederick I may mention one to which I can connect some remark about the constitution of the Empire which occupied me on former occasions and again in March 1890.

The Emperor Frederick was inclined to refuse his consent to the law prolonging the period of the legislative assembly from three to five years in the Empire and in Prussia. As regarded the Reichstag, I explained to him that the Emperor as such was no factor of the legislature, but that his co-operation took place only as King of Prussia by the Prussian vote at the federal council; he did not possess by the imperial constitution a veto against unanimous resolutions of the two legislative assemblies. This explanation was sufficient to determine his Majesty to complete the document by which the publication of the law of March 19, 1888, was ordered.

To the question of his Majesty in what position the matter stood as regards the Prussian constitution, I could only answer that the King had the same right of adopting or rejecting every project of law as either of the two houses of the Prussian Parliament. His Majesty then for the time refused his signature, reserving his decision. The question then arose how the ministry of state which had requested the royal consent must behave. I supported the view that for a time we should not insist on a discussion with the King, since he was exercising an undoubted right; since, moreover, the project of law had been introduced before the change of ruler; and lastly, since we must avoid intensifying, by raising cabinet questions, the situation which, even without this, was sufficiently difficult on account of the illness of the monarch. My view was adopted. The end of the matter was that his Majesty, of his own accord, sent to me on May 27 the Prussian law also completed.

In practice people have been accustomed to regard the Chancellor as responsible for the whole policy of the government of the Empire. This responsibility can only be maintained if we admit that the Chancellor is justified first in refusing to countersign, then in rendering inoperative the imperial messages by means of which proposals of the allied governments find their way to the Reichstag (Art. 16). The Chancellor himself, if he is not at the same time a Prussian plenipotentiary at the imperial council, would, according to the text of the constitution, not even have the right personally to take part in the debates of the Reichstag. If, as has hitherto been the case, he has at the same time a Prussian commission for the federal council, then he has by Art. 9 the right of appearing in the Reichstag and being heard at any time. No clause of the constitution gives this right to the Imperial Chancellor as such. If, therefore, neither the King of Prussia nor any other member of the confederation provides the Chancellor with a commission for the federal council, he is entirely without any constitutional claim to appear in the Reichstag; he presides indeed in the federal council by Art. 15, but without a vote, and the Prussian plenipotentiaries would be just as independent of him as those of the other allied states.

Supposing the existing relations were altered so that the responsibility of the Chancellor was limited to the ordinances of the imperial executive power, and the qualification, let alone the duty of appearing and taking part in the discussions of the Reichstag, were withdrawn from him, it is obvious that this would be not merely a formal change, but would essentially alter the centre of gravity of the factors of our public life. I considered the question whether it was desirable to discuss eventualities of this kind at the time when, in December 1884, I found myself opposed to a majority in the Reichstag which consisted of a coalition of the most varied elements—of Social Democrats, Poles, Guelfs, the French party in Alsace, the Radical Crypto-Republicans, and occasionally also the discontented Conservatives at Court—the coalition which, for example, refused the vote for a second director at the Foreign Office. The support which I found at Court, in parliament and elsewhere against this opposition was not unconditional, and was not free from the co-operation of grudging supporters who were trying to

push their way in the world as my rivals. At that time
I for some years considered, both alone and with others,
whether the amount of national unity which we had
attained did not require for its security another form than
that which prevailed at the time, which had been delivered
to us by the past, had been developed by active life and
compromise between governments and parliaments; my
opinion on the pressing importance of this often wavered.
At that time I have, as I think, also hinted in public
speeches [1] that the King of Prussia might see himself
compelled to lean for stronger support on the foundations
which the Prussian constitution afforded him, if the
Reichstag carried its hindrance to the monarchical establishment beyond the limits of what was possible. At
the restoration of the imperial constitution I feared that
danger to our national unity was in the first place to be
feared from the separate interests of the dynasties, and
had therefore set myself the task of winning the confidence
of the dynasties by an honourable and friendly maintenance of their constitutional rights in the Empire, and
I had the satisfaction that the prominent princely houses
more especially found at the same time their national
feeling reconciled with their particular rights. In the
feeling of honour which always inspired the Emperor
William I towards his allies I always found an understanding for what was politically necessary, which in the
end outweighed his own strong dynastic feeling.

On the other side I had calculated on setting up a
bond of union in the common public institutions, especially
in the Reichstag, in finances based on indirect taxes, and
in monopolies, the receipts of which would only remain
available if the permanence of our connexion were

[1] *Political Speeches*, vol. xi. p. 468.

assured, and that this bond would be sufficiently strong
to resist the centrifugal movements of certain of the allied
governments. Notwithstanding all the bad will which I
had had to combat in the Reichstag, at Court, in the
Conservative party, and from the *declaranten* at the end of
the 'seventies, I had not yet been confirmed in the conviction that I was mistaken in this calculation, that I had
underestimated the national feeling of the dynasty, and
overestimated that of the German voters, electors, or the
Reichstag. Now I have to ask pardon of the dynasties;
history will some day decide whether the group-leaders owe
me a *pater peccavi*. I can only bear witness that I lay to
the charge of the parties more blame for the injury done
to our future than they themselves feel, and I include in
this the idle members who shunned their work as much
as those ambitious men in whose hands lay the leading
and the votes of their followers. 'Get you home, you fragments,' says Coriolanus. The Centrum is the only party of
which I can say it has not been incapably led; but it is
calculated for the destruction of the disagreeable edifice
of a German Empire with a Protestant Emperor; at elections and divisions it accepts the assistance of every party,
hostile though it may be in itself, but which for the
moment is working in the same direction, not only of the
Poles, Guelfs, and French, but also of the Radicals.
The leaders alone would be able to judge how many of
the members work consciously for ends hostile to the
Empire, and how many do so from the limitations of their
intellect. Windthorst, politically a latitudinarian, in religion an unbeliever, was by accident and the blunders of
the bureaucracy driven on to the side of our enemies.
Notwithstanding all, I still hope that in times of war the
national feeling will rise high enough to tear asunder the

web of lies in which the party leaders, ambitious orators, and party newspapers hold the masses during times of peace.

Any one who recalls the period in which the Centrum (relying less on the Pope than on the Jesuits), the Guelfs (not merely from Hanover), the Poles, the French Alsatians, the people's party, the Social Democrats, the Freethought party, and the Particularists, linked together only by hostility to the Empire and the dynasty, held under the leadership of the same Windthorst, who before and after his death was made a national saint, a firm and commanding majority against the Emperor and the allied governments, and who is also in a position fully to judge the situation of that time and the dangers which threatened us to East and West, will find it natural that an imperial chancellor who was responsible for the final results should have thought of meeting possible foreign combinations, and an alliance of them with internal dangers, with no less independence than we had undertaken the war in Bohemia, without considering political feelings, and often in opposition to them.

Of the Emperor Frederick's private letters I add one, for his sake and for mine, as an example of his character and his method of writing, and also to overthrow the legend that I have been an enemy of the army.

' Charlottenburg: March 25, 1888.

' To-day, my dear Prince, I think with you of the fifty years which have gone by since you entered the army, and I am genuinely glad that the *Garde Jäger* of that time can look back with so much satisfaction to this half-century which has gone by. I will not to-day enter on long considerations on the political services which have for ever enwoven your name with our history. One thing I must lay stress on, that where it was a question of the welfare of the army, of bringing it to full strength and readiness, you never failed to fight out the struggle and carry it through.   The army therefore thanks you for the blessings attained, which it will never forget ; at its head the war-lord who but a few days ago was called to take up that office after the departure of him who never ceased to carry in his heart the welfare of the army.

'Yours most truly,

'FREDERICK.'

INDEX

—— • ⟨ • ——

END OF THE SECOND VOLUME

PRINTED BY

SPOTTISWOODE AND CO., NEW STREET SQUARE

LONDON

SMITH, ELDER, & CO.'S PUBLICATIONS.

SIR FRANK LOCKWOOD: a Biographical Sketch. By AUGUSTINE
BIRRELL, Q.C., M.P. Third Edition. With 2 Portraits, 10 Full-page Illustrations, and 2 Facsimile Letters. Large crown 8vo. 12s. 6d.

'A book to be read with pure enjoyment.'—ILLUSTRATED LONDON NEWS.

COLLECTIONS AND RECOLLECTIONS. By 'One Who Has Kept
a Diary.' Sixth Impression. With Frontispiece. Demy 8vo. 16s.

'"Collections and Recollections" will rank high among the books of recent years which have added to the gaiety of the nation. It is the best jest-book which has been published for a long time.'—REVIEW OF REVIEWS.

'The most interesting diary that has been published for years.'—TRUTH.

MR. GREGORY'S LETTER-BOX, 1813-30. Edited by Lady GREGORY.
With a Portrait. Demy 8vo. 12s. 6d.

'Lady Gregory's pages bristle with good stories. Indeed, the great difficulty of a reviewer in dealing with this fascinating book is the plethora of good things that clamour for quotation.'—WORLD.

EGYPT IN THE NINETEENTH CENTURY; or, Mehemet Ali
and his Successors until the British Occupation in 1882. By DONALD A. CAMERON, H.B.M.'s Consul at Port Said. With a Map. Post 8vo. 6s.

'This is a book which was distinctly wanted. As a book of reference it should prove invaluable to journalists, and as a lucid account of how Egypt became what she was when England took her in hand, it will be instructive to every intelligent reader.'—SATURDAY REVIEW.

THE AUTOBIOGRAPHY OF ARTHUR YOUNG. With Selections from his Correspondence. Edited by M. BETHAM EDWARDS. With 2 Portraits and 2 Views. Large crown 8vo. 12s. 6d.

'Miss Edwards has done her task with a reserve and succinctness to be much commended. She deserves well of all who hold in honour the memory of one who ever strove manfully to make two blades of grass grow where one grew before.'—TIMES.

THE LIFE OF SIR JOHN HAWLEY GLOVER, R.N., G.C.M.G.
By Lady GLOVER. Edited by the Right Hon. Sir RICHARD TEMPLE, Bart., G.C.S.I., D.C.L., LL.D., F.R.S. With Portrait and Maps. Demy 8vo. 14s.

'Written with noteworthy tact, ability, and discretion by his widow. . . . One of the best and most satisfac ory biographies of its class produced within recent years.'—WORLD.

DEEDS THAT WON THE EMPIRE. By the Rev. W. H. FITCHETT
(' Vedette'). Seventh Edition. With 16 Portraits and 11 Plans. Crown 8vo. 6s.

'There is no bluster, no brag, no nauseous cant about a chosen people; but there is a ringing enthusiasm for endurance, for dashing gallantry, for daring and difficult feats, which generous-hearted boys and men will respond to quickly. There is not a flabby paragraph from beginning to end.' – BOOKMAN.

THE STORY OF THE CHURCH OF EGYPT: being an Outline of
the History of the Egyptians under their successive Masters from the Roman Conquest until now. By E. L. BUTCHER, Author of 'A Strange Journey,' 'A Black Jewel,' &c. 2 vols. crown 8vo. 16s.

'Mrs. Butcher is to be congratulated on the ability, thoroughness, and research which she has brought to the accomplishment of her formidable task.'—CHRISTIAN WORLD.

RELIGIO MEDICI, and other Essays. By Sir THOMAS BROWNE. Edited,
with an Introduction, by D. LLOYD ROBERTS, M.D., F.R.C.P. Revised Edition. Fcp. 8vo. 3s. 6d. net.

'Dr. Lloyd Ro¹ erts gives an excellent selection, edited with the loving care of a true bibliophile, which leaves no phase of Browne's genius unrevealed.'—MANCHESTER COURIER.

GABRIELE VON BULOW. Daughter of Wilhelm von Humboldt. A
Memoir Compiled from the Family Papers of Wilhelm von Humboldt and his Children, 1791-1887. Translated by CLARA NORDLINGER. With Portraits and a Preface by Sir EDWARD B. MALET, G.C.B, G.C.M.G., &c. Demy 8vo. 16s.

'Miss Nordlinger's excellent translation gives English readers an opportunity of becoming acquainted with a very charming personality, and of following the events of a life which was bound up with many interesting incidents and phases of English history.'—TIMES.

ELECTRIC MOVEMENT IN AIR AND WATER. With Theoretical Inferences. By Lord ARMSTRONG, C.B., F.R.S., LL.D., &c. With Autotype Plates. Imperial 4to. £1. 10s. net.

'One of the most remarkable contributions to physical and electrical knowledge that have been made in recent years. . . . The illustrations are produced in a superb manner, entirely worthy of so remarkable a monograph.'—TIMES.

London: SMITH, ELDER, & CO., 15 Waterloo Place, S.W.

SMITH, ELDER, & CO.'S PUBLICATIONS.

SIR CHARLES HALLÉ'S LIFE AND LETTERS. Being an Autobiography (1819-60), with Correspondence and Diaries. Edited by his Son, C. E. HALLÉ, and his Daughter, MARIE HALLÉ. With 2 Portraits. Demy 8vo. 18s.

'The volume is one of the most interesting of recent contributions to the literature of music.... A strong sense of humour is manifest in the autobiography as well as in the letters, and there are some capital stories scattered up and down the volume.'—TIMES.

THE MEMOIRS OF BARON THIEBAULT (late Lieutenant-General in the French Army). With Recollections of the Republic, the Consulate, and the Empire. Translated and Condensed by A. J. BUTLER, M.A., Translator of the 'Memoirs of Marbot.' 2 vols. With 2 Portraits and 2 Maps. Demy 8vo. 28s.

'Mr. Butler's work has been admirably done.... These memoirs abound in varied interest, and, moreover, they have no little literary merit.... For solid history, bright sketches of rough campaigning, shrewd studies of character, and lively anecdote, these memoirs yield in no degree to others. — TIMES.

PREHISTORIC MAN AND BEAST. By the Rev. H. N. HUTCHINSON, Author of 'Extinct Monsters,' 'Creatures of Other Days,' &c. With a Preface by Sir HENRY HOWORTH, M.P., F.R.S., and 10 Full-page Illustrations. Small demy 8vo. 10s. 6d.

'A striking picture of living men and conditions as they once existed.... It combines graphic description with scientific accuracy, and is an admirable example of what a judicious use of the imagination can achieve upon a basis of established facts.'—KNOWLEDGE.

SHAKSPEARE COMMENTARIES. By Dr. G. G. GERVINUS, Professor at Heidelberg. Translated, under the Author's superintendence, by F. E. BUNNETT. With a Preface by J. F. FURNIVALL. Fifth Edition. 8vo. 14s.

THE LIFE OF GOETHE. By GEORGE HENRY LEWES. Fourth Edition. Revised according to the latest Documents, with Portrait. 8vo. 16s.

HOURS IN A LIBRARY. By LESLIE STEPHEN. Revised, Re-arranged, and Cheaper Edition, with Additional Chapters. 3 vols. crown 8vo. 6s. each.

A HISTORY of ENGLISH THOUGHT IN THE EIGHTEENTH CENTURY. By LESLIE STEPHEN. Second Edition. 2 vols. demy 8vo. 28s.

LIBERTY, EQUALITY, FRATERNITY. By the late Sir JAMES FITZJAMES STEPHEN, K.C.S.I. Second Edition, with a new Preface. Demy 8vo. 14s.

NEW AND CHEAPER EDITION OF 'GARDNER'S HOUSEHOLD MEDICINE.'
Thirteenth Edition. With numerous Illustrations. Demy 8vo. 8s. 6d.

GARDNER'S HOUSEHOLD MEDICINE AND SICK ROOM GUIDE : a Description of the Means of Preserving Health, and the Treatment of Diseases, Injuries, and Emergencies. Revised and expressly adapted for the Use of Families, Missionaries, and Colonists. By W. H. O. STAVELEY, F.R.C.S.Eng.

'Fully succeeds in its object, and is essentially practical in its execution.'—LANCET.

'It is difficult to conceive that its valuable information could be presented in a better form.'
DAILY TELEGRAPH.

London: SMITH, ELDER, & CO., 15 Waterloo Place, S.W.

STANDARD EDITIONS.

ROBERT BROWNING'S COMPLETE WORKS. New and Cheaper
Edition. Edited and Annotated by AUGUSTINE BIRRELL, Q C., M.P., and FREDERIC G. KENYON.
2 vols. large crown 8vo. bound in cloth, gilt top, with a Portrait-Frontispiece to each volume.
7s. 6d. per volume.
'Not only a cheap, but a handy, useful, and eminently presentable edition. . . . Altogether a
most satisfactory and creditable production.'—GLOBE.

*** Also the UNIFORM EDITION of ROBERT BROWNING'S WORKS, in 17 vols. crown 8vo.
bound in Sets, £4. 5s.; or the volumes bound separately, 5s. each.

ELIZABETH BARRETT BROWNING'S POETICAL WORKS.
New and Cheaper Edition. 1 vol., with Portrait and fac-simile of the MS. of 'A Sonnet
from the Portuguese.' Large crown 8vo bound in cloth, gilt top, 7s. 6d.

*** Also the UNIFORM EDITION, in 6 vols. small crown 8vo. This Edition contains
Five Portraits of Mrs. Browning at different periods of life, and a few Illustrations.

MISS THACKERAY'S WORKS. Uniform Edition. Each Volume
illustrated by a Vignette Title-page. 10 vols. large crown 8vo. 10s. each.
CONTENTS. – Old Kensington—The Village on the Cliff—Five Old Friends and a Young Prince—To
Esther, &c.—Bluebeard's Keys, &c.—The Story of Elizabeth; Two Hours from an Island—Toilers
and Spinsters—Miss Angel; Fulham Lawn—Miss Williamson's Divagations—Mrs. Dymond.

LIFE AND WORKS OF CHARLOTTE, EMILY, AND ANNE
BRONTË. LIBRARY EDITION. 7 vols. each containing 5 Illustrations, large crown 8vo. 5s.
each.
CONTENTS.—Jane Eyre—Shirley—Villette—Tenant of Wildfell Hall—Wuthering Heights—The
Professor; and Poems—Life of Charlotte Brontë.

*** Also the POPULAR EDITION, in 7 vols. small post 8vo. limp cloth, or c cth boards, gilt
top 2s. 6d. each. And the POCKET EDITION, in 7 vols. small fcp. 8vo. each with a Frontispiece,
bound in cloth, with gilt top, 1s. 6d. per volume; or the Set, in gold-lettered cloth case, 12s. 6d.

MRS. GASKELL'S WORKS. Uniform Edition. 7 vols. each containing
4 Illustrations. 3s. 6d. each, bound in cloth.
CONTENTS.—Wives and Daughters—North and South—Sylvia's Lovers—Cranford, and other
Tales – Mary Barton, and other Tales—Ruth, and other Tales— Lizzie Leigh, and other Tales.

*** Also the POPULAR EDITION, in 7 vols. small post 8vo. limp cloth; or cloth boards, gilt
top 2s. 6d. each. And the POCKET EDITION, in 8 vols. small fcp. 8vo. bound in cloth, with gilt
top, 1s. 6d. per volume; or the Set, in gold-lettered cloth case, 14s.

LEIGH HUNT'S WORKS. 7 vols. fcp. 8vo. limp cloth; or cloth boards,
gilt top, 2s. 6d. each.
CONTENTS.—Imagination and Fancy—The Town—Autobiography of Leigh Hunt—Men, Women,
and Books—Wit and Humour—A Jar of Honey from Mount Hybla—Table-talk.

SIR ARTHUR HELPS' WORKS. 3 vols. crown 8vo. 7s. 6d. each.
CONTENTS.—Friends in Council, 1st Series—Friends in Council, 2nd Series—Companions of My
Solitude: Essays written during the Intervals of Business; an Essay on Organisation in Daily Life.

W. M. THACKERAY'S WORKS. The Standard Edition. 26 vols.
large 8vo. 10s. 6d. each. This Edition contains some of Mr. Thackeray's Writings which had
not previously been collected, and many additional Illustrations.

W. M. THACKERAY'S WORKS. The Library Edition. 24 vols. small
demy 8vo. handsomely bound in cloth, £9; or half-russia, marbled edges, £13. 13s. With
Illustrations by the AUTHOR, RICHARD DOYLE, and FREDERICK WALKER.
*** The Volumes are sold separately, in cloth, 7s. 6d. each.

W. M. THACKERAY'S WORKS. The Popular Edition. 13 vols. large
crown 8vo. with Frontispiece to each volume, scarlet cloth, gilt top, £3. 5s.; or in half-morocco,
gilt, £5. 10s.
*** The Volumes are sold separately, in green cloth, 5s. each.

W. M. THACKERAY'S WORKS. The Cheaper Illustrated Edition.
26 vols. crown 8vo. bound in cloth, £4. 11s.; or handsomely bound in half-morocco, £8. 8s.
*** The Volumes are sold separately, in cloth, 3s. 6d. each.

W. M. THACKERAY'S WORKS. The Pocket Edition. 27 vols. bound
in cloth, with gilt top, 1s. 6d. each.
*** The Volumes are also supplied as follows :—

THE NOVELS. 13 vols. in gold-lettered cloth | THE MISCELLANIES. 14 vols. in gold-
case, 21s. | lettered cloth case, 21s.

*** Messrs. SMITH, ELDER, & CO. will be happy to forward a copy of their CATALOGUE
post free on application.

London : SMITH, ELDER, & CO., 15 Waterloo Place, S.W.

SMITH, ELDER, & CO.'S PUBLICATIONS.

MRS. E. B. BROWNING'S LETTERS. Edited, with Biographical
Additions, by FREDERIC G. KENYON. Fourth Edition. 2 vols. With Portraits. Crown 8vo.
15s. net.

'These volumes are the first adequate contribution which has been made to a real knowledge of
Mrs. Browning. . . . The inestimable value of the collection is that it contains not merely interesting critical writing, but the intimate expression of a personality.'—ATHENÆUM.

THE LIFE AND LETTERS OF ROBERT BROWNING. By
Mrs. SUTHERLAND ORR. With Portrait and Steel Engraving of Mr. Browning's Study in
De Vere Gardens. Second Edition. Crown 8vo. 12s. 6d.

POT-POURRI FROM A SURREY GARDEN. By Mrs. C. W. EARLE.
With an Appendix by Lady CONSTANCE LYTTON. Fifteenth Edition. Crown 8vo. 7s. 6d.

Dean Hole, in an article upon the work in the *Nineteenth Century*, says:—'There is no time
for further enjoyment of this sweet, spicy "Pot-Pourri"; no space for further extracts from this
clever and comprehensive book; only for two more earnest words to the reader—Buy it.'

SONGS OF ACTION. By CONAN DOYLE. Second Impression. Small
crown 8vo. 5s.

'Dr Doyle's "Songs" are full of movement. They have fluency, they have vigour, they have
force. Everybody should hasten to make acquaintance with them.'—GLOBE.

NEW AND CHEAPER EDITION OF 'THE RENAISSANCE IN ITALY.'

In Seven Volumes, large crown 8vo. With Two Portraits.

THE RENAISSANCE IN ITALY. By JOHN ADDINGTON SYMONDS.

1. THE AGE OF THE DESPOTS. With a
Portrait. Price 7s. 6d.
2. THE REVIVAL OF LEARNING. Price
7s. 6d.
3. THE FINE ARTS. Price 7s. 6d.

4 and 5. ITALIAN LITERATURE. 2 vols.
Price 15s.
6 and 7. THE CATHOLIC REACTION. With
a Portrait and an Index to the 7 vols.
Price 15s.

FRANCE UNDER LOUIS XV. By JAMES BRECK PERKINS, Author of
'France under the Regency.' 2 vols. Crown 8vo. 16s.

'A very good book. . . . Mr. Perkins's tracing out of the foreign policy of France through the
wars which did so much to break down her power and the prestige of her crown is very clear and
intelligent, and his judgment appears to be generally sound.'—TIMES.

PUBLISHED UNDER THE AUTHORITY OF THE SECRETARY OF STATE FOR INDIA.

Third and Standard Edition, with Map. Demy 8vo. 28s.

THE INDIAN EMPIRE: its Peoples, History, and Products. By Sir
W. W. HUNTER, K.C.S.I., &c.

THE MAMELUKE OR SLAVE DYNASTY OF EGYPT,
1260-1517 A.D. By Sir WILLIAM MUIR, K.C.S.I., LL.D., D.C.L., Ph.D. (Bologna), Author of
'The Life of Mahomet,' 'Mahomed and Islam,' 'The Caliphate,' &c. With 12 Full-page Illustrations and a Map. 8vo. 10s. 6d.

London: SMITH, ELDER, & CO., 15 Waterloo Place, S.W.

NEW EDITION OF W. M. THACKERAY'S WORKS.

IN COURSE OF PUBLICATION IN THIRTEEN MONTHLY VOLUMES.

Large crown 8vo. cloth, gilt top, 6s. each.

THE BIOGRAPHICAL EDITION

OF

W. M. THACKERAY'S COMPLETE WORKS.

THIS NEW AND REVISED EDITION COMPRISES

ADDITIONAL MATERIAL and HITHERTO UNPUBLISHED LETTERS, SKETCHES, and DRAWINGS

Derived from the Author's Original Manuscripts and Note-Books,

AND EACH VOLUME INCLUDES A MEMOIR IN THE FORM OF AN INTRODUCTION

BY MRS. RICHMOND RITCHIE.

Contents of the Volumes :—

1. **VANITY FAIR.** With 20 Full-page Illustrations, 11 Woodcuts, a Facsimile Letter, and a New Portrait. [*Ready.*
2. **PENDENNIS.** With 20 Full-page Illustrations and 10 Woodcuts. [*Ready.*
3. **YELLOWPLUSH PAPERS, &c.** With 24 Full-page Reproductions of Steel Plates by GEORGE CRUIKSHANK, 11 Woodcuts, and a Portrait of the Author by MACLISE. [*Ready.*
4. **THE MEMOIRS OF BARRY LYNDON; THE FITZBOODLE** PAPERS, &c. With 16 Full-page Illustrations by J. E. MILLAIS, R.A., LUKE FILDES, A.R.A., and the AUTHOR, and 14 Woodcuts. [*Ready.*
5. **SKETCH BOOKS : THE PARIS SKETCH BOOK, THE IRISH** SKETCH BOOK, NOTES OF A JOURNEY FROM CORNHILL TO GRAND CAIRO, &c. With 16 Full-page Illustrations, 39 Woodcuts, and a Portrait of the Author by MACLISE. [*Ready.*
6. **CONTRIBUTIONS TO 'PUNCH,' &c.** With 20 Full-page Illustrations, 26 Woodcuts, and an Engraving of the Author from a Portrait by SAMUEL LAURENCE. [*Ready.*
7. **THE HISTORY OF HENRY ESMOND, and THE LECTURES.** With 20 Full-page Illustrations by GEORGE DU MAURIER, F. BARNARD, and FRANK DICKSEE, R.A., and 11 Woodcuts. [*Ready.*
8. **THE NEWCOMES.** With 20 Full-page Illustrations by RICHARD DOYLE, and 11 Woodcuts.
9. **CHRISTMAS BOOKS, &c.** With 97 Full-page Illustrations, and 122 Woodcuts, and a Facsimile Letter. [*On December 15.*
10. **VIRGINIANS.** With 20 Full-page Illustrations.
11. **THE ADVENTURES OF PHILIP; and A SHABBY GENTEEL STORY.**
12. **DENIS DUVAL, ROUNDABOUT PAPERS, &c.**
13. **MISCELLANIES, &c.**

THE BOOKMAN. —' In her new biographical edition Mrs. Richmond Ritchie gives us precisely what we want. The volumes are a pleasure to hold and to handle. They are just what we like our ordinary every-day Thackeray to be. And prefixed to each of them we have all that we wish to know, or have any right to know, about the author himself ; all the circumstances, letters, and drawings which bear upon the work.'

THE ACADEMY. —' Thackeray wished that no biography of him should appear. It is certain that the world has never ceased to desire one. Hence the compromise effected in this edition of his works. Mrs. Ritchie, his daughter, will contribute to each volume in this edition her memories of the circumstances under which her father produced it. Such memoirs, when complete, cannot fall far short of being an actual biography.'

THE DAILY CHRONICLE. —' We shall have, when the thirteen volumes of this edition are issued, not, indeed, a biography of Thackeray, but something which will delightfully supply the place of a biography, and fill a regrettable gap in our literary records.'

*** *A Prospectus of the Edition, with Specimen Pages, will be sent post free on application.*

London : SMITH, ELDER, & CO., 15 Waterloo Place, S.W.

POPULAR NOVELS.

Each Work complete in One Volume, crown 8vo. price Six Shillings.

By HENRY SETON MERRIMAN:
RODEN'S CORNER 3rd Edition.
IN KEDAR'S TENTS. 8th Edition.
THE GREY LADY. With 12 Full-page Illustrations.
THE SOWERS. 19th Edition.

By A. CONAN DOYLE:
THE TRAGEDY OF THE KOROSKO. With 40 Full-page Illustrations.
UNCLE BERNAC. 2nd Edition. With 12 Full-page Illustrations.
RODNEY STONE With 8 Full-page Illustrations.
THE WHITE COMPANY. 18th Edition.

By S. R. CROCKETT:
THE RED AXE. 2nd Edition.
CLEG KELLY, ARAB OF THE CITY. 33rd Thousand.

By Mrs. HUMPHRY WARD:
HELBECK OF BANNISDALE. 4th Edition.
SIR GEORGE TRESSADY. 3rd Edition.
MARCELLA. 16th Edition.
ROBERT ELSMERE. 27th Edition.
THE HISTORY OF DAVID GRIEVE. 9th Edition.

By STANLEY J. WEYMAN:
THE CASTLE INN. With a Frontispiece. 2nd Edition.

By Miss THACKERAY:
OLD KENSINGTON.
THE VILLAGE ON THE CLIFF.
FIVE OLD FRIENDS AND A YOUNG PRINCE.
TO ESTHER, and other Sketches.
BLUE BEARD'S KEYS, and other Stories.
THE STORY OF ELIZABETH; TWO HOURS; FROM AN ISLAND.
TOILERS AND SPINSTERS; and other Essays.
MISS ANGEL: Fulham Lawn.
MISS WILLIAMSON'S DIVAGATIONS.
MRS. DYMOND.

By CLIVE PHILLIPPS-WOLLEY:
ONE OF THE BROKEN BRIGADE.

By ALEXANDER INNES SHAND:
THE LADY GRANGE.

By the Rev. J. E. C. WELLDON:
GERALD EVERSLEY'S FRIENDSHIP: a Study in Real Life. 4th Edition.

By ARCHIE ARMSTRONG:
UNDER THE CIRCUMSTANCES.

By the Rev. COSMO GORDON LANG:
THE YOUNG CLANROY: a Romance of the '45.

By W. CARLTON DAWE:
CAPTAIN CASTLE: a Story of the South Sea. With a Frontispiece.

By Mrs. DE LA PASTURE:
DEBORAH OF TOD'S. 4th Edition.

By ANNA HOWARTH:
KATRINA: a Tale of the Karoo.
JAN: an Afrikander. 2nd Edition.

By FRANCIS H. HARDY:
THE MILLS OF GOD.

By HAMILTON DRUMMOND:
FOR THE RELIGION.

By ARCHER P. CROUCH:
SEÑORITA MONTENAR.

By J. A. ALTSHELER:
A SOLDIER OF MANHATTAN.

By OLIVE BIRRELL:
THE AMBITION OF JUDITH.

By PERCY FENDALL and FOX RUSSELL:
OUT OF THE DARKNESS.

By A. E. HOUGHTON:
GILBERT MURRAY.

By ADAM LILBURN:
THE BORDERER.

By Mrs. BIRCHENOUGH:
DISTURBING ELEMENTS.

By PERCY ANDREAE.
THE SIGNORA: a Tale.
THE MASK AND THE MAN.

By R. O. PROWSE:
A FATAL RESERVATION.

By LORD MONKSWELL:
KATE GRENVILLE.

By SARAH TYTLER:
KINCAID'S WIDOW.

By LADY VERNEY:
LLANALY REEFS.
LETTICE LISLE. With 3 Illustrations

London: SMITH, ELDER, & CO., 15 Waterloo Place, S.W.